The Political Theatre of David Edgar

David Edgar's writings address the most basic questions of how humans organise and govern themselves in modern societies. This study brings together the disciplines of political philosophy and theatre studies to approach the leading British playwright as a political writer and a public social critic. Edgar uses theatre as a powerful tool of public discourse, an aesthetic modality for engaging with and thinking/feeling through the most pressing social issues of the day. In this he is a supreme rationalist: he deploys character, plot and language to explore ideas, to make certain kinds of discursive cases and model hypothetical alternatives. Reinelt and Hewitt analyse twelve of Edgar's most important plays, including *Maydays* and *Pentecost*, and also provide detailed discussions of key performances and critical reception to illustrate the playwright's artistic achievement in relation to his contributions as a public figure in British cultural life.

JANELLE REINELT is Professor of Theatre and Performance at the University of Warwick. She was President of the International Federation for Theatre Research from 2003 to 2007, and is a former editor of *Theatre Journal*. Her books include *After Brecht: British Epic Theatre, Critical Theory and Performance* with Joseph Roach, *The Performance of Power* with Sue-Ellen Case and *The Cambridge Companion to Modern British Women Playwrights* with Elaine Aston. She is the series editor, with Brian Singleton, of Studies in International Performance.

GERALD HEWITT is Professor Emeritus of Philosophy and Political Science at the University of the Pacific in Stockton, California, and Research Fellow in the School of Theatre, Performance and Cultural Policy Studies at the University of Warwick. He was a founding faculty member of the School of International Studies at the University of the Pacific and Department Chair of the Department of Political Science. His areas of expertise include political theory, jurisprudence and modern European history and politics.

# CAMBRIDGE STUDIES IN MODERN THEATRE

Series editor
David Bradby, *Royal Holloway, University of London*

Advisory board
Martin Banham, *University of Leeds*
Jacky Bratton, *Royal Holloway, University of London*
Tracy Davis, *Northwestern University*
Sir Richard Eyre
Michael Robinson, *University of East Anglia*
Sheila Stowell, *University of Birmingham*

Volumes for Cambridge Studies in Modern Theatre explore the political, social and cultural functions of theatre while also paying careful attention to detailed performance analysis. The focus of the series is on political approaches to the modern theatre with attention also being paid to theatres of earlier periods and their influence on contemporary drama. Topics in the series are chosen to investigate this relationship and include both playwrights (their aims and intentions set against the effects of their work) and process (with emphasis on rehearsal and production methods, the political structure within theatre companies and their choice of audiences or performance venues). Further topics will include devised theatre, agitprop, community theatre, para-theatre and performance art. In all cases the series will be alive to the special cultural and political factors operating in the theatres examined.

*Books published*

Maria DiCenzo, *The Politics of Alternative Theatre in Britain, 1968–1990: the Case of 7:84 (Scotland)*
Jo Riley, *Chinese Theatre and the Actor in Performance*
Jonathan Kalb, *The Theatre of Heiner Müller*
Richard Boon and Jane Plastow, eds., *Theatre Matters: Performance and Culture on the World Stage*
Claude Schumacher, ed., *Staging the Holocaust: the Shoah in Drama and Performance*

Philip Roberts, *The Royal Court Theatre and the Modern Stage*

Nicholas Grene, *The Politics of Irish Drama: Plays in Context from Boucicault to Friel*

Anatoly Smeliansky, *The Russian Theatre after Stalin*

Clive Barker and Maggie B. Gale, eds., *British Theatre between the Wars, 1918–1939*

Michael Patterson, *Strategies of Political Theatre: Post-War British Playwrights*

Elaine Aston, *Feminist Views on the English Stage: Women Playwrights, 1990–2000*

Gabriele Griffin, *Contemporary Black and Asian Women Playwrights in Britain*

Loren Kruger, *Post-Imperial Brecht: Politics and Performance, East and South*

David Barnett, *Rainer Werner Fassbinder and the German Theatre*

Mary Luckhurst, *Dramaturgy: A Revolution in Theatre*

Scott Boltwood, *Brian Friel, Ireland, and The North*

Gerwin Strobl, *The Swastika and the Stage: German Theatre and Society, 1933–1945*

Gene A. Plunka, *Holocaust Drama: The Theater of Atrocity*

Nadine Holdsworth, *Joan Littlewood's Theatre*

William Storm, *Irony and the Modern Theatre*

Janelle Reinelt and Gerald Hewitt, *The Political Theatre of David Edgar: Negotiation and Retrieval*

# The Political Theatre of David Edgar

## Negotiation and Retrieval

Janelle Reinelt and
Gerald Hewitt

CAMBRIDGE
UNIVERSITY PRESS

**CAMBRIDGE**
**UNIVERSITY PRESS**

University Printing House, Cambridge CB2 8BS, United Kingdom

One Liberty Plaza, 20th Floor, New York, NY 10006, USA

477 Williamstown Road, Port Melbourne, VIC 3207, Australia

314-321, 3rd Floor, Plot 3, Splendor Forum, Jasola District Centre, New Delhi - 110025, India

79 Anson Road, #06-04/06, Singapore 079906

Cambridge University Press is part of the University of Cambridge.

It furthers the University's mission by disseminating knowledge in the pursuit of education, learning and research at the highest international levels of excellence.

www.cambridge.org
Information on this title: www.cambridge.org/9781108701617



First published 2011
First paperback edition 2018

*A catalogue record for this publication is available from the British Library*

*Library of Congress Cataloging in Publication data*
Reinelt, Janelle G. The political theatre of David Edgar / Janelle Reinelt, Gerald Hewitt.
p. cm. – (Cambridge studies in modern theatre)
ISBN 978-0-521-50968-8 (hardback)
1. Edgar, David, 1948– Criticism and interpretation. 2. Political plays, English – History and criticism. 3. Politics and literature – Great Britain – History – 20th century. I. Hewitt, Gerald. II. Title. III. Series.
PR6055.D44Z84 2011
822′.914–dc22 2010053222

ISBN 978-0-521-50968-8 Hardback
ISBN 978-1-108-70161-7 Paperback

# Contents

*List of illustrations* *page* viii
*Acknowledgements* x

1 Introduction: political commitment and performative practice 1
2 Intervening in public discourse: Edgar as commentator and activist 35
3 Things fall apart: after ideology in *Maydays* and *Continental Divide* 63
4 Governing memberships: *Destiny*, *Playing with Fire*, and *Testing the Echo* 103
5 'A legend in your own time': *The Jail Diary of Albie Sachs*, *Mary Barnes*, and *Albert Speer* 154
6 Socialism's aftermath: *The Shape of the Table*, *Pentecost*, and *The Prisoner's Dilemma* 205

*Afterword* 265
*Notes* 270
*Selected bibliography* 295
*Index* 308

# Illustrations


1 David Edgar. Courtesy David Edgar. *page* 36

2 The cover of *Race & Class*, pamphlet no. 4, 1977. Courtesy of the Institute for Race Relations. Photographer: Mark Rusher. 55

3 *Maydays* (1983). This photo, used also as our cover art, was used in the design of the poster and publicity for the RSC production at the Barbican. Every effort has been made to contact copyright holders; the publishers will be glad to make good in any future editions any errors or omissions brought to their attention. 70

4 *Continental Divide* (2003), Berkeley Repertory Theatre and Oregon Shakespeare Festival, director Tony Taccone. Photo courtesy of Berkeley Repertory Theatre and kevinberne.com 88

5 *Continental Divide: Mothers Against* (2003), Berkeley Repertory Theatre and Oregon Shakespeare Festival, director Tony Taccone. Photo courtesy of Berkeley Repertory Theatre and kevinberne.com 97

6 *Destiny* (1976), The Other Place, Stratford and the Aldwych, London, director Ron Daniels. Courtesy Joe Cocks Studio Collection © Shakespeare Birthplace Trust. 114

7 *Playing with Fire* (2005), Olivier Theatre (NT), director Michael Attenborough. Courtesy of the National Theatre and photographer Catherine Ashmore. 130

8 *Testing the Echo* (2008), Out of Joint on tour, director Matthew Dunster. Courtesy of Out of Joint and Jon Bradfield (artist). 152

9 Self-portrait of Mary Barnes, with permission of Joseph Berke, from *Mary Barnes: Two Accounts of a Journey Through Madness*, by Mary Barnes and Joseph Berke. 180
10 Poster design for the Swedish production of *Albert Speer* (2001). Courtesy of the Göteberg Stadsteatern and Photographer Aorta. 190
11 *Albert Speer* (2000), Lyttelton Theatre (NT), director Trevor Nunn. Courtesy of the National Theatre and photographer John Haynes. 203
12 *The Shape of the Table* (1990), Cottesloe Theatre (NT), director Jenny Killick. Courtesy of the National Theatre and photographer Knobby Clark. 219
13 *Pentecost* (1997), Berkeley Repertory Theatre and Oregon Shakespeare Festival, director Tony Taccone. Courtesy of the Berkeley Repertory Theatre and photographer Ken Friedman. 232
14 *Pentecost* (1997), Berkeley Repertory Theatre and Oregon Shakespeare Festival, director Tony Taccone. Courtesy of the Berkeley Repertory Theatre and photographer Ken Friedman. 240
15 *The Prisoner's Dilemma* (2001), The Other Place, Stratford and the Barbican, London, director Michael Attenborough. Courtesy John Haynes, © Royal Shakespeare Company. 253

# Acknowledgements

We would like to thank friends and colleagues who have helped us research and write this volume. Special thanks and appreciation first and foremost to David Edgar for sharing his time and his archives so generously during these past years, and to David and Stephanie Dale for their ongoing friendship; to Tony Platt, for reading the manuscript and commenting extensively, and to Tony and Cecilia O'Leary for their friendship and their political and academic acumen. To our Warwick colleagues, Jim Davis, Milija Gluhovic, Yvette Hutchison, and Silvija Jestrovic, who read chapters and offered their insights, our grateful thanks. Also to head of department Nadine Holdsworth for understanding and supporting our work by allocating study leave during 2010. Thanks to Tony Taccone, Michael Attenborough, and Robyn A. Rodriguez for their interview insights about working with David Edgar. Thanks also to our editor at Cambridge University Press, Vicki Cooper, and our line editor, Rebecca Taylor, who were always helpful and willing to work with us on any difficulties on this project.

This book is dedicated to the late David Bradby, with love and respect.

# 1 Introduction

## Political commitment and performative practice

> Anybody who used to call themselves a Marxist now has fairly intense self-definitional problems.
>
> David Edgar (1994)[1]

> He is an optimist who has been around.
>
> John Peter (1994)[2]

Of the distinctive voices in the contemporary British theatre, David Edgar's provides the most comprehensive articulation of major political questions. His career spans more than four eventful and politically complex decades, and encompasses every variety of writing for performance, including agitprop and touring pieces; community plays; radio, film and television plays; and large-scale plays produced in major national venues such as the Royal Shakespeare Company and the National Theatre.[3] In addition, Edgar has maintained a high profile as a public intellectual, engaging in depth with a wide variety of political issues through newspaper opinion pages, journal essays, and book reviews, as well as via frequent public speaking engagements before a variety of organizations, including the Commission on Racial Equality; the Royal Society of Arts, Manufacturing and Commerce; the Fabian Society; and the annual Marxism conference. Thus, well beyond his own creative work, Edgar has been a central figure in British public life, particularly with regard to the relationships among the arts, government, and society.[4]

Edgar has been politically on the Left since he was a young man at university, attracted by the idea of Marxist revolution.[5] What it means to be on the Left, however, has changed dramatically over the years – for Edgar as for most others. Maintaining a sceptical attachment to Trotskyism during the 1970s, Edgar joined the Labour Party in 1981,[6] and two years later wrote a kaleidoscopic critique of the history of the Left (*Maydays*, 1983), which explained in part why he had turned from revolutionary socialism to social democratic parliamentary politics, but which also anatomized certain left-wing defectors who had moved all the way to the reactionary Right. It was already characteristic of Edgar to stage the contradictions through which he and his generation were currently living; and he has continued to forge a theatre that embodies the social predicaments of modernity as they have developed from the Second World War to the new millennium.

All of Edgar's writings, plays as well as other forms, address the most basic questions of how humans organize and govern themselves in modern societies; in this regard he is a consummate political writer. His *oeuvre* stands as a kind of illustrative compendium of the leading conceptual puzzles of political theory. In studying the politics of his work here, we have concentrated on twelve of his most important plays and organized our discussion thematically, linking the plays to their overarching problematics. For example, we discuss the two plays that make up his diptych *Continental Divide* (2003) alongside *Maydays* (1983) because together these plays attempt to track the decline of the Left (and the rise of neo-conservatism) through a sweep of history, and at the same time confront situated moments in recent party politics in the United States (*Continental Divide*) and British seventies radical left politics (*Maydays*). Thus seemingly different plays, separated by twenty years, are joined by their representation of the failure of ideological visions as well as by the impact of blighted history on idealistic activism. The twelve plays explored here address issues such as the relationship between politics, government, and the state, as well as difficulties of democratic practice and conflict over definitions of public interest. Each play, however, creates a different encounter for spectators with the fictionalized reality of these conundrums and the human beings who live and work within them. As we move through the volume, a cumulative notion of Edgar's political architecture, his convictions, insights, and blind spots will emerge along with an examination of his success and challenges in placing these before his audiences in different theatrical productions. The plays selected for detailed examination include *Destiny* (1976), *The Jail Diary of Albie Sachs* (1978), *Mary Barnes* (1978), *Maydays* (1983), *The Shape of the Table* (1990), *Pentecost* (1994), *Albert Speer* (2000), *The Prisoner's Dilemma* (2001), *Continental Divide* (*Mothers Against* and *Daughters of the Revolution*) (2003), *Playing with Fire* (2005), and *Testing the Echo* (2008).

The decisions about which plays to focus on and which to treat only indirectly reflect our judgments and interests, but also the necessity of choosing from among a large number of works which would require several volumes to survey adequately. We focus on theatre works rather than Edgar's substantial body of television and radio plays, paying most attention to his plays from the 1990s onwards, which serve as a means of thinking through our recent history and daily sociality.

Thus Edgar's most successful box office hit, *Nicholas Nickleby* (1980), is not extensively discussed here because we have limited our focus to plays whose subject matter is the contemporary world. We acknowledge, however, *Nickleby's* importance within Edgar's career and within British theatre history.[7] Representing a significantly large investment of resources and artistic talent by the Royal Shakespeare Company, Edgar's adaptation of Charles Dickens's novel featured over one hundred characters and originally played over two (long) nights. It proved hugely successful in London and on Broadway, winning the 1980 Best Play Award from the Society of West End Theatres and the Lawrence Olivier Award, and in 1982 the Tony Award for Best Play.[8]

To illuminate the twelve plays that are our central concern, our collaboration on this book brings together the disciplines of political philosophy and theatre studies to approach Edgar primarily as a political writer and a public social critic. We believe he merits serious critical attention that combines a complex analysis of the socio-political context of the plays in relation to a sustained discussion of the formal political problems figured in the texts and in his related body of public writing. In addition, his dramaturgy and theatrical stylistics are both integral to the subjects he explores and independently valuable in their own right as a subject for aesthetic investigation and judgment.

The detailed material situations and characters of Edgar's dramaturgy embody and configure a key political concern that has grown increasingly present during modernity: the gap between wide-ranging, sometimes utopian visions of political theory and the always more limited actual human practice, often not even coming close to the desired good. Indeed, in some ways Edgar is an elegiac writer because he most often stages such failures to achieve satisfactory human social arrangements. Yet Edgar's purpose in exploring so many ways of falling short becomes clear in the demonstration of his will to persist, reinvent, begin again. Thus, it is no surprise that most of his plays end in simultaneous disillusionment with a given project and recommitment to social purpose, and have as their major dramatic actions the negotiation and retrieval central to the playwright's vision of polity. In this volume, we have attempted to foreground the nature and quality of *negotiation* as a method of political praxis and *retrieval* as the appropriate response to failure. Edgar, taking his cue from the great modernist writers (Brecht's 'long anger' and Beckett's injunction to 'fail better'), is supremely committed to celebrating quotidian human gestures of re-engagement with polities and failed political initiatives.

Edgar's work has been important to us (and of course to many others) not only because it humanizes the large abstractions of political theory, but also because it confronts the specific pressing issues of contemporary life in Britain and the West: the rise and threat of fascism in the moment of pre-Thatcher reaction (*Destiny*, 1976); the impossibility of sustaining 1960s-style utopian collectives (*Mary Barnes*, 1979); the emergence of 'Fortress Europe' and the predicament of refugees after the fall of the Wall (*Pentecost*, 1994 and *The Prisoner's Dilemma*, 2001); race relations and community relations at the end of New Labour and in the aftermath of 9/11 and 7/7 (*Playing with Fire*, 2005). These and other extremely topical and specific socio-political problems are taken up to be embodied, imagined, and worked through in dramatic form. Edgar uses theatre as a powerful tool of public discourse, an aesthetic modality for engaging with and thinking/feeling through the most pressing social issues of the day.[9]

In this, he is also unrepentently rationalist: he deploys character, plot, language to explore ideas, make certain kinds of discursive cases, model hypothetical alternatives. He is, in this sense, a rhetorical playwright: he lives for engagement with spectators who will not necessarily agree with him, but who will use his theatrical figures to think through their own understandings of the dilemmas he stages. An audience deep in political argument on its way out of the theatre is his highest mark of a successful play.

From the perspective of British theatre trends in the second decade of the twenty-first century, Edgar can sometimes be perceived as being 'out of fashion'.[10] His theatrical style is mostly based on language and rhetoric rather than the now ascendant 'physical theatre' or in Hans-Thies Lehmann's term, 'post-dramatic theatre'. Actually, Edgar's plays offer a robust reminder of the values of narrative, discursive exploration of character and situation, and above all capacious thinking about social reality. By investigating his work in depth, we hope here to argue for a reconsideration of some of these recently undervalued concepts. In addition, as we argue concerning competing definitions of political theatre in the following pages, a pluralistic set of aesthetic modes and styles is a sign of a healthy theatre, and there is room for many overlapping and complementary forms. As Edgar moves into the fifth decade of his writing career, he continues to transform his vision and his dramaturgy to suit the changing times. We see him as a major contributor to a polyvocal theatre scene in the UK and beyond, where a variety of dramaturgical strategies successfully coexist to form a vibrant theatrical panoply of performances about our lives in common, and our attempts to improve them.

In the rest of this chapter, we tackle the key questions that must be answered in any sustained investigation of Edgar's work, especially those that cluster around the central concern: what is political theatre today? This term is often used in common parlance, as if everyone is agreed on its meaning, but we think consensus is far afield. Recent theatre scholarship has challenged the term 'political theatre' and also the discourses around politics (especially democracy), changing previously familiar sources and formulations. Much of this work is extremely valuable and provocative, and contributes to a renewal of our scholarship appropriate to widespread changes in the wake of neo-liberalism, globalization, the 'war on terror', and the breakdown of confidence in fiscal and parliamentary institutions. We will discuss it here with both sympathy and critique in equal measure, and explain how we see Edgar participating in the changing spectrum of theatrical performances with political valences.

## What is political theatre?

> I sometimes think I've spent my life sitting on the same panel in the same black box theatre above the same pub, debating whether British political theatre has a future. The fact that I have spent so long addressing the question implies the answer.
>
> David Edgar (2010)[11]

There is a persistent and perhaps escalating attempt to uncouple or bracket off the term 'political' from theatre, especially within the academy. Critiques of the concept come from several different quarters, and have serious and compelling analyses to offer as to why this might be desirable. We oppose this tendency, which is frequently simplified in the press and other journalism, but even to state this opposition is to presuppose a stable, unified concept around which to wrangle with others. Therefore, first, we need to know what the concept entails.

Political theatre is often discussed without any real delineation of the meaning of the term 'political'. Newspaper critics label this or that performance 'political' readily enough, but scholars also often assume we all know (and agree on) what the term means. Edgar's witty polemic quoted above points to the perennial recurrence of the claim that political theatre is in eclipse. What inevitably happens, however, is that several critics and scholars point out that the terms of engagement have changed under the pressure of contemporary events, and that we need to understand what it means to be political in a new and revised way. Then we can designate as 'political' performances that stage the new conjuncture or interrogate the new uncertainty.

The 'in-yer-facers' of the 1990s are a specific case in point.[12] Graham Saunders, in introducing an excellent collection of essays on the period, *Cool Britannia? British Political Drama in the 1990s*, takes up the critical assessment of Sarah Kane, Mark Ravenhill, Nick Grosso, Jez Butterworth and others who came into their ascendancy towards the end of the eighteen years of Conservative rule (1979–97). Arguing that by the mid nineties 'there appeared to be a disengagement and dismantlement from recognizable forms of political engagement', Saunders then carefully rehabilitates key plays of these writers. He suggests that critics such as Aleks Sierz, scholars such as Patrice Pavis, and the dramatists themselves (quoting Mark Ravenhill's *Shopping and Fucking* [*1996*] and David Eldridge) recognized that the new playwrights were reacting to shifts in the British political scene but also 'to the impact of globalization, technology, and theories posited by postmodernist thinkers such as Baudrillard and Lyotard, who questioned the nature and veracity of "reality" – and with it the viability of eliciting social or political change'.[13] Quoting Pavis in a pronouncement that Ravenhill's *Some Explicit Polaroids* differs from the past because it is a '"problem play" rather than a "thesis play"', Saunders advances a careful judgment that what was familiar as political theatre had changed as new forms and new content appeared, appropriate to a transformed situation. In the same breath, however, Saunders still marked the 'naive sentimentality' of many of the plays, as well as noting that some were superficial, self-absorbed, and fetishized violence and shock value.[14] He also pointed out that in the new millennium new forms of explicitly political theatre reappeared, especially verbatim, as the global situation changed dramatically once again.

A recent and very sophisticated version of this argument has been made by Dan Rebellato. It will be considered further below on other grounds, but here we wish to highlight the tendency to redefine 'political' in order to retain its meaning in relation to theatre. In an essay that delineates a shift from politics understood through 'state-of-the-nation' plays to politics understood through the staging of globalization's effects, Rebellato writes:

> I want to argue that the political context in which the state-of-the-nation play was developed has changed, and as a consequence political theatre has changed. I want to suggest that British playwriting continues to respond to its political surroundings with remarkable imaginative power and that the critics, with their outdated dramaturgical models, are looking for political theatre in all the wrong places.[15]

The problem with these otherwise useful and complex discussions of changing times and theatre styles is that they assume that while 'politics' may be different in any historical moment, there can be only one corresponding theatrical style to suit the times. Thus for Saunders, the new writers of the nineties were forging a style that was in some cases, but not all, political; and for Rebellato, the state-of-the-nation play no longer suits the political state of affairs under globalization. This is also the problem with journalism that periodically asserts that political theatre is dead – it privileges only one conception of political theatre. In order to propose a different way of configuring the relation between politics and theatre, we would suggest separating politics and theatre, only to rejoin them again by analysing their relationship as a third term as mobile and processual as both of the others.[16]

A definition of politics or the political must be general enough and flexible enough to serve as a theoretical platform for analysis of a range of human interactions from parliamentary participation to gender behaviour. Politics configures human relations through structures of social meaning and organization, and these structures are ubiquitous and always present, although they are also chimerical and fluid. Referencing precisely these structures keeps them visible and prevents them from going unremarked, naturalized as ideology. (As examples, 'identity politics' is in disfavour now in part because it has become ideological, and likewise the popular charge that politics has become too corrupt and unseemly is also dangerously close to becoming naturalized as an unexamined judgment.)

What, then, do we think politics actually is?[17] The best articulation of politics we know comes (ironically) from a conservative political theorist, Michael Oakeshott, who nonetheless offers a mobile, nitty-gritty definition inviting deep engagement and not a little reflexivity:

> Politics is the activity of attending to the general arrangements of a collection of people who, in respect of their common recognition of their manner of attending to its arrangements, compose a single community ... This activity, then, springs neither from instant desires, nor from general principles, but from the existing traditions of behaviour themselves. And the form it takes, because it can take no other, is the amendment of existing arrangements by exploring and pursuing what is intimated in them.[18]

What is especially valuable here is the recognition that people find themselves in certain relations with others *in media res*, and then attempt to rearrange, transform, or in some cases strengthen the existing arrangements, and this effort is always a negotiation with sociality, even if it might be violent or unilateral. It can describe a high-level legislative deliberation in a democratic state, or it can describe a dispute over a back fence or a tower block or a blog with an opponent one does not know, who speaks a different language half way across the world. Looking at these arrangements as arrangements that proceed through both micro and macro practices, one finds small adjustments and occasionally huge seismic shifts in the ways these politics work. We seek to map this notion of politics on to theatre and performance.

Looking at theatre as its own separate practice, what can we say about its apparatus of self-reflexivity and 'ontological queasiness'?[19] Following from Oakeshott's definition of politics, theatre is a micro-political practice in that it invites its spectators to pay close attention to a number of relations between the performers and spectators, and among all the humans participating in the event. To quote Nicholas Ridout's description of the politics of theatre, 'Theatre's failure, when theatre fails, is not anomalous, but somehow, perhaps constitutive ... It is precisely in theatre's failure, our discomfort with it, its embeddedness in capitalist leisure, its status as a bourgeois pastime that its political value is to be found'.[20] The failure he has in mind is theatre's inevitable failure to evade or transcend capital, as well as more pedestrian but ubiquitous failures that follow from such theatrical imperfections as 'corpsing' (uncontrollable laughter), stage fright, or children's and animals' tendency to rupture the expectations of performance conditions. All of these things can be made sense of if Oakeshott's is the model for what constitutes the political; it is more difficult if the model is Machiavelli's or Marx's.

Our line of thinking argues for a connection between the presence of political relations in the apparatus of the theatrical machine itself as well as its ability to stimulate awareness of the fundamental political situations developing elsewhere. Theatre attends to the amendment of existing arrangements by exploring and pursuing what is intimated in them, both reflexively on a metatheatrical level and with reference to other 'arrangements', through metaphor, allegory, modelling, or mimesis. In the fluctuation of history, both politics and theatre change significantly, and the third term, 'political theatre', changes its meanings and form as well. If any one of these terms is taken to be fixed, the result is inaccurate and unsatisfying.

Of course, what Machiavelli and Marx add to the equation are the distinctions of value, power, and justice. Oakeshott's formulation is value-neutral – as is theatre's political process. Politics is attending to those arrangements in the name of some values over others – struggling as much as attending in most cases. For example, 'equality' understood as the demand for equal treatment under the law is different from the demand for equal respect in the workplace, or equality in a primary classroom, where teachers may achieve equality by treating students differentially according to each one's particular combination of intellectual and personal attributes. Joe Kelleher, in his short, thoughtful book *Theatre and Politics* turns to Stefan Collini to define politics as 'the important, inescapable, and difficult attempt to determine relations of power in a given space'.[21] This version is also value-neutral, but it does underline, as Kelleher points, out that 'shaping and determining these questions is not straightforward and is likely to be contested', and also that Collini's 'inescapable' insists 'that whatever this or that image or this or that theatre is capable of provoking, and however we are capable of responding as spectators and as participants, the politics is unavoidable, is bound to come round sooner or later'.[22] We think this is a nice addendum to Oakeshott's slightly too breezy and genteel formulation.

In order to engage the relationship between theatre and politics in a historicized fashion, it becomes necessary to take up this concrete level of attending to the particularities of specific arrangements. David Edgar, for example, is commonly considered a 'left-wing' playwright and is associated with the early decades of his career when, in the 1970s, he worked toward revolutionary change and thought he knew what it would look like. The fact that his own political positions have changed significantly since then notwithstanding, this is often the aspect of Edgar's work that is sometimes considered passé. To examine this perspective, however, involves thorough consideration of the recent work (which we do in the coming chapters). As a place holder against a more extensive analysis of plays such as *Playing with Fire* or *Testing the Echo*, we return to Dan Rebellato's claim that 'we're looking for politics in the wrong places'.[23]

In addition to this assertion in *The Guardian*, written in the wake of a number of new plays that were produced in the run up to the May 2010 general elections, Rebellato has mounted a fuller argument in the essay quoted earlier, 'From the State of the Nation to Globalization: Shifting Political Agendas in Contemporary British Playwriting'. Rebellato describes the state-of-the-nation play (SON) as a model of political theatre developed in the 1970s, identifying a number of plays by David Edgar as well as Howard Brenton, David Hare, and others (men), that involve

> (a) large-cast plays, with (b) a panoramic range of public (and sometimes private) settings, employing (c) epic time-spans (years rather than hours or days), and (d) usually performed in large theatres, preferably theatres with a national profile. The grand scale of these plays represents a belief that the domestic rooms of mainstream naturalist theatre represent a conservative and highly individualistic view of the world.[24]

These SONs were/are no longer viable, according to Rebellato, not only because Thatcher made large plays too expensive, or because their sexual politics were inadequate, but because the world changed to render the terms of SON obsolete. Rebellato, in a rhetorical sleight of hand, substitutes 'nation-state' for 'state of the nation', and suggests that the technique of the seventies SONs worked only as long as nation and state were co-joined. He describes the state as the institution of 'public political organization', with its responsibility for justice, reason, and law, while nation 'binds people together through shared temperament, language, history, culture, landscape and so on'.[25] Since SON plays worked by combining the agitprop conception of judicial generality at the level of the state with the realism equivalent to the 'sensuous particularity of the nation', the coordination of nation and state to private and public was the way the plays staged 'recognizable human beings against the background of the historical and social forces that carry them forward'.[26] Once the connection between state and nation began to break down, with the emergence of globalization, the connection between private and public could not be sustained: global capital has overtaken states and nations have fragmented, becoming 'unbundled from state'.[27]

At this point it is pertinent to quote David Edgar in terms of what he himself perceived socialist plays to have been doing in the SON heyday: 'The political plays of the 1970s shared a number of characteristics, of which the most important were a hostility to domestic and familial settings, a determination to write plays set in present-day England ... and a shared model of what had made that England what it was.'[28] So, fair enough, in terms of Rebellato's linkage of these traits to the SONs. However, the rhetorical turn of 'state-of-the-nation' to 'nation-state' is less fair, and produces a more rigid geometry than that which applies to SONs, then or now. The state–nation distinctions Rebellato is using are versions of the terms *dēmos* and *ethnos* in political theory, which have an intellectual history that extends well beyond the present context. In Chapter 4 below we cite Etienne Balibar's use of the terms to discuss the geopolitical situation of the changing configuration that is Europe. In other words, a *dēmos* (or a state) could be either a small community, like a city-state (read Athens), or a federation of larger units (read Europe). Not only does this make 'state' a term that might signify beyond its linkage to nation;

it also makes nation more loosely a 'people' (the meaning of *ethnos*) who share history, kinship, language, culture, and so on, not necessarily joined to particular territory – think diaspora peoples. Furthermore, a state-of-the-nation play can be one that deals with the *condition* of the nation rather than, more narrowly, the relation of the nation to the formal institutional forms of its governance through the state. The Merriam Webster Dictionary offers eight definitions of 'state', and the first given is 'a mode or condition of being'. Only in its fifth definition does it offer the meaning of a literal political body – 'a politically organized body of people usually occupying a definite territory'.[29]

The point is that the unfortunately popular term 'state-of-the-nation' caught on as shorthand for political theatre, much as 'in-yer-face' caught the zeitgeist of the plays it purported to describe in the 1990s, but also severely limited their description. Michael Billington is probably the main source of the popularization of the SON term. The left-leaning *Guardian* reviewer championed the form during forty-five years of reviewing (ongoing), and identified it in his 2007 retrospective on postwar theatre as the 'obsessive concern with using the stage to symbolise and analyse the state of the nation that was to become the animating force in British drama over the next fifty years'.[30] Rebellato comes by the term honestly and mounts his attack with sophisticated attention to the impact of globalization on life within nation-states. For him, the nation-state could no longer be the source of possible 'hope and liberation' because the state had been by-passed by capital while the nation had 'widened to the state level', losing the particularity of the individual.[31]

However, in Rebellato's view this dissociation produced new dramaturgies that identified and engaged with the new conditions: he champions Caryl Churchill's *This is a Chair* and *Far Away* because they stage explicitly the 'experience of radical dissonance and an affirmation of the desire to build connections between the general and the particular'.[32] Employing a Kantian notion of the sublime, he finds the plays that stage sublime dissonance nevertheless 'affirm the desire to express ethical judgment in the world, and the possibility of this judgment even against overwhelming odds'.[33]

We would suggest, however, that *This is a Chair* and *Far Away* can also be seen as SONs, in the sense that they confront the state-in-the-sense-of-condition of collective life in the *dēmos*, where there is a doubleness of the United Kingdom as *dēmos* on the one hand but the global surround as *dēmos* on the other, and where the 'people' are both configured (through language, British casting, venue, etc.) as British *ethnos* but also citizens of the world. The double references actually strengthen the politics of the pieces because they ask spectators to consider their own situatedness locally and globally together. In addition to these plays and the others Rebellato singles out, we would then add to the mix a play focused on governing elites such as David Hare's *Stuff Happens* as well as David Edgar's *The Prisoner's Dilemma*. A different style of play featuring a cross section of British society, Edgar's *Testing the Echo* also operates within this double referential scheme. Its comparison of citizenship tests from Canada, Australia, and the US builds a critique of 'Britishness' along with other national constructions, and calls for cosmopolitan citizenship (or, at least, individual membership in multiple overlapping communities) – a problematic that might touch the Kantian sublime. The point is that the SON label can describe new plays with different dramaturgies; different dramaturgies approach the current SON differentially.

Perhaps it is useful to remember that Caryl Churchill is herself an accomplished SON writer of the type identified with the 1970s: *Cloud 9* (1979) and *Top Girls* (1982) are, as Reinelt argues in her book on British epic theatre, cut from the same cloth as the big SON plays by Hare, Brenton, and Edgar.[34] In addition, a number of early SON plays already pictured the state and nation severed, and looked to a global frame of reference to oppose (dialectically) the state. David Edgar's *Maydays* is surely one of these plays, as much as is Hare's *A Map of the World*, praised by Rebellato. Produced in the same year (1983), both of them ask for audiences to look from an international perspective at more parochial values associated with the state, through the eyes of their protagonists. Surely Brenton's *Weapons of Happiness* (1976) also ruptures the cosy marriage of state and nation by making the Czech communist minister, Josef Frank, come back from the dead as a key protagonist in that work, allowing history and memory to undermine any nation-state exclusivity in its concerns. The truth is that the particular forms of revolutionary socialism that many of these playwrights then entertained were international (or, perhaps better, extra-state) in character: Edgar along with his colleagues was at that time influenced by Marxism. All of them thought about the United Kingdom in relation to a larger geopolitical map, since Marxism believed that contemporary states were simply creatures of the capitalist power structure, and would wither and die once the revolution had come and they no longer had any function. The terminology of SON is the real problem because it covers up a multiplicity of subject matters and dimensions of 'attending to arrangements'.

The other important rejoinder to Rebellato's argument is that the concern with linking the individual to the larger body politic (*dēmos* or *ethnos*, but in any case collective interaction and not inner psychological states abstracted from the social) continues to be a defining imperative of political theatre. Saunders parses his judgments about the in-yer-face writers of the 1990s along these lines, and even in her most abstract plays Churchill never abandons the representation of subjects-in-context (where the context is a set of relations linking her personages to history, to forms of *dēmos*, to conflictual relations of gender, sexuality, race, and class). Mark Ravenhill has written plays set in domestic space without territorial markers, but his characters are still 'types' in a Lukácsian sense, seen against a socio-political context. We are not denying theatrical styles that are anti-realist here, but we are saying that 'political theatre' attends to individuals who are in some sense typical *in situ*, or else imagines alternative worlds that exist in tension with what we know to be the current state of affairs, getting its effects thereby. This need to move beyond the individual subject is acute because it is precisely under neo-liberalism and the ideology of global capitalism and consumerism, that the celebration of the individual has become almost unchallenged in popular western culture. To attempt to offset that atomism is a political aesthetics worth struggling over.

What is no longer tenable, and certainly David Edgar knows it, is a programmatic approach to problems in our contemporary arrangements of sociality. Most of his plays, as he has said repeatedly, are about failure of vision or programme to deliver on emancipation or justice or freedom. From *Maydays* to *Playing with Fire*, Edgar stages the recurrent breakdowns of human attempts to cooperate and legislate – attempts to improve upon arrangements. He has written that his great theme is disillusion, 'the political consequences of disillusion'.[35] Although this remark refers especially to *Maydays*, he returned to this formulation in 2006, when interviewed by Peter Billingham:

> I think the overall theme for me . . . is of coming to terms with the failure of Socialism to live up to the ambitions of its founders. Each new generation comes to terms with that in different ways. But also, why did the idea of a more equal society and – more and more – a society that enables people to emancipate themselves and discover themselves prove to be so unrealisable? How can one get over the waves of disillusionment and avoid the kind of retreat into cynical despair or the defector's march to the Right?[36]

Edgar belongs to a particular age and a generation – that much is true – and his generation developed what came to be called the 'state-of-the-nation' play in the 1970s. Yet looking at work that transcends nation and state from *Mary Barnes* to *Pentecost*, and in Pavis's formulation noted above, most of his plays from *Destiny* onwards are 'problem plays' rather than 'thesis plays', and it seems that he and most of the other major writers of his group transcend the limitations of the category.

Focusing on the details of his political landscape, we find that Edgar's writings address the most basic questions of how humans organize and govern themselves in modern societies. The thematics of his work match up their classical formulations in studies of politics, international relations, and democratic theory. In writing this volume and surveying Edgar's work, we have identified the following list of key problematics:

1. The basic relationships among individuals and society, and how these are shaped by the way people organize (or are coerced by) their lives together to provide security and material benefit.
2. How contemporary modes of such organization – 'nations' and 'states' – create authority, require legitimacy, and generate power.

3. How these forms are institutionalized through constitutions that detail relationships by specifying membership in the group, and the rights and duties of members to one another, embodied in systems of law and justice.
4. How constitutions detail the methods through which the system will be actualized, providing for representation, practical democracy, and some way to pursue public goods.
5. How such institutions protect and balance competing values central to political systems, such as freedom, tolerance, equality, social justice, and welfare.
6. How political communities deal with change, either repressing it, pursuing it through orderly means, or experiencing violent and revolutionary transformation.
7. How opposing regimes deal with one another.

In the second half of this chapter we will take a closer look at Edgar the dramatist, tracing a genealogy that links him to the great modern writers such as Ibsen, Brecht, and Shaw, but also to his contemporary colleagues. We will also discuss Edgar's critical reception in the press, and comment on the typical challenges of his work for producers and audiences.

## Edgar the playwright in theatrical context

> Throughout my writing career, but particularly since the fall of the Berlin wall, I have been fascinated by the process of politics: by negotiations, the drafting of documents, strategising, roleplay and ceremony . . . In the same way that David Mamet's *Glengarry Glen Ross* is about selling real estate but also about ambition, deception and dread, I felt that the deaths of communism, apartheid and Yugoslavia were not just processes it was important to understand . . . but also sites for rich drama about human beings confronting their bitter enemies, risking their own futures and playing for the highest stakes.
>
> David Edgar (2003)[37]

In looking for an entry point to begin to describe David Edgar's dramaturgy, we thought Edgar's passion for political processes came close to capturing the unique focus of his playwriting *oeuvre*. In this statement, he not only identifies some of the theatrical aspects of concrete politics (obvious in role play and ceremony, but equally suggestive as negotiation or strategy) but, in the comparison with the David Mamet play, he highlights the connection between the emotions, psychic investments, and personal struggles of dramatic protagonists and the concrete historical configurations within which they live. He indicates that 'flesh-and-blood' dilemmas of living in global times are important, in fact central, to his concerns, and he affirms once again a political commitment to investigating the present arrangements to which we must attend.

The link to David Mamet here is ironic, because, of course, while Mamet has been admired by some British left-wing playwrights, his true reactionary streak became painfully clear in his 2008 'conversion story', 'Why I am no longer a "brain-dead" liberal'.[38] Edgar cites him in 2003, however, to directly address the possibility that the kind of gritty three-dimensional characterization associated with Mamet's work might also apply to his own.

Edgar has his own narrative about the development of his aesthetics, which moves from an agitprop period to a social realist period to an eclectic mix of styles, sizes, and structures. In numerous accounts, he has written or spoken about his agitprop years with General Will (1971–4), the theatre company in Bradford that he joined after university and for whom he wrote a number of plays in agitprop style. He explains the rationale at the time in terms of an opposition between descriptive agitprop and representational naturalism with its 'individualist assumptions'. Television's domination of popular culture sharpened this difference: 'the dominant form of television drama is naturalism, which shows people's behaviour as conditioned, primarily or exclusively, by individual and psychological factors. The socialist, on the other hand, requires a form which demonstrates the social and political character of human behaviour'.[39] Susan Painter's study of Edgar includes a detailed discussion of the techniques he developed in the plays he wrote for General Will, but for our purposes the most useful part of her discussion is about the techniques of craft he developed which remain useful to him even in the present.[40]

These dramaturgical techniques involved adaptations of Piscator's early documentary theatre strategies, as Painter points out, but seem to us most clearly an adaptation of Brechtian epic techniques for the English stage: juxtaposition of scenes with clear, independent images and actions; economical representation of complex ideas through using images, symbols or gestures; borrowing from other theatrical styles to parody or create satire that carried explanation (such as Victorian melodrama, used to explain the Housing Finance Act in *Rent or Caught in the Act* [1972]). When Edgar abandoned agitprop, his skills in these techniques were still useful in order to communicate complex information economically and to historicize the events of narratives by juxtaposition and episodic structure. In fact, all of the major characteristics of Brechtian epic – episodic structure, historicizing the incidents, use of *Gestus*, and alienation or distanciation effects (Brecht's celebrated *Verfremdungseffekt*) – have been retained and refined in Edgar's corpus of work subsequent to this period. The larger, truly epic plays, such as *Maydays* and *Albert Speer*, probably contain the greatest number of these strategies, but many of the other plays, such as *Pentecost* or *The Prisoner's Dilemma*, also utilize these playwriting techniques to keep prominent the analytic and socio-political elements of the narrative.

Edgar has cited *Destiny* (1976) as the breakthrough play in which he achieved a new style that combined agitprop with realism in a synthesis that historicized individual experiences.[41] Telling the story of four figures, three military men and an Indian servant, whose lives intersect thirty years after Indian independence in the local politics of a midlands by-election, Edgar pointed up the possible rise of fascism within a country that had fought to defeat it in the Second World War. In fact Dan Rebellato quotes Edgar's programme note for *Destiny* in order to set up his perception that in the state-of-the-nation play (of which *Destiny* was the prototype) the state was equated with 'public' and agitprop while the nation was equated with 'private' and realistic characterization.[42] By the time Edgar wrote the introduction to his collected *Plays: One* (1987), he mentioned agitprop in terms of a negation: '*Destiny* is not an agitprop play'.[43] While we analyse *Destiny* in Chapter 4 below in terms of its epic characteristics, it is perhaps more important here to explicate Edgar's understanding of the uses of realism, and to describe his deployment of it. It is as if he gets this term (agitprop) out of the way to make space for the discussion of characterization he wants to develop, based mainly on the theories of Georg Lukács.

Earlier, in 1978, Edgar had turned to John Berger's version of Lukács in *Art and Revolution* (1969) to describe realism in opposition to naturalism (which attempts a faithful representation of the surface of human behaviour) as selectively striving towards the typical. Edgar wrote: 'The actions of people are presented within a "total" context' the central character's actions are felt 'as part of the life of his class, society, and universe'.[44] In the piece from 1987, he identifies *Destiny* (and also *The Jail Diary of Albie Sachs* and *Mary Barnes*, which we discuss in Chapter 5 below) as 'social-realist pieces'. He elaborates:

> That is, unlike symbolist or absurdist or agitprop plays, they present what aspires to be a recognisable picture of human behaviour as it is commonly observed – but, unlike naturalistic drama, they set such a picture within an overall social-historical framework. The characters and situations are thus not selected solely because that's how things are – but because they represent a significant element in an analysis of a concrete social situation. The most popular definition of this endeavour is by Lukács, who said that social-realism presents 'typical' characters in a 'total' context.[45]

The post-structuralist and postmodern critique has developed, however, and 'typical' and 'total' are not exactly edifying concepts today. 'Typical' tends to be read as 'stereotypical', and is criticized for exaggeration and shallowness that often entails bigotry; 'total' sounds like the grand narratives of progress, democracy, the Enlightenment, Modernity – in other words, all the 'totalizations' that Lyotard, Derrida, and Deleuze and Guattari, among many others, have dismissed as oppressive and falsifying. Of course communism is one of these forms of totalization, and Lukács was a Marxist literary critic. However, rather than dismissing his formulation by acknowledging that Edgar and other writers on the Left have moved away from revolutionary socialism, we think it is important to spend a little more time with Lukács in order to argue that he meant something much more nuanced by these terms, and that they in fact can continue to have strong descriptive powers in the contemporary situation.

In the preface to *Studies in European Realism*, Lukács wrote a full account of his idea of realism. We quote two critical passages:

> The central category and criterion of realist literature is the type, a peculiar synthesis which organically binds together the general and the particular both in characters and situations. What makes a type a type is not its average quality, not its mere individual being, however profoundly conceived; what makes it a type is that in it all the humanly and socially essential determinants are present on their highest level of development.

> True great realism thus depicts man and society as complete entities, instead of showing merely one or the other of their aspects. Measured by this criterion, artistic trends determined by either exclusive introspection or exclusive extraversion equally impoverish and distort reality. Thus realism means a three-dimensionality, an all-roundness, that endows with independent life characters and human relationships.[46]

This description of realist dramaturgy still works pretty well – it calls for seeing individuals in their particularity, embedded in the historical context within which they live. In some formulations, it can be a deterministic vision (these individuals behave this way *because* of the conditioning factors in their milieu), but in more sophisticated formulations, arguably from Ibsen and Chekhov to Edgar and Churchill, Hare and Brenton, the dynamic interplay between individuals and their contexts creates effects and affects reciprocally. Playwrights such as Harold Pinter or even Samuel Beckett are sometimes discussed as realist writers because, although they attenuate their representations to a sublime minimalism, aspects of the three-dimensional character *in situ* remain a strong feature of their dramaturgy. Many newer British writers could be called realist in this sense (Roy Williams, Tanika Gupta, David Greig, and Lucy Kirkwood, for example). After *Destiny*, Edgar's next two major plays both featured individual psyches and interiorities as a central focus of the drama. Albie Sachs and Mary Barnes not only gave their names to the plays, they animated the plays. During this period Edgar honed his craft for the ability to achieve this kind of characterization without losing the larger public canvas so important to keeping the focus on the social relations unfolding in an historical moment with attention to their arrangements. *Mary Barnes* embeds Mary within the typical (for the times) attempt to form a utopian community, using the particularity of the psychiatric profession and her remarkable true story to stage the contradictions and aspirations of this type of experiment in living out a set of egalitarian principles. *The Jail Diary of Albie Sachs* dramatized, as we argue in Chapter 4 below, a crisis of leadership within progressive white South African politics at the beginning of apartheid while concurrently examining one person's prison experiences as a test of his political commitments and personal resoluteness.

The skills developed during this period, roughly 1976 to 1979, have remained with Edgar throughout all of his subsequent writing for the stage. The plays that followed take several different forms – for that reason, we do not think the labels 'epic' writer or 'realist' writer are adequate to describe him. He has worked with a canvas that includes aspects of both in different proportion, but there is a third stylistic that also plays a strong role in determining his signature: David Edgar is a rhetorician.

All writers pay attention to words and language – it is what they do. Thus in saying that Edgar's work is especially marked by rhetoric, defined as an emphasis on language and speech in order to create rhetorical effects (where 'rhetoric' is simply 'the art of speaking or writing effectively'),[47] we have not said very much about what is unique to his work, or indeed to any writer's. However, David Edgar privileges words and language as the major scaffolding of his playwriting, and although he also develops image, scene, plot, action, character, and many other aspects of dramaturgy, his major strength lies in the discursive strategies of shaping the meanings and melodies of his stage plays. Of his closest colleagues, Howard Brenton is a stronger poet in the theatre; David Hare writes more emotionally detailed characters; David Edgar writes better dialogue designed to carry argument and conceptual complexity. He does this by employing the craft of rhetoric, ranging from conventions of emplotment to devices such as pointing or echoing. He is the only one of the three who could have written *How Plays Work*, because he is the only one who has systematically and self-consciously developed a compendious knowledge and classification system for dramaturgy across the western canon – not only Shakespeare, whom he can deftly anatomize, but Sheridan, Ibsen, Brecht, and Wilde as well as Brian Friel and Alan Ayckbourn.[48]

Edgar writes clever, witty banter that encodes a deeper thematic meaning (see Chapter 6 below, on *Pentecost*), repetitions with a difference that add up to a final 'drop line' (*Maydays* as well as *The Prisoner's Dilemma*), plots that resemble or invoke detective fiction as their genre motor (or well-made plays with their dependence on secrets from the past) – such as *Speer*, *Playing with Fire*, and *Continental Divide*. All of these and many more 'devices' allow Edgar to represent a double layer of meaning, the general and the particular, or in another formulation, the fiction and the analogous 'real'. Much of the comedy in Edgar's work delights through irony, word play, even punning – this is a writer who loves language and treats it playfully as well as seriously. Although romantic comedy does not come immediately to mind when one thinks of Edgar, scenes of erotically charged low-level flirtation occur in many of the recent plays, including *Pentecost*, *The Prisoner's Dilemma*, and *Playing with Fire*. His adaptation of Ibsen's *The Master Builder* (2010) perfectly realizes the difficult first scene between Solness and Hilde by balancing its combination of playful and menacing eroticism.[49]

The more important exhibition of skilful dialogue occurs in scenes which explicitly deal with negotiation. In negotiations, the drafting of documents, strategizing, role play, and ceremony, his skill at parsing group negotiations through precise attention to dialogue and word choice shines through. In *Destiny*, his version of a community-based political meeting is both funny and frightening as the small irritations of community-based organizing detail typical meeting behaviour and ceremonies, while the gradual amalgamation of positions quite different to each other (high Tory vs petit bourgeois) result in a forged unity under the concept of 'patriotism', actually masking fascism. In *The Shape of the Table*, in which the main action *is* negotiation, the whole regime changes – a peaceful turnover which could not have been predicted at the beginning of the play, but which inch by inch comes to pass through words struggled over at the negotiating table (see Chapter 6 below). In fact, looking at Edgar's plays since *Destiny*, every one of them that we discuss here contains a scene of public negotiation turning on the way words are used, from Albie Sach's interactions with his jailers around testimony and law, to the positions fought over by the gubernatorial candidates in *Daughters of the Revolution* (*Continental Divide*) concerning the wording of the fictional Proposition 92 – the 'Oath of Allegiance'. The specific difference words make is an overarching thematic in Edgar's work, as is complex multifaceted jockeying for position within democratic deliberation. In these negotiations, the ways people communicate through words, and the word choices themselves, are highlighted as a particularly powerful way of 'attending to social arrangements'.

## Edgar and Shaw

> Shaw's ideas may have begun as jokes, but they didn't end there.
>
> David Edgar (2006)[50]

It is probably not surprising that the great modernist playwright who most reminds us of David Edgar is George Bernard Shaw. Superficially, we might note that, like Shaw, Edgar favours prefaces and afterwords or publishes accompanying articles and essays for the plays, contributing a good deal of additional material as background for his dramatic depiction. Edgar has even written an introduction to a volume of Shaw's *Plays Unpleasant.*[51] Shaw, of course, was canonized for his 'theatre of ideas' or his 'discussion plays' (a term he developed in *The Quintessence of Ibsenism* to describe Ibsen's reliance on discussion scenes, but as Christopher Innes has pointed out, it self-described 'the basis for Shaw's drama in a far more direct way').[52] And there are few modern dramatists with lengthier disquisitions than Shaw in a play like *Man and Superman* (although Edgar's *Nicholas Nickleby* and *Continental Divide* also stretch the stage-time of conventional British theatre).

However, if the Shaw and Edgar comparison is to yield any substantial insights, it must come at a deeper level of connection. Edgar himself puts his finger on this affinity when he writes that 'Shaw's great subject was disenchantment, though, as he pointed out, you can't be disenchanted unless you're enchanted first'.[53]

Edgar, of course, has studied Shaw's work, as he has Ibsen's and Brecht's, in great detail. He knows so much about Shaw that he was able to write a comparative review essay for the *London Review of Books* on the 2005 Shaw biography, *Bernard Shaw: A Life*, by A. M. Gibbs, assessing it against Michael Holroyd's multivolume standard. This long essay begins by contrasting Gibbs and Holroyd concerning interpretations of Shaw's sexuality, comments on Shaw's view of the discussion play in Ibsen ('a little dubious'), and moves on to offer Edgar's own view of the heart of Shaw's dramatic gifts, that Shaw 'was able to address the contradictions and difficulties that all thinking socialists come up against, but rarely feel able to articulate'.[54] In what follows, we recognize the great overlap between the socialist dramatist of disenchantment and the socialist dramatist of disillusion: 'The gap between what people believe and the way they live' and 'The fear that, as currently constituted, the masses aren't up to the tasks history has set them'.[55] Discussing the internal contradictions between Shaw's Fabian utopian socialism and his later 'flirtation with Italian Fascism and full-blown dalliance with Soviet Communism', Edgar finds that Shaw's paradox is that 'the deformations of Stalinism both implied and resulted from a rejection of individual emancipation as a socialist goal'.[56] In the following chapters, as we develop as a major theme of Edgar's writing the coming to terms with his generation's disillusionment with revolutionary socialism, we shall have cause to remember that the comparison to Shaw does not only turn on the rhetorical nature of dramatic technique, but also on the pessimism of the intellect and the optimism of the will.

## Edgar and the critics

Journalists love and hate the plays of David Edgar in almost equal measure. Contrast these estimations of *The Prisoner's Dilemma:*

> *The Prisoner's Dilemma* is a clever-clever bloodless drama penned by a boffin.[57]

> This is one of the most urgent and intellectually committed political plays of the past two decades, and it should be seen by everybody who wants to understand the world of wars we live in.[58]

> There are moments when Edgar, who has clearly digested a stack of conflict-resolution handbooks, bombards us with one too many intellectual paradoxes. But in contrast to *Albert Speer*, his last play, which groaned with historical detail, here his erudition and appetite for major subject-matter have paid off. This must be seen.[59]

These three reviews pretty well sum up what David Edgar has come to expect from journalist reviewers – there are some who are overtly hostile and anti-intellectual from the start; there are some who fully appreciate his engagement with the contemporary world, and there are some (maybe the majority) who seem often to give credit with one hand and take it away with the other. In the course of researching this book, we have read most of the press reviews for the twelve original productions of the plays considered here, and along with this range of responses we have also noticed that most reviewers either do not grasp the main thrust of the play's thematics or else describe it rather badly. Part of this is due, no doubt, to the pressures of reviewing that call for instant reactions and written responses to what may be complex events of multilayered theatrical signification; part of it reflects the task of journalism in the increasingly shorter form of review for the general public – quick judgments and showy adjectives to tell a person scanning the review whether or not they should go to the show. Still, the overwhelming impression of the cache of Edgar's reviews is that most often the response of the critics has been genuinely mixed for his most ambitious and densely packed works.

This archive seems to reflect a judgment about how much intellectual content is appropriate to art – rather than a judgment about the politics under review. (Indeed, Michael Billington is one of the critics who often gives Edgar mixed notices, or writes positively of the play in question, but withholds one or two stars so that the quick verdict looks like 'so-so'.) On the other hand, we could find little evidence that certain reviewers always praise or loathe Edgar's work, and that seems like a positive finding since it means that at least they consider each play on its own merits.[60] In the chapters that follow, we quote from these reviews as they highlight or illustrate a point we are making or where the impression of the audience seem critical to our topics, but we do not deal with them extensively. We are much more interested in the longer scholarly considerations that theatre studies colleagues have given the work, because at least, even when the reaction is quite negative, as in the case of Alan Read to *Playing with Fire*, (see Chapter 3 below), it is placed within a full and thoughtful discussion of the grounds for judgment.

In the light of our preceding analysis of Edgar's rhetorical skill and affinity to Shaw, it is amusing and ironic that the two writers have been compared – and not altogether favourably – in several critics' pieces. A key example would be Benedict Nightingale's review of the original production of *Pentecost* at the Other Place, Stratford. The subheading to 'History below the surface' already warns of the mixed verdict: 'Benedict Nightingale reviews the RSC's staging of a "fascinating but flawed" new play by David Edgar'. The first paragraphs are taken up with the (not insignificant) task of describing the premise and action of the play's first act. Apart from the 'fascinating but flawed' pronouncement in the first paragraph, it looks like it will be a largely positive review, and it is. However, here comes the Shaw comparison: 'Indeed, the play sometimes seems likely to turn into a neo-Shavian argy-bargy, asking what's meant by culture, nationhood, West, East, and other grand concepts. It is not until the second half that Edgar transforms those ideas into living suffering people and brings them pell-mell onto Robert Jones's set.'[61] This is the sort of criticism-by-association that the Shaw/Edgar duo elicit: too many words, too many 'grand concepts'. The review continues to connect *Pentecost* with Nightingale's reading of Shaw by way of *Man and Superman*, and concludes in favour of Shaw: 'What we are watching is a demonstration – less lucid, admittedly, than Shaw would have made it – of the tribal mess and muddle that is our world now.'[62] In the last paragraph,

Nightingale does in fact write that he likes Edgar's play: 'I like the idea that human diversity and the complexities of history have their up as well as their down sides.' This sum-up is an illustration of the glib remarks that often characterize press reports on Edgar plays.

For now, we would like to acknowledge an ambivalence in both critical and popular response to Edgar's work. We lack the systematic analysis of audiences that would allow us to generalize about those responses further. However, in closing this section, we would like to discuss some of the factors that can typically affect reception of an Edgar play in production. We have seen multiple productions of *Pentecost, The Prisoner's Dilemma, Continental Divide,* and *Testing the Echo,* and have attended a workshop performance as well as the full production of *Playing with Fire.* Thus at least with regard to Edgar's more recent work, we have some comparative impressions about the impact of venue, casting, staging choices, and the historical moment of production upon the performance and reception of the plays. While we comment on those experiences in the chapters below, it might be helpful to present a short overview here of some viewing experiences that throw light on some aspects of Edgar's plays in concrete production circumstances.

Audiences at Edgar plays need to be able to 'hear' the play at least as much as to see it. It should not be surprising that clarity of diction and speech is at a premium in plays where words matter as definitively as they do in the negotiations of *The Shape of the Table* or *The Prisoner's Dilemma,* or the political arguments in *Continental Divide* or *Testing the Echo.* The complexity of the plots and themes involved, and the emphasis on wit and rhetoric, mean that the language of the plays carries their main valences. If one cannot hear the actors or finds the action muffled or blurred, this surely hurts the play – and the production as a whole. As in staging Shakespeare, 'speaking the speech trippingly on the tongue' is as essential as evoking location through sculpting actors in space (something Edgar's plays need too, especially the large epic plays such as *Maydays).* Two examples, from *Pentecost* and *Testing the Echo,* pertain specifically to the auditory aspects of production and underline this feature.

*Pentecost* brings together a desperate set of refugees from many countries who take hostages in a central European church. Waiting for a response to their demands for safe passage to an EU country and the right to remain, the group begins to tell each other stories, each in his or her own language. The 'Pentecost' scene plays on the biblical idea of speaking in tongues, and depends on an extremely well-orchestrated unfolding of stories which gradually brings the characters into a kind of brief community, as they understand each other across language barriers.

The ease with which a mishandling of this scene can wrong-foot the play was very clear in an otherwise inventive and well-executed production in Los Angeles in 2002. A young and innovative company, the Evidence Room, made ingenious use of a large warehouse-like space, seating the audience on two sides of the rectangle, which served as an excellent spatial approximation of the large, empty church Edgar designates for the setting of the play. A site-specific quality enhanced the realism of the situation, as actors raced down the long length of the room in response to the action. However, because the actors were often speaking with their backs to the audience, it was sometimes difficult to hear the text. Furthermore, in the critical 'Pentecost' scene, the presence of drumming intended to provide rhythm and counterpoint to the stories actually drowned out some of them. The acoustics of the venue were no doubt partially responsible for this problem, in addition to a slip-up in the otherwise crisp direction by Bart DeLorenzo.[63]

The Evidence Room problems created a false impression of the play itself, as was evident when the *Los Angeles Times* critic wrote, 'Only once does Lorenzo's staging falter, in a painfully leisurely sequence evidently meant to induce a trance-like, tribal atmosphere'.[64] Apart from a questionable, even offensive choice of descriptors, the judgment shows how this crucial aspect of the text depends on timing and precision for its effect. A counter-example, when the brief utopian moments of the scene were fully recognized, came in Tony Taccone's excellent productions in Ashland, Oregon, and Berkeley, California (co-produced by the Oregon Shakespeare Festival and the Berkeley Repertory Theatre in 1997).

A gifted director at home with improvisation, Taccone also had a solid voice and text director, Nancy Benjamin, who was part of the artistic team from Oregon who regularly work with Shakespeare productions as their major assignments. The challenge of polyglot speech as well as the wit and rhetoric of a typical Edgar play set many challenges for actors who are not well trained vocally. American actors are often faulted for not handling language well when it is verse or otherwise complex. This ensemble was very good as a result of their combined efforts. Taccone describes some of the rehearsal process:

> The actors came into the rehearsal room and the only person they saw was the stage manager. They were blindfolded, put in a van, and for the rest of the day they didn't hear a single language that they understood. We drove them to a place they did not know, and we had hired two actors who they didn't know who spoke Russian and Polish. They were split up and the rule was they couldn't speak in English to anybody; their stuff was taken from them, and according to the hierarchy of the play, the troublemakers got isolated right away. We had this fantastic speech coach [Benjamin], and she had these different coloured yarns, and she connected everybody in the cast according to who could understand who. They had to develop a vocabulary with the others who understood them.[65]

The result in production was a clarity of diction, rhythm, and pacing which orchestrated the scene to an emotional high – partly because of the sense of urgency that communication was essential to these characters struggling with their own fear and need.

Another example of the difference ensemble work makes to complex verbal interactions comes from the dinner party scene in *Testing the Echo*. In this play, a group of friends and relatives argue among themselves, while the scene is intercut with another scene in which the hostess of the party argues with one of her (Egyptian) students from the ESOL school where she teaches. The dialogue is composed of overlapping speeches (Edgar gives a slash notation in the text to help clarify how this should work). The original Out of Joint production toured the UK, and we followed its progression. As we discuss in more detail in Chapter 4 below, the execution of this scene varied from muddy and unfocused to sharp and clear juxtaposition of character and argument. The role of rhetoric and speech stood out as most important, even in a play such as this one, which is more fluid and less discursive than much of Edgar's earlier work.

The other factor that seems to influence Edgar's reception is the ratio of complexity to clarity on offer within a single viewing. As we have pointed out, many reviewers complain about Edgar's detail and depth as being too intellectual or ambitious, or sometimes just too long. If people cannot follow the action, they sometimes feel patronized or wrong-footed. Michael Attenborough, who is David Edgar's most important British director (along with Ron Daniels for the earlier work), describes this aspect of working with Edgar very specifically:

> There is nobody, David Hare included, who writes with such density and complexity as David [Edgar] does. If he comes to a subject, he comes with research manuals as thick as *War and Peace* – to an awesome degree, he brings a wealth of knowledge, understanding, and perception. The challenge for me as director is to say to David, 'We are rehearsing for five weeks (as happened with *Playing with Fire*), the audience can't read it, and will only hear it the once.' The extraordinary thing about David – the most fascinating thing about working with him – he doesn't have easy political answers, he finds paradox, contradiction, ambiguity, like Shakespeare. The political is circular, not a straight line; this is true about the world, the lives we live, and human personalities. But it can be confusing for audiences, when their brains are being teased. Unconsciously they are waiting for the result; he rarely gives them a result. When you are looking at something so burningly relevant, people say, 'What went wrong? Tell me how to make it work.' [66]

We think that the tension between the sensible experience of performance, where in one short exposure audiences must take in all that is on offer, and the experience of a written text, which can be read, consulted several times and the words parsed, is a classical problem that is more acute in contemporary times when habits of listening have changed and audiences are often not made up of similar language communities or performance traditions. As we move through the discussions of Edgar's *oeuvre*, we will be asking about the capacity of audiences to process the playwright's creations, and also about the nature of the playwright's expectations of his audiences.

In the chapters that follow, we look in Chapter Two at Edgar's adjacent writings and political activism to establish a fuller picture of him as a public intellectual, attending in a number of ways to the arrangements of the British polity and also to a more global cosmopolitan imagined community. This second chapter will draw heavily on Edgar's writings and speeches to establish the extra-dramatic interventions he has made into public discourse on a wide variety of topics from Islamophobia to contemporary politics, censorship, and the need for the NHS to treat overweight people the same as others.[67] The chapter argues that his writings, whether they are in the form of creative work or in review essays for the *London Review of Books* or op/ed pieces in the *Guardian*, need to be read intertextually, as they are part of a deliberate configuration of his persona as an engaged artist participating in activist practice.

Edgar continually experiments with dramatic forms, and Chapter Three begins with his juxtaposition of epic and realist dramaturgies: *Continental Divide* (2003) is actually two plays intertwined around a single focusing event (a fictional political contest for the governorship of a western US state). One play focuses on the political Right, the other on the Left, but they are not mirror images of each other. *Mothers Against*, the one on the Right, is an Ibsenite family drama with a 'secret' centred around preparing a candidate for a campaign debate; the one on the Left, *Daughters of the Revolution*, is the 'quest' adventure of a former political activist seeking to understand what really happened in his past, and takes the form of a Brechtian epic. The two plays are united by their depictions of what has happened to the political idealism of the US sixties – both right and left – as it devolved at the end of the century. In this, they are compared to *Maydays (1983)*, Edgar's exploration from twenty years earlier of how the English Left dealt with the decline of international socialism between 1945 and Thatcher's ascendancy. These three plays, then, represent a large historical canvas, and share a common concern with how individuals respond to events that disillusion them over time, often through various kinds of defection from the movements they originally joined, but in other cases through a faithfulness to the ideals that originally motivated them but that now seem to require another form of behaviour.

Chapter Four on *Destiny* (1976), *Playing with Fire* (2005), and *Testing the Echo* (2008) centres on issues of racial conflict, citizenship, reaction, and reform. This chapter will allow us to look at how Edgar views the impact of thirty years of generational change, immigration and assimilation, economic development, and evolution of political style on the nation's self-concept – in three different incarnations. In the process, this chapter will also allow us to explore another characteristic dimension of Edgar's dramaturgy: these plays involve large casts of characters and no clear protagonist, a compositional strategy used to avoid presenting issues in black and white or some other schematic polarity.

The fifth chapter will group together *Mary Barnes* (1978), *The Jail Diary of Albie Sachs* (1978), and *Albert Speer* (2000) as plays dealing with problems of leadership, but the chapter will go far beyond this obvious feature to question the problems of communitarianism, the effects of isolation on human nature, and the limits of moral defence based on acts of omission. These plays problematize humans' ability to see themselves clearly in relation to their social roles. They also provide major insights into Edgar's dramaturgical style through the way in which his use of Albie Sachs, Joe Berke (Mary's psychiatrist and a leader of the alternative therapeutic community) and Albert Speer, as paradigmatic individuals, develops and then departs considerably from a 'social realist' way of approaching characterization.

Three plays, sometimes considered a trilogy, in which Edgar confronts Europe after communism are the subject of Chapter Six. Beginning with *The Shape of the Table* (1990), which takes place on the very cusp of change, representing negotiations to replace one regime with another – a so-called 'velvet revolution' – Edgar asks what is worth salvaging from the old system and what totally new options are possible in a time of radical change, as well as what can confer legitimate authority on leadership in a situation where most are compromised one way or another by involvement with the former regime. By *Pentecost* (1994), the second play in this group, the disillusionment of those who believed that democracy would quickly translate into a new, just society is the main concern, but this problem is investigated in tandem with several related issues, especially those surrounding the question of how much commonality (linguistic, cultural, historical, etc.) is necessary for a functioning polity (and what size and shape of immigration threatens such necessary homogeneity). *The Prisoner's Dilemma* (2001) searches for a realistic solution to years of ethnic conflict and outside intervention in a fictional country in the Balkans (or a region like the Caucasus). In our treatment of that play, we look at theories of conflict resolution explored through the play and what is possible versus what is likely when the rationalistic processes of something like game theory are applied to human life. In the background, however, are questions of whether the wrongs of the past can ever be righted by devices like truth and justice commissions or must inevitably result in complete separation of the former oppressors and victims; whether 'liberal interventionism' ever really serves the interests of those in whose country the intervention takes place; and how much the outcome of public processes may often owe to private projects and motivations, frequently unrelated to those public events.

In the Afterword to the volume we will return to the subtitle 'Negotiation and Retrieval' in order to read the project of Edgar's career in terms of his determination to persist in finding ways of continuing to attend to the arrangements of the polity by amending them in whatever fashion possible, since 'the form [politics] takes, because it can take no other, is the amendment of existing arrangements by exploring and pursuing what is intimated in them'.[68]

# 2 Intervening in public discourse

## Edgar as commentator and activist

In his role as a public intellectual, David Edgar combines a robust and unique blend of technical skills, creative talent, comprehensive understanding, passionate conviction, linguistic wit, and a capacity for sheer hard work. He grew up in a theatre family, his father an actor and stage manager at Birmingham Rep and then a television producer for the BBC. His mother was an actor and radio announcer, and his aunt Nancy Burman was a theatre administrator, running Birmingham Rep in the 1960s and 1970s. In such a family, Edgar learned early the nature and value of performance and the need to be performative – as well as some of the costs of doing so.[1]

Edgar attended Oundle public school near Peterborough in Cambridgeshire, and then read English Literature at the University of Manchester, reinforcing and developing a lifelong enjoyment of words, rhetoric, wit, and language. He was editor of the college newspaper and developed his political commitments protesting against the Vietnam war and university exam policies. His first employment was as a reporter on the Bradford *Telegraph and Argus*.[2] (Good) journalism entails reporting on, and intervening in, public events and discourse, emphasizes fact-based evidence behind positions, and retrieves significant disclosures from seemingly commonplace phenomena – all valuable skills for a lifetime of writing and activism.

Even as Edgar grew into his playwriting career, he continued to contribute to public discourse through writing for significant periodicals, newspaper opinion sections, and other forums. He has now

Fig. 1 David Edgar.

written over sixty performed and published plays with an extraordinary variety of genres, styles and subject matter. And at the same time that he has produced this body of work, he has contributed articles, columns, and reviews on a wide range of subjects to various periodicals, began and taught the UK's first course on playwriting at the University of Birmingham and paralleled that with his activities to co-found a union for playwrights, which he has lead through several successful kinds of negotiations.[3] He also continues to be a regular participant in political activities, involving everything from the anti-fascist and anti-racist struggles of the seventies to the anti-Islamophobia challenges of the present, as well as more conventional party politics. All of these activities embody his dedication to making/changing the world through committed socio-political endeavour – identifying him as a public intellectual.[4]

We find it useful to consider Edgar's public figure under three primary manifestations: as a prolific creative writer, a respected and skilful analyst of the contemporary world, and as a powerful advocate of complex cultural and political positions. Obviously, these categories inevitably overlap, and this formulation does not assume they will ever be completely separate; but we shall see that Edgar regards the public function of plays and other creative endeavours to be distinct from those of political investigation and analysis, and both in turn – for him – are seen as different from outright advocacy.

In the last chapter, we commented on David Edgar's playwriting *oeuvre*, its main themes and dramaturgical strategies, and placed it in relation to both modernist precursors and contemporary colleagues. In this chapter, we describe the nature of his non-dramatic writings and commentary, and also outline his political activism – the better to complete the portrait of this artist and intellectual.

For Edgar, the play is a unique, supple, and rich art form, which can enhance human understanding of the intricacies of life – especially life in common – through its capacity to dramatize conflict and feeling, to allow audiences to understand complex developments through empathizing with those undergoing them, to override distances in space and time so that the essentials of a situation can be grasped and thought about. Although he acknowledges a certain level of advocacy in his very choice of subject matter, his aim is to explore complexity, to concretize the fact that there are more than two sides to most issues, to leave audiences debating without easy answers. As Edgar says, 'Theatre loves open endings because they can be completed by the audience.'[5] This view of drama informs all of his creative work – scripts for the stage, radio and TV plays, libretti, cinema screenplays, community plays and short stories. Historian and journalist Misha Glenny, speaking of Edgar's *Playing with Fire*, says that 'His blend of unresolved individual political dilemmas against a background of big issues such as community relations and the relationship between central and local government is one of the most mature pieces of political theatre in a long while.'[6] Such fictional endeavours differ from much of his writing for journals, such as the *London Review of Books, Marxism Today, Race & Class*, and the *New Statesman*; or the opinion pages or weekly magazines of papers such as the *Guardian* or the *Independent*. Here the extremely detailed research Edgar has undertaken (frequently in preparation for writing a play) has enabled him to present lucid and insightful analyses of contemporary domestic and international problems, and to 'translate' his understanding of the politics of countries he knows well (such as the US) for the benefit of those with less background. He can serve as the obvious 'expert' to review major new studies in fields such as the massive political change in eastern/central Europe (ECE) in 1989, to explore official reports on fields such as 'arts policy', or to provide witty and incisive commentary on aspects of popular culture. Indeed, in the first half of 2010, to take an example, he published articles on civil liberties, the Labour leadership contest, the BBC, coalition politics in Europe, a comparison of novel-writing and playwriting, censorship and the arts, new playwriting, and a review of studies of patriotism and 'Britishness'.[7]

Related to these activities has been Edgar's effort to help all concerned to understand playwriting as a craft and an art form: developing and teaching (for a decade) the first British postgraduate course on playwriting at the University of Birmingham, organizing conferences on the subject which enhanced dialogue among practitioners and academic researchers, always working with casts and directors of his plays in the progressive development of final scripts. In addition, in 2007 he organized a new initiative to continue this work as a cooperative under the banner of the British Theatre Consortium. Among its projects was the 2009 commission from Arts Council England to survey the state of playwriting during the decade.[8] The report ran to 150 pages of methodological framework, collected data, and extensive analyses, and produced a number of surprising conclusions, the chief of which was that new writing was actually doing much better than anyone suspected: not only were over 70 per cent of plays produced in the last ten years new pieces, but they were increasingly being performed in larger theatres (undercutting the presumption that new plays did not fill seats and were typically relegated to the ghetto of 'studio' theatre).[9]

Lest these endeavours seem an obvious and expected extension of a playwright's career, Edgar ruefully observes: 'Playwrights are not really expected to write about their own business (Brecht has suffered particularly on this score); certainly, they are not encouraged to stray from aesthetics into the fields of public comment and political controversy, and, if they do so, they find their pretensions mocked rather than their arguments contested.'[10]

Finally, there is Edgar the activist and controversialist. From the beginning, Edgar had been a promoter, an activist, a campaigner. In the early years, activism and playwriting were one and the same activity for him – his plays were essentially, and unashamedly, agitprop theatre. But a change occurred during the time he wrote *Destiny*:

> *Destiny* was important to me because it gave me a political life above and beyond political theatre. In the early 1970s, the two were indistinguishable ... In the late 1970s, it was liberating to discover that politics and theatre could operate not simultaneously but in parallel; that I could treat British neo-fascism in one way in the theatre, and in quite another way in articles and speeches for the anti-racist and anti-fascist movement.[11]

Edgar sees his plays as attempts to understand comprehensively how certain phenomena occur. As one result, he has been accused of making characters too sympathetic to those whose positions he abhors (e.g., neo-fascists) – but it is critical to his playwriting that his audiences see how it is possible for someone who fought against Nazi Germany could turn to fascism only two decades later. His writing and speaking about fascism, however, show no such sympathy: there he is concerned to state his opposition in the strongest possible terms. Advocacy and playwriting each have their own place, and each should be positioned to accomplish its particular purpose. His clarity about these different realms seems ironic in the face of critics who, depending on their own politics, fault his plays both for the moral ambiguity of his characters, on the one hand, or for being too doctrinaire or prescriptive, on the other.

All three of these lines of endeavour – playwriting, commentary, and advocacy – then, combine and complement each other in a variety of ways, as Edgar performs the public intellectual.[12] In the end, his aim is 'political' in the very broadest sense, the pursuit of the good for the community, 'amending the arrangements' of the polity: 'He writes, from the New Deal via European post-war social democracy to the desegregation of the American south, the great democratic achievements of the 20th century were brought about by an alliance between the intelligentsia and the dispossessed.'[13]

## Edgar's commentary and advocacy

From the mid 1970s to the time of this study, Edgar has published more than 150 original articles, commentaries, and columns (in addition to an equal number of book reviews, many of the latter being review essays). Somewhat more than half of these are 'advocacy' pieces, about half of that group relating to theatrical/playwriting topics, the other half to a more general range of contemporary issues or subjects. It is beyond the scope of this study to consider all of these writings, so we have selected some major topics which are present – in one form or another – throughout Edgar's career, in order to investigate the way he develops these writings. The topics include: the role of arts in society; political disillusionment; racism/immigration/Islamophobia; censorship and the arts; and the critique of governing bodies and laws.

### *Arts policy*

We begin with an illustration of the kind of commentary and political intervention Edgar can make in the area of national arts policy. In April of 2004, the then Labour Minister for Culture, Tessa Jowell, published a 'personal essay' on public policy and the arts which she said she hoped would initiate an extensive discussion on this subject.[14] Two months later, there had not yet been much public response when David Edgar published a commentary on her essay in the *Guardian*.[15] He began by suggesting that this lack of response was due to its thesis about the value of the arts, one most people already accepted. He then argued that while that might well be the case, her position still represented a major shift in official attitudes towards the arts and arts policy, from market populism to 'traditional' values, and should be examined.

He traced the history of public positions on arts policy, beginning in the postwar era and marked by a patrician attitude to the arts, through to the (different) instrumentalist approaches of the Thatcher and New Labour governments. His conclusion from this brief survey was that Jowell's position represented a very commendable new departure for the government, and ought to be valued as such – up to a point. Edgar charged that 'Jowell edges uncomfortably close to a new social mission for the arts when she argues that culture has an additional part to play "in defining and preserving our cultural identity – of the individual, of communities, and of the nation as a whole".'[16] He interpreted her position thus, showing up its assumptions: 'Jowell defines the purpose of art in defiantly premodern terms as the exploration of the internal world we all inhabit – the world of individual birth, life and death, of love or pain, joy or misery, fear and relief, success and disappointment, revealed to us by artists who can show us things we could not see for ourselves'.[17] There was just one problem, from Edgar's point of view: what artists show us may not be what we want to see. Edgar argues that a central function of art is to be provocative, to 'make things strange', to ask the hard questions. It is when art does that that objections to it arise, and special care must be taken to protect (and support) this vital role. He sums up this rejoinder to Jowell: 'If the arts are to have the centrality to our human experience that Jowell rightly expects of them, the inevitably patrician institutions that provide them need to be challenged and held to account by the spirit of provocation rather than flattened out by the market.'[18]

A number of letters and columns were published in succeeding days debating the merits and demerits of Edgar's position and of Jowell's original arguments. Edgar's piece had succeeded in provoking extended public discussion of this issue. In later *Guardian* articles, playwright Steve Waters commented on both positions, arguing: 'The state cannot prescribe or dictate aesthetics; what they can and must do is secure zones of play and freedom from the homogenising tendencies of the market. Jowell's rallying cry for complexity needs beefing up, but it should be fought for and urgently'. James Fenton, regular *Guardian* columnist, poet, and former correspondent for *Socialist Worker* and the *New Statesman*, meanwhile, took a more belligerent position against instrumentalism:

> It descends from Stalinism, from the old questions of the form: 'What has your string quartet done, comrade, to further the cause of revolution?' One might have expected such perverse rhetoric to die with Stalinism. Instead it morphed into a social-democratic 'instrumentalism' – the arts were to be judged as instruments of social change. The oboe concerto was expected to help young mothers escape the poverty trap.[19]

A month later, Edgar addressed the National Campaign for the Arts conference and rehearsed the debate with Jowell, gaining more exposure for the issues.[20] And later, in June 2006, Tessa Jowell and David Edgar shared the podium as speakers at the Institute for Public Policy Research, where the issues from their previous dialogue were discussed a final time in relation to the conference theme, 'Identity, Culture and the Challenge of Diversity'. Through all of these sources, a full-bodied discussion of the role of art within culture, its relationship to the nation and to its citizens unfolded as a result of Edgar's first intervention.

### *Political 'defectors'*

Another parallel case of 'attending to arrangements' (read stirring things up) from a more recent time involves Edgar's campaign in 2008 to criticize Left sympathizers and activists who had gone over to the (far) Right. This was not a new theme for him; *Destiny* and *Maydays* dramatized how people can make this journey. Indeed, it was one of the central dramaturgical axes in both plays, and following the premiere of *Maydays*, Edgar responded to a negative review by *Guardian* columnist Peter Jenkins, who accused him of exaggerating the defection of his central character, and indeed, the importance of the far left in Britain. Edgar wrote a letter to the editor of the *Guardian* that shows some of his more rhetorical street-fighting skills as well as elaborating on this concern, pointing out that the word 'fascist' appears only once in his play while it appears five times in Jenkins's review (a 'cheap shot' in response to what he considered Jenkins's deliberate misreading of his play). He then restates his main concern with defectors:

> What this sleight-of-hand does is to allow Mr Jenkins to attack the significance and indeed the credibility of my argument, which is that contemporary conservatism, in Britain and elsewhere, cannot be understood without understanding the role of defectors within it. The influence or significance of former left-socialists who have become fascists is of course limited (if any such people exist). The importance of left socialists who are now *conservative* [italics in the original] – from Sherman, Johnson, Valzey, Thomas, Levin in this country to Kristol, Glazer, Bell, Podhoretz in the States ... is another matter altogether.[21]

In this fashion, Edgar took advantage of an opportunity within the context of the discourse around his play to make direct political points about the contemporary situation of key figures on the Right. In newspaper parlance, he parlayed 'culture' into 'politics'.

The political intervention concerning defection was much more direct in 2008, although it again turned on a playwright. As we mentioned above in Chapter 1, David Mamet had renounced being a self-described 'brain-dead liberal' and formally moved to the Right in March 2008. In April, David Edgar published a long essay in the Saturday Review section of the *Guardian* designed to provoke a fresh debate about defectors from the Left. Entitled 'With Friends Like These ...', it did no more than mention the Mamet defection, while its wide scope took up both an historical and a present moment examination of the implications of disengagement from previously held progressive positions by several generations of former Leftists. The thesis of the article appears in its second paragraph:

> Just as past generations sought to reposition the fault-lines of 20th-century politics (notably, by bracketing communism with fascism as totalitarianism), so now, influential writers seek to redraw the political map of our own time. And, intentionally or

> not, they are undermining the historic bond between progressive liberalism and the poor.[22]

Dating his own interest in the topic of defection to the time of *Destiny*, when the Labour government was falling apart and a number of former socialists and communists 'contributed to proto-Thatcher tirades', Edgar mentions Kingsley Amis, Max Beloff, Reg Prentice, Paul Johnson, and Alun Chalfont. He locates a new moment of mass defection in the 2008 present, noting Nick Cohen, Andrew Anthony, Ed Husain, and Melanie Phillips as 'self-confessed deserters'. All had recently published books that had attracted significant attention, and as three of the four were also regular newspaper columnists, Edgar was clearly picking a fight.

The essay he puts forward contains a history of Left defectors responding to what he calls 'Kronstadt moments' (from the 1921 Bolshevik suppression of a sailors' uprising at Kronstadt, the port of St Petersburg). These are times when extreme events provoke communists and radical socialists to renounce their former commitments, such as the Stalinist purges in the thirties, the 1939 Nazi–Soviet pact, the full exposure of Stalin by Khrushchev and the invasion of Hungary in 1956. For Edgar, 9/11 and 7/7 have become present-time 'Kronstadt moments'.

Edgar explored explicitly and at some length the reasons why many activists leave Leftist organizations: 'their authoritarianism and manipulation, their contempt for allies as "useful idiots", their insistence that the end justifies the means and that deceit is a class duty ... and most of all, their dismissal as "bourgeois" of the very ideals that draw people to the left in the first place'.[23] However, he also accused those who have turned to the Right of turning against the people they originally felt moved to defend – usually the poor. The reason for this dis-alliance with the oppressed is, according to Edgar, a kind of anger that these victims do not turn out to be heroic or ideal enough to sustain the wish to defend them. Here, the biting rhetoric of the activist rather than the commentator takes aim: 'The discovery that the poor do not necessarily respond to their victimhood with uncomplaining resignation is as traumatic as the complementary perception that they don't always behave in a spirit of selfless heroism'. This sarcastic derision is then followed up with an account of famous defectors in the UK and the US, detailing the rancour of their revised positions. Irving Kristol's *On the Democratic Idea in America*, according to Edgar, 'blamed the free market for encouraging unreasonable appetites in the working class'; Norman Podhoretz, who once wrote approvingly about the beat generation, now finds 'homosexuality was a death wish and feminism a plague'; Kingsley Amis turned from communist to supporter of Thatcher, opposing the expansion of higher education because 'more will mean worse'.[24]

The real point of the essay, however, was to engage the recent defectors over the Islamophobia apparent in most of their defections. As Edgar perceives it, Muslim Pakistanis and Bangladeshis in Britain were being persecuted and discriminated against, 'particularly during Cohen, Aaronovitch and Anthony's formative years'. Quoting their anti-Muslim statements and attacks on multiculturalism, he charges: 'the culture of betrayal has blinded contemporary defectors to the significant achievements of the alliance between British Muslims and the left'.[25] In so doing, they end up splitting the alliance between intellectuals and the group that is under sustained political attack, the comparatively poor and racial 'outsiders' in a *faux* imperial Britain. Edgar's grievance is that the persuasive power of those who have 'the authority of the convert' influence people away from 'the vocabulary of alliance that has done so much good in the past and is so necessary now'.[26]

Edgar certainly met with quick response and forensic engagement. Andrew Anthony responded on the same day (he must have seen Edgar's column in advance?) with a broadside that engaged the rhetoric as much as the substance; his opening matched every bit of Edgar's derision: 'Do we get the idea that describing the Soviet model, with its vast network of gulags and millions of state murders and total party control as "totalitarian" was a historical error? Certainly that's the suggestion left hanging like a two-pig-owning kulak.'[27]

By 25 April 2008, when Edgar posted his own response to Commentisfree, Oliver Kramm and Denis MacShane had also fiercely attacked the piece. He spends the first few paragraphs directly refuting the claims of his detractors ('I do not think and did not say that totalitarianism was an incorrect description of the Soviet Union [Anthony], but that communism and fascism aren't the same thing').[28]

The most interesting collateral effect from this exchange was the appearance of hundreds of blog comments – it really did provoke a debate over substantial social issues. A lot of the blog comments might appear stupid or pointless, but the majority of them weigh in (on one side or another) in an attempt to parse out the most important elements in the debate.[29] Indeed, we think the democratic struggle that makes democracy real can be seen in the 'long anger' of this debate, as an illustration of what political theorist Chantal Mouffe has repeatedly insisted is a key feature of any democratic political community – 'agonistic pluralism' – the friction and clash that 'clearly differentiated positions and the possibility of choosing between real alternatives' constitutes democracy at its most embodied and real.[30]

We find Mouffe's formulation compatible with Edgar's conception of a suitable performance of public intellectuals: they ought to be prepared to survey the social, economic, political, cultural, and intellectual environment, and contribute to our better understanding of it – partly by providing informed background, context, and perspective; partly by advancing controversial evaluations or critiques; partly by pointing out unconscious assumptions or stereotypes. These kinds of contributions are essential to the general discourse that shapes public opinion.

Most writers experience social pressure to perform such a role, but many shun away from it because it does not reflect their self-understanding of themselves as writers. Edgar, on the other hand, sees the role of public commentator as central to his own vocation as a writer, at least partly because he began his writing career in journalism. It is possible, of course, to make too much of Edgar's early training as a journalist, but it should certainly not be overlooked. While not a narrow empiricist, he does show – in his plays, his commentaries, and his argumentative work – a constant concern for the facts of a case. A journalistic training in interview techniques and information gathering which emphasized the need for hard evidence for conclusions is certainly essential for someone who wished to affect the public conversation about important issues in a persuasive way. Sometimes Edgar's journalistic practice shades his activist agenda. His rhetorical skills mean he can make a clever comment or puncture an opponent's argument in ways that feature verbal dexterity and wit at the expense of the close argument he pursues on other occasions. (These balance out for us, if regarded from a full cognizance of his multiple 'performances'.)

## *Edgar and the academy*

One result of Edgar's endeavours to produce well-grounded examinations of current issues based on significant research is that his work is used extensively by theatre historians as evidence for their own research work. Studies by theatre scholars such as John Bull, Stephen Lacy, Simon Jones, and Baz Kershaw cite Edgar as part of their historical surveys.[31] Graham Saunders, in *Cool Britannia*, begins with Edgar's version of political theatre history as a succession of waves signalling renewal (if only to question it) and later he makes extensive use of Edgar's theorizing about 'faction', his term for drama which is completely fact-based but not necessarily tied to history 'exactly as it happened'.[32] Edgar's published work in *New Theatre Quarterly* and *Contemporary Theatre Review* have also put his ideas into academic discourse, as have his frequent lectures at academic conferences. His collection of essays, *The Second Time as Farce: Reflections on the Drama of Mean Times* (1988) made a major contribution to cultural history with a series of essays on the pre-Thatcher era and the Thatcher years, reflecting on the theatre's development during this period but also commenting on the wider political scene. The volume's essays on fascism come from the period following *Destiny* but are not limited to a playwright's perspective; the analysis of the New Left and its contradictions is the work of a political commentator who happens to be a playwright. The original sources of these essays ranged from the *New Socialist* to the *Listener*, and from *Race & Class* and *Marxism Today* to the *Guardian* and the *Times Literary Supplement*.

Actually, Edgar gained credence in the academic world by partially joining it. Already by the mid seventies he was contributing to the work of undergraduates at the University of Birmingham through a fortnightly seminar on playwriting, and by the late 1980s he had developed this into a full-blown course as part of the M.Phil. at Birmingham. Typically, he did not frame this work primarily as an attempt to invade academia, but as an extension of work he and others were already engaged in to support and assist playwrights, especially beginning ones (through the Theatre Writers' Union and subsidiary organizations):

> The most prominent self-help group was the Manchester-based Northwest Playwrights, founded in Manchester in 1982 by the local branch of the Theatre Writers' Union. There were also groups in the North East, and, later, in the West Midlands. Three of the underlying principles of the Birmingham course, then and now – that it is taught by practising playwrights, that it combines theoretical exploration with work on student texts, and that it involves live performance of students' work – were principles that defined the self-help movement.

Edgar taught the course from 1989 to 1999, when he passed it on to other playwrights, and some 115 students took it over this decade, a number going on to work as dramatists themselves – including Steve Waters, who now runs the M.Phil. at Birmingham in addition to his creative work, Sarah Wood, Lucy Gough, Amy Rosenthal, Charles Muleka, Fiona Padfield, Clare Bayley, Helen Blakeman, Ben Brown, and Edgar's partner, Stephanie Dale. Sarah Kane was also enrolled on the course, though not felicitously – as Edgar has commented: 'And, sure, I'm proud of Sarah Kane, who was not polite about the course, but who came to Birmingham determined that the only dramatic form of any worth was the monologue and left having written a three-hander called *Blasted* (the world premiere of the first half of which was her performance piece).'[33] Edgar also eventually revised and published the material he used in the course as *How Plays Work* in 2009, and it has become a university text in a number of courses. Its approach reflects the fact that Edgar believes playwriting to be partly a product of individual creativity, and partly a set of skills to be learned, individually or socially. He discusses the western canon in terms of its basic dramaturgical elements (action, character, genre, structure of scenes and plots, and special devices). The best parts of the book are his close readings of how key scenes work in Shakespeare or Sheridan, Brenton or Churchill, showing once again his command of the entire anglophone theatrical tradition. We point out some of the ways Edgar's own plays make use of his 'devices', especially in *The Prisoner's Dilemma* (see Chapter 6).

In tandem with this course, Edgar organized and put on an annual conference on playwriting and theatre at the University of Birmingham, with topics such as 'new writing', 'regional theatre', 'theatre and nationalism', and 'the role of text in theatre'. These conferences, in both their presentations and their invited attendance, deliberately joined together practitioners of theatre – writers, actors, directors – with academics, as Edgar felt such cross-fertilization was not only vital but long overdue. He published a collection representing ten years of these discussions in *State of Play: Playwrights on Playwriting* (1999), beginning with an extended historiographic essay putting theatre of these years in the larger postwar context ('Provocative Acts: British Playwriting in the Post-war Era and Beyond').[34] This essay has also been much cited by theatre scholars, such as Stephen Lacy.[35]

## *Research offshoots*

Some of Edgar's work has received a wide hearing as a result of its appearance before the public in various forms. As we pointed out in Chapter 1, the essay 'Ten Years of Political Theatre, 1968–1978' had three formal publications in two journals and a book (*Second Time as Farce*). Another example of Edgar's ideas appearing in several places for different audiences occurs with his account of the splintered harmony between street theatre, social realism, and performance art towards the end of the seventies. He put forward his ideas in a talk at the annual conference of the Political Studies Association and offered a version to the English faculty at Oxford University, published it in the *Times Literary Supplement* (1982), and finally published it in the introduction to *State of Play* (1999).[36]

As we have indicated, Edgar's plays are extremely well researched. A side effect of that research skill is that Edgar is often asked to provide book reviews in fields where reviewers are ordinarily chosen for their academic expertise. When the *Guardian*, for example, wanted a reviewer for the flood of new studies of eastern and central Europe that came out in the year following the 1989 events in that region, Edgar was the one to contribute an extensive and informed review essay on the subject.[37]

For the 2009 Arts Council report 'Writ Large', Edgar drafted the historical overview of the fate of new writing for the English stage and the evolution of institutional responses and support (or lack of it) for new plays. Most of what was known – and debated – about this subject was impressionistic or anecdotal, and the group's report set out empirically what the state of play really was.[38]

Allied to these efforts for both the general public and the more specific public of theatre-oriented people was Edgar's effort in organizing and promoting the work of playwrights. In 1975, for the first time, what had been expanding levels of subsidy for theatre work were clearly going to be cut back. Edgar was part of a group that met to consider that policy shift, and was involved in co-founding the Theatre Writers' Union as a response. He was active in this group from the start, eventually becoming its president, as it sought to negotiate what its membership saw as a much needed revision in the way playwrights were paid for their work. This union work provided Edgar with an insider's look at the nature of negotiations and the relationship among the activities of negotiation, the problems of representation of the larger membership, and the outcomes of such talks, which would later inform some of his plays; but in the short run he also learned a lot of practical skill in promoting the interests of his colleagues and himself. Eventually, the Theatre Writers' Union proved to be too small to accomplish its aims, and so he led the group into the larger Writers' Guild, where it now resides. He first became president of the Writers' Guild in 2007, and was re-elected in 2009, a term that will last until 2013.

## Edgar as activist

David Edgar was 20 and at university in 1968. Like many others of his generation, he was caught up in the surge of political optimism of that moment, and shared in the generally leftist analysis of the ills of existing society and the dreams for a comprehensively better future. For many, such ambitions made for some amalgam of the late sixties' counterculture approach to human community blended with a Marxist analysis of socio-economics. 'I was trying to find ways to write about socialism, about the working class, from my own background ... What I could offer was a reasonably analytical mind and a talent for research ... There was a very conscious, a very strong feeling: what can I do, what contribution can I make?'[39] In Britain, such endeavours on the Left took a particular turn at the beginning of the seventies because the British economy weakened seriously in those years, while the trade union movement became much more active. It seemed to many on the Left that some kind of workers' revolutionary activity might be possible after all. Since Soviet-style Communism did not seem promising (especially after the Red Army crushed the Prague Spring in 1968), these factors pushed those with revolutionary ideas towards Trotskyist thinking, since from that ideological perspective it was possible to criticize the USSR from the Left while still holding out hope of an eventual worldwide workers' revolution. Edgar's efforts to make a 'contribution' in these circumstances led him to write a large number of agitprop plays, dramas deliberately kept simple to put across Marxist ideas and motivate the working class for action. The problem with this work, he discovered, was that although agitprop was aimed at the working class, the audiences his plays were finding were distinctly middle class and already seemed mildly sympathetic to his perspective. They did not need to be won over; he was singing to the choir.[40]

As we have seen above, writing *Destiny* in the mid seventies provided an answer to the dilemma this raised. Although this play was not entirely clear of agitprop elements, its success as a fully formed drama enabled Edgar to see that he could work in the future in parallel: write plays to explore the complexities of contemporary political developments and at the same time pursue other activities – journalism, organizing, speech-making, marching, debating – that might have more of a chance of influencing the political future of the working class. *Destiny* also provided a principal focus for his early development of these aims: the interconnections among racism, xenophobia, and fascism. In the mid seventies this was a powerful focus, as the National Front had gained considerable ground by emphasizing issues of immigration and 'law and order' during the decade.

So Edgar went to work, not only writing *Destiny* but also publishing six other articles on the National Front, anti-Semitism, racism, neo-Nazism, and immigration by the end of the decade. He helped organize demonstrations, made speeches, and pursued other forms of political activism. Such endeavours began to challenge some of his Marxist outlook. Whether in traditional or Trotskyist form, a Marxist analysis began and ended with class struggle: issues such as racism or feminism were definitely epiphenomenal, or some form of 'false consciousness', produced to hide the real importance of class. But the politics Edgar was dealing with no longer seemed to be structured along the single axis of class. The working class was slowly evaporating in advanced industrial countries by then, anyway, while phenomena such as racism and, later, feminism and environmentalism seemed to have an independent valence all their own. Marxism would remain a bedrock starting point of political analyses for Edgar, even down to the present; but it became more and more clear that the overall political problems of the day stemmed from far more complicated causes – and their solutions, if they had any, would require far more complex visions than those of Marx and Engels in 1848. As Edgar says, looking back from the present:

> Where do I position myself now? I'm a left-wing social democrat in a tradition that goes back through the twentieth century; I'm very much reminded of the Fabian tradition within British Labour and left-wing politics. I always hesitate now when people ask me, 'Are you still a Marxist?' Well, no, I'm not a Marxist in that it's not serious to say – as did the original Communist Manifesto – that 'Workers of the world unite, you have nothing to lose but your chains.' I'm not a Marxist because I don't believe that solution is workable. Am I a Marxist in terms of do I think that Marx is right and that he gets righter and righter and righter in terms of his analysis of capitalism, imperialism and

> globalization? In that sense I still am, but thinking that there remain severe and dramatic limitations.[41]

This kind of change in Edgar's political outlook has happened over a number of years, but it was already underway by the late seventies. In practical terms, it meant that he could focus his political activities on separable critical issues of the day (without always needing to refer them back to the class struggle) and could make alliances in action with individuals and groups that a Marxist more concerned with his ideological purity might disdain. By 1981, Edgar would even become a member of the Labour Party (which, it should be remembered, still had a serious left wing to it at that time).

At the time he wrote *Destiny*, Edgar's conception of what the appropriate tactics for political activism should be were built on the premise that a people like the British, who had recently endured an horrific war against Nazism, would not knowingly take up Nazism for itself. His conviction was that the majority of the voters did not realize the extent of the connection between the National Front and Nazism, and that if they understood the true nature of the party, they would reject it. Therefore it is not surprising that his activism during this time took the form of working with the Committee Against Racism and Fascism and the Anti-Nazi League, including serving as a speaker at over fifty of their events during the decade.[42] The Anti-Nazi League was created in 1977 in an alliance between the Socialist Workers Party and several trade union groups to bring together left and liberal activists to fight the rise of right-wing groups. Along with marches and organizing, Edgar devoted a good deal of energy to writings with titles such as 'The National Front *Is* a Nazi Front'[43] and 'Achtung!',[44] aimed at informing the public about the real aims and structure of the National Front; or writing for a US periodical that primarily addressed itself to a Jewish audience (*Present Tense*), in which he emphasized both the hidden anti-Semitic agenda of the National Front and the fact that as its aims and activities were becoming better known in Britain, opposition to it had been growing.[45]

He could also see the merit in activities such as the Anti-Nazi League's 'Evening of Music and Comedy Against Racism', a blend of cultural event and politics that a more traditional Marxist might find illegitimate or compromised. The Anti-Fascist League sponsored a huge carnival/rock concert in 1978 with the intention of targeting young people with their message. Edgar spoke about these activities some years later (1982) to the National Anti-Klan Network Conference in Atlanta, Georgia:

> I am convinced that the Anti-Fascist League and its carnival achieved three major successes. One was to convince the country that the National Front was really a fascist organization. Second, to pare down the National Front vote to the absolute hard core of its racist supporters in the general election. And third, it prevented, if only for a while, the Nazis from making significant inroads into working-class white youth.[46]

His writings during this period were polemical – written with rhetorical skill to accuse, underline, and create an impression, not necessarily to argue carefully and systematically – this is the activism part of the writing. For example, in October of 1978, in the run up to the general election, Edgar wrote an opinion piece for *The Sunday Times* which argued that the BBC should cancel coverage of the National Front campaign and not give it neutral, uncritical attention. For someone like Edgar, for whom freedom of speech was/is a primary value, this was a strong statement. He details the programme of the National Front and compares its racial policies to the Nazis, stressing that the NF believed in an international Jewish conspiracy and that 'the Black, Asian and Jewish "races" represent a *threat* to the existence of the British nation' (italics in the original). The argument against allowing the NF election coverage hinges on their ideology based on biology, and Edgar insists that 'broadcasting companies cannot and should not be neutral about racialism (of this form or any other)' and quotes the BBC's testimony to the Annan Committee that a racially intolerant person does not have the right to the same treatment as a person who condemns racial intolerance.[47] In all of his writing on this issue, Edgar stressed that the National Front was a Nazi party with no redeeming virtues (see Fig. 2). He reviewed a number of books on the National Front between 1977 and 1982 that were, in his opinion, insufficiently

Fig. 2 The cover of *Race & Class*, pamphlet 4 (1977).

critical or accurate in their portrayal of the party. Besides the specifics of his criticism of authors Martin Walker, Paul Wilkinson, Stan Taylor, and Nigel Fielding,[48] Edgar always inserted his own analysis of the specifics of the National Front history and ideology to make the pieces arguments in their own right against the party. All of these ways of combating the threat of fascism in Britain added up to a strong activist contribution to the anti-racism struggle.

Looking back on these activities of the seventies from twenty years later, Edgar argued:

> I wrote a play, called *Destiny*, which is about the rise of the National Front in the late 1970s. It contributed as a minor part of an overall campaign to persuade the public that the National Front was not just an anti-immigration pressure group, it was a Nazi organization. That campaign, along with a number of other factors such as the election of Margaret Thatcher and our electoral system, created a much more arid climate for the extreme right – one of the reasons why it has done so badly here compared to some other European countries.[49]

At other points in later years, Edgar emphasized the fact that the anti-National Front campaigners in the seventies did not see how powerful the appeal of Margaret Thatcher's own anti-immigration positions would be – had they understood that at the time, they might have been somewhat less concerned about the threat posed by the front, since the Tories appeared to gain a lot of electoral support from precisely the groups that might have been susceptible to the front's appeal.

By the early eighties, Edgar's activism, combined with the direction of domestic politics in that decade (Thatcher in the UK, Reagan in the US), led him increasingly towards the support of those movements – multiculturalism, feminism, environmentalism – he and others on the Left judged progressive, without regard to their immediate connection to industrial struggle (although he supported the miners' strike, and wrote *That Summer* in 1987).[50] In 1985 he felt obliged to provide a qualified defence of the Live Aid Concert,[51] and to articulate the better outcomes of the sixties against backlash from both the Right and the Old Left in 'It wasn't so naff in the 60s after all'.[52] In these defensive pieces, he had begun to pinpoint the attacks on progressive movements from those who had once led and supported such movements, but who had now moved to the centre or all the way to the right in their politics. On the creative side, such an interest in the politics of defection – combined with his personal experience of revising his own views on the incipient revolution – led directly to *Maydays* in the early eighties.

In more recent times, his strong conviction that intellectuals must intervene and criticize the post-9/11 patriotism which has conceptually re-divided the world into a binary 'us and them' around 'the clash of civilizations' between the West and Islam has found Edgar engaged both intellectually, as in his 2008 defectors essay and other pieces of journalism, and creatively in his plays about multiculturalism and Britishness in the late noughties: *Playing with Fire*, *Testing the Echo*, and his contribution, 'Black Tulips', to the plays about Afghanistan at the Tricycle under the umbrella title *The Great Game.* However, some aspects of the campaign against Islamophobia have put severe pressure on other areas of Edgar's committed practice, as is nowhere more evident than the '*Behzti* affair' in his own Birmingham 'back garden'.

In his accounts of the postwar history of the British theatre, Edgar has always identified abolition of official stage censorship in 1968 (after 250 years of such control) as a crucial element in the flowering of drama in the last half-century. Recurrently, over the years following, he has found himself writing and joining with others in protests to defend freedom of expression in the theatre and outside, as new challenges have appeared. Indeed, among his signature positions is the championship of freedom of speech. So, in 2004, when the Birmingham Rep cancelled the run of Gurpreet Kaur Bhatti's play *Behzti* after only ten performances due to mob violence,[53] he had – he thought – pretty well mapped out his position on this issue: a Voltaire-style defence of absolutely free expression. However, in the major essay he wrote for *Race & Class* to reconsider the overall issue,[54] he confessed he 'found [him]self unexpectedly, uncomfortably and unusually tempted by the fence [i.e., a position in the middle]'.

The *Behzti* events became a flashpoint for debate concerning not only censorship, but also the criteria for good governance in a multicultural society. The play had been in rehearsal at the Birmingham Repertory Theatre (BRT), and the theatre had recognized that the material would be controversial for the substantial Sikh community that lives in the city. The play depicted rape and murder within a Sikh temple (Gurdwara), and criticized the hypocrisy of Sikh elders and the complicity of some women in their own oppression. It also portrayed a young woman fighting against her own abuse at the hands of her family and friends, and also against the institutional repression of the Gurdwara while maintaining her Sikh faith. In the run up to the premiere, the theatre consulted with members of the Sikh community, and made a number of modifications in the staging and script, supporting, however, the playwright in her judgments about what could be changed and what was essential for the play, as she saw it.[55] Nevertheless, when the play opened there was significant dissent expressed through protests outside the theatre. Over the next ten days these grew, and on 18 December 2004 there was a riot which injured five policemen and damaged the theatre and backstage area considerably.[56] The theatre took the decision to cancel the rest of the play's run on the grounds they could not guarantee the health and safety of patrons, and the playwright received a number of death threats. This situation was immediately seized upon by the press and media, and the debate over 'censorship' went on across most organs of the British public sphere. The difficulty, of course, was that the issues were not clear-cut, and the principles invoked were seemingly contradictory. As Helen Freshwater characterized it, 'The heat generated over the closure of *Behzti* surely indicates that we have to face up to the tension between the liberal ideals of freedom of expression and respect for cultural difference ... Evidently, finding a balance between competing commitments to freedom of expression and respect for cultural difference is difficult to achieve'.[57]

For David Edgar, years of living in a south Asian neighbourhood, deep political involvement in city and community politics, and long-time connections to BRT meant that he was an insider to these issues in a very direct way. When he confessed a divided mind about this issue, he went on to locate his 'unease', primarily in the hypocritical way in which a number of sources were using the argument for free speech basically to put down minority communities (in this case, Sikhs) and argue for the superiority of European culture, religion, and politics. While Edgar rejects absolutely the belief that to represent is to enact, which he argues is the ground of many contemporary arguments to censor or limit speech, he also realized that the events at BRT were not simple by any means, and that theatres and theatre artists needed to address 'knottier questions about how theatres who want to represent the communities around them should respond when parts of those communities don't like what they hear'. In his essay 'Shouting Fire: Art, Religion and the Right to be Offended', Edgar parsed the relative values at stake within French democratic ideals: 'So, lest we forget: while *liberté* is a necessary condition of social wellbeing and justice, it is not a sufficient condition. Indeed, in the absence of *egalité* and *fraternité*, there are circumstances in which *liberté* can be a tool of rejection and exploitation. While individual free speech is an absolute (though, in its current form, a very recent gain), it does not stand alone.'[58] Collective action is necessary, Edgar said, first of all to protect freedom, but secondly to determine a community's true position on an issue. In the end, it may be right to be offended, but being offended sometimes may be the price of living in society. He challenged the 'smug, self-satisfied and patronizing' attitudes of German and British journalists in response to the Danish cartoon affair, and recognized, especially, a tendency that he had criticized repeatedly in those he considers 'defectors':

> When we read progressive and liberal thinkers condemning young Muslims and Sikhs for attacking free speech, don't we hear echoes of previous generations of progressives who felt betrayed by the people they were standing up for and used that feeling of betrayal as an excuse for abandoning them? In particular, aren't we reminded of the first generation of American neo-conservatives, who used what they saw as the excesses of the late 1960s – particularly the criminalisation of the Black Panthers – as an excuse for abandoning the civil rights struggle?[59]

This line of argument, however, is not the main message of the essay. It is a qualm which Edgar acknowledges and struggles with, but in the end he reasserts the overwhelming need for the principle of freedom of speech to trump these concerns. The early part of the essay lists a number of cases of unofficial censorship or suppression that came about because people confused portrayal (representation) with enactment and/or approval. His examples range from the Christian campaign against *Jerry Springer: the Opera* to the firing of *Daily Mail* reporter Jane Kelly for painting a picture of Myra Hindley as well as a number of other recent and more historical examples.

Edgar is here building an argument that the disappearance of *official* censorship is being supplanted by numerous forms of *unofficial* censorship – including self-censorship – or that limits to expression are now coming from other, perhaps well-intentioned quarters (e.g., banning hate speech). Some of these unofficial forms are particularly threatening to theatre, because, among other things, well-made plays represent evil skilfully on stage: 'Without the comforting authority of the [novelist's] voice, playwrights find themselves in even more difficult territory ... not only is it hard to draw the line between presenting, defending, and promoting a character (or a relationship) but often that ambiguity is at the very heart of the dramatic project.'[60] That 'life is a tale told by an idiot, full of sound and fury and signifying nothing', may or may not have been Shakespeare's own view. We only encounter it as the speech of one of his characters and have to understand it with all the particularities of its location in the play, and, indeed, in the world.

In the end, although perhaps far from Voltaire, Edgar finds he must still opt to defend as broad a freedom of expression as possible, because it is essential to story-telling, especially dramatized stories. Humans, he claims, need such freedom for at least four major reasons: (1) to imagine other worlds and other times than our own; (2) to be able to plan future lives by being able to see what the consequences of different courses of action might be; (3) to be able to empathize, even with those called evil or monstrous – being good is not possible without knowing what evil is possible; (4) to be able to imagine what the world looks like through another's eyes – to escape in limited ways from the imprisonment of our own subjectivities. In this way, freedom of expression and story-telling are vital to our lives together as humans, because they develop the skills necessary for interaction in society, especially the ability to see things from another's point of view. Freedom of expression is even more important for the listener than the speaker, and therefore for the entire society.[61]

We have certainly not attempted to survey all of Edgar's performances as a public intellectual here, but rather to give some useful sense of the range, calibre, and purpose of his endeavours in this regard. Like many of the Left, he seems committed to the idea that much that is harmful in human public life is the result of ignorance (partial or full), and so the primary thing needed for improvement is solid knowledge and deep understanding, both leading to the possibility of genuine empathy and solidarity. The extent and the nature of his activities as a commentator and as an advocate strongly embrace this orientation, reflecting an optimism about socio-political improvement perhaps not fully supported by much recent history. His preoccupation with disillusionment comes from just such impossible-to-resolve dilemmas and conflicting values. If the anti-Nazi struggle of the 1970s was unambiguous and unassailable in its goals and aims, the complexities of the politics of difference as they have unfolded during the past three decades have made simple positions impossible, but principled interventions no less important.

Following 9/11 and 7/7, the upsurge of anger and discrimination against Muslims has turned Edgar once again towards activism, and although the debates are complex and fraught, he has spoken and written a good deal in an attempt to persuade left and liberal members of the public to maintain what he considers their historic alliance with the poor and oppressed. His criticism of defectors in 2008 – that they were giving up on the poor through their Muslim-bashing disregard for the most oppressed members of their society – is the core of Edgar's attack on Islamophobia. It involves him in some matters such as the *Behzti* affair that strain against clear partisanship, and push against his ability to champion both freedom and equality in the same breath. In this case, he does not satisfactorily resolve the contradictions, and we cannot agree with the weight he affords the principle of free speech, believing that the relative values of any particular speech act are held in tension with the values of context and moment. We do share Helen Freshwater's conclusion that 'The debate over *Behzti* indicates that the application of the abstract principle of freedom of expression is fraught with provisionality and conditioned by context'.[62] Nonetheless, it is overwhelmingly clear that David Edgar has made – and continues to make – an extensive and intensive impact on public understanding and public dialogue on an impressively wide range of matters over the last four decades. The persistence with which he argues his case(s) and challenges the blind spots of dominant hegemony establish him as a formidable presence in British public life. The study of his plays, to which we now turn in detail, needs to be viewed continuously together with his other contributions to popular discourse, if a full portrait of the artist is to emerge.

# 3 Things fall apart

## After ideology in *Maydays* and *Continental Divide*

> Socialism is an international movement which does not demand a rigid uniformity of approach. Whether Socialists build their faith on Marxist or other methods of analysing society, whether they are inspired by religious or humanitarian principles, they all strive for the same goal – a system of social justice, better living, freedom and world peace.
>
> The Frankfurt Declaration (1951)[1]

Throughout all of David Edgar's work, there runs a red thread of political commitment to democratic socialism. He does not advance it so much as he assumes it: social justice, emancipatory movements, class analysis, critique of capitalism – all of these values and practices underpin his creative writing as well as his non-theatrical works. This list of qualities is, however, carefully chosen – our readers will notice we list class analysis, not class struggle; critique of capitalism, not Marxism-Leninism; emancipatory movements, not revolution; and social justice, not collective ownership of the means of production. In short, we are looking at a fairly capacious definition of socialism that can be attributed to Edgar throughout his career, to cover a powerful continuity of outlook. Of course, at various moments along the way the particular political vision he has held and the particular allegiances or practices that seemed efficacious were more radical, perhaps, but as his politics has evolved, these values fundamentally remain.

What characterizes the kind of politics Edgar embraces is indicated by his age: born in 1948 and coming of age in the 1960s, Edgar belongs to a generation who redefined the meaning of the term 'Left' from an earlier era of pre-war and wartime activity more closely tied to Soviet-style Communism and the earlier formulations of Marxism seen in Leninism and Trotskyism. The cause-driven movements of the sixties, beginning in the fifties with anti-nuclear (UK) and civil rights campaigns (US), blossomed in various combinations and amalgamations, many with Marxist or socialist socio-economic agendas. The promise of that time was precisely to create new ways of living together, new organizations of life in common that could encompass a variety of goals and achieve a new political order. The experiences of many of us, however (as we are also of Edgar's generation), proved that while some considerable positive changes in the situations of women, blacks, gays, the poor and former colonials were realized (and arguably the Vietnam war ended as the result of activism), they were accompanied by considerable disillusionment and substantial failure in terms of any lasting structural changes in the apparatus of advanced capitalism; nor were there any truly revolutionary achievements on view in matters of state organization and function. Furthermore, the sectarian battles among the Left and the internal divisions in, for example, the women's movement and black power struggles caused many to face up to the difficulty of acting in common, defining and implementing policies or even platforms that could result in really existing changed circumstances – call it socialism, racial and/or gender equality or sexual freedom.

As this generation began to move into middle age sometime in the late seventies or early eighties, the central preoccupation of many became the analysis of how the emancipatory vision had gone bad. With the collapse of the Soviet system and the dissolution of the cold war, those who identified with the Left began to painfully piece out what could be salvaged, and in what form, from a project that in its statist manifestations had utterly failed, but in its aspirations, aspects of its analysis, and some accomplishments, remained valuable and necessary. The plays discussed in this chapter, together with those of Chapter 4 (and aspects of Chapter 5), demonstrate David Edgar's historical project of dramatization, critique, and retrieval of the political vision of this period.

An additional aspect of Edgar's own biography marks his perspective. Classically, the Left has always been perplexed by the role of the intellectual in making the revolution. While Edgar's class position is basically that of a petty bourgeois intellectual (from a theatre family), that is precisely the stratum from which many of the New Left theorists and commentators in fact emerged. This group often also included 'red diaper' babies from working-class backgrounds as well as children of teachers and librarians, who took advantage of new educational opportunities and became professionals or academics imbued with a sense of responsibility to improve the society from which they came, and they emphasized the analytic and communication skills they had obtained. In Edgar's writing for the theatre from *Destiny* onwards, he is addressing mainly the white-collar public sector and the political commentariat – the intellectuals, middle managers, lecturers, artists, teachers, and middle-class civil servants who give weight to public sphere debates about politics and society, and for whom newspapers, books, theatre, film, television, and recently the Internet offer ways of comprehending their world and imagining new ways of engaging or changing it. This orientation means that in plays such as *Maydays* and *Continental Divide*, especially, the political ideas that characters hold and the rhetorical construction of their expressions carry the impetus of political struggle. For a wordsmith such as Edgar, *how* something is said is almost as important as the saying itself. This emphasis on rhetoric manifests itself through the importance of the articles written in the various revolutionary newspapers, or the slogans used on banners, or the play on words in the difference between Lennon and Lenin, which a character may miss but an audience is expected to catch. Thus we will pay particular attention to rhetoric in the plays, both as a matter of content and as a matter of form – beginning with the observation that political speeches work metatheatrically in all three plays discussed in this chapter. Both political and theatrical discourses are prepared for delivery to an audience, and the two forms of address are linked together by the technical purpose of rhetoric: to persuade.

Before turning to an extended analysis of the plays in question, it may be helpful to review a brief chronology of the twentieth-century Left in Britain and the (somewhat different) United States. We have divided it into three periods and give most attention to the second, which concerns the plays directly. The first of these eras spans the early days of socialism/communism from the Russian revolution through the Second World War and into the late fifties; second comes the fragmentation which intensified in the fifties with Khruschev's 'secret speech' attacking Stalin and the Soviet invasion of Hungary, and continues with the Soviet intervention in Czechoslovakia, the rise of the New Left in the sixties, as well as the backlash in the late seventies when Margaret Thatcher and Ronald Reagan came to power; and third is the period since the eighties, with the collapse of the Soviet system as well as the exhaustion of most of the ideological ferment on the Left. While these three divisions may appear somewhat arbitrary at first glance, we think they capture three moments of development and evaluation of the Left: one, a first period of project, optimism, and commitment; two, a fundamental challenge to and rethink of the original positions; and three, a time of decline and reformulation (or for some, abandonment) of the original project.

Of these three, the crucial period for Edgar's work considered in this chapter (and, to some extent, Chapter 4 as well) is the middle one – the mid fifties through the mid eighties – because the plays deal with these times, either explicitly or through their consequences in the lives of characters. However, the British and US political landscapes differ from each other in the second period . Thus we will need to recall how these histories diverged in order to understand the differences as well as the parallels between the two contexts dramatized in *Maydays* and *Continental Divide.*

Communist parties (and associated splinter groups) developed quickly in both the US and UK in the 1920s, following the Russian revolution and through the early years of the Soviet Union, with its utopian vision of a new and better world. In the economic troubles of the thirties, parties in both countries got a new boost as they worked with the more radical elements in the labour movement in both locations, and both the ideology and practice of this period came to be generally labelled the 'Old Left'. Trouble developed for dedicated members in the latter half of the decade, however, as Stalin's purges began to increase and be publicized, but the 'united front' mentality of the Spanish Civil War era merging into the Second World War papered over some of these problems. As the war ended, however, the narrative of the UK Left diverged significantly from the US.

In the UK (and, of course, most of western Europe) throughout the postwar period, the Communist Party (CP) (and many other small Marxist-Leninist groups)[2] remained a legal political party, even electing two Members of Parliament in 1945 and formally renouncing violent revolution as a pathway to political leadership in 1952. The CP never became a mass political party in Britain (top membership in about 1943 was 60,000, while the French CP had over 800,000 members and the Italian CP peaked at about 1.7 million), and so – given the two-party bias of political systems such as the British – it never had a chance of gaining any real political power.[3] Like all of the Marxist-Leninist Left in Europe during this period, it offered an account of history and socio-economics that claimed scientifically certain knowledge of the meaning of current events and the future of human social, economic, and political organization.

This dogmatic approach had always caused problems for members (notably the 1939–41 see-saw of the Party on Germany and fascism), but the Soviet invasion of Hungary and the related revelation of the extent of Stalin's crimes shattered many members' faith in the infallibility of the party and reduced the ranks of the CPGB by about a half. People in Britain in their thirties and forties in 1960, then, had either found a way to accommodate these shifts in party doctrine/ practice and remain members of the Left, (although many left the party), or had renounced Marxism-Leninism and shifted to the Labour Party, or had gone all the way to the Right. However, it is important to see that for those coming of age in 1960s Britain, there was still a 'Left' (comprised of many small but intense groupings) that had a coherent history stretching back fifty years with numerous spokespersons.[4]

The picture in the US was quite different. Even while the Left was expanding its activities within the labour and civil rights struggles of the thirties, Roosevelt's (moderate) New Deal programmes were being denounced by opponents as 'communist'. Although this 'anti-communism' was muted a bit during the Second World War, it spawned a process of McCarthyism well before Senator McCarthy's opening shot in February 1950. As a result, the CP in the US was not a legal organization; Leftists were driven from positions of union or political leadership (or even their very jobs in teaching, the media, etc.), and the major progressive development of the fifties, the civil rights movement, did its best to keep clear of any leftist 'taint'.

In its early years, the CPUSA had been a strong supporter of campaigns to improve the political, legal, and economic positions of African-Americans, but the complexities and zigzags of Stalin's Comintern policy undercut its ability to appeal substantially to others involved in these struggles. The party was probably most successful in the mid 1930s, in its penetration of labour organizing, its support for the Scottsboro Boys (targets of racist prosecutions), and in the fact that the US contribution to the international campaign to support Spain's popular front government against fascism in the Spanish Civil War – the Abraham Lincoln Brigade – was the first integrated US 'military' unit in its history. On the other hand, the main US civil rights organizations, such as the NAACP and later the SCLC, SNCC,[5] and others, had different aims than the CP, and were (to different degrees) suspicious of its long-term goals, both because of McCarthyism and because of the fact that most of the leading African-American organizations had their foundations and leadership in the Christian churches. In Martin Luther King's last years, as he increasingly saw that racial justice was inextricably tied up with economic justice, he moved clearly to the left, but at the cost of general support among both white and black publics.[6]

As a result, younger people in the US, coming of age in the sixties, experienced a discontinuity on the left – they themselves might even be the children of old Leftists, but could be unaware of their parents' political leanings because they were dangerous in the US environment. Thus the New Left in the US in the sixties was 'new' in a different way to the New Left in Europe, and a US college student, opting politically for the Left in the Sixties, would already be viewing the Old Left as past history, rather than dealing with movements and people who embodied the continuities with the past. Although the movements which came out of the sixties in both the UK and the US are usually labelled 'New Left', they show significant differences, many of which begin with this different history prior to the sixties.

Thus, it should not be surprising that *Maydays*, with its focus on the British Left (and those who left it), begins formally in 1945, and stretches into the mid eighties, while the two plays of *Continental*

*Divide* start their back stories with the US in the mid sixties. Both plays examine what happens to youthful idealism and passion over several eventful decades, and are centrally concerned with how individuals and groups handle the inevitable disillusionments that history brings.

## *Maydays*

> Any play attacked by both Peter Jenkins and Tariq Ali must have something going for it.
>
> Michael Billington[7]

> But surely, the most anticipated and publicized opening of the year was to be the RSC's first new play (as opposed to first new *musical*) to be staged at the Barbican, by the same author whose last *new* play was almost the last new script ever to be presented at the Aldwych (before the RSC became timid about presenting anything new other than in a studio space).
>
> David Roper (italics in original)[8]

*Maydays* (1983) was the first new play produced on the large stage at the Barbican. Appearing at a time when second-term Tory cuts to the arts were widely expected, an immense production (both in budget and dramatic scope) on the main stage of one of the country's two premier subsidized theatres dealing with revolutionary socialism was bound to cause controversy. Much of the public debate mirrored the range of political positions and postures examined and sometimes mocked within the play, illustrating the very theatricalization of politics therein embedded at a metatheatrical level.

By the time David Edgar wrote *Maydays* he had been a member of the Labour Party for two years, and Margaret Thatcher had recently celebrated her second-term victory (a landslide win, partially because of the recent popular war in the Falklands/Malvinas).[9] Like *Destiny*, *Maydays* offers a certain kind of warning to those who would heed it, but unlike *Destiny*, *Maydays* is more about being caught between a rock and a hard place. While Labour was routed in the general election of 1983, having lost hugely (in parliamentary seats) to a combination of Conservative votes and the coalition of Social Democrats and Liberals, who took 25 per cent of the vote, the extraparliamentary left parties and groups that earlier seemed like viable alternative choices to mainstream politics also appeared to Edgar to offer little hope for a better world.[10] Rather than giving in or giving up, Edgar set out to shake up complacency by demanding a thorough rethink of the Left's accomplishments and failures in order to determine a (political) way forward. The resulting drama was voted the London Theatre Critics' 'Best New Play' for 1983. (See Fig. 3.)

At the time, the play was hotly debated and discussed: those on the right maintained that a play so focused on the preoccupations of the far left had no place on stages subsidized by public funds (Jenkins's main point),[11] while those to the left of Edgar claimed that he had offered a caricature of the far left for the ridicule of the establishment,

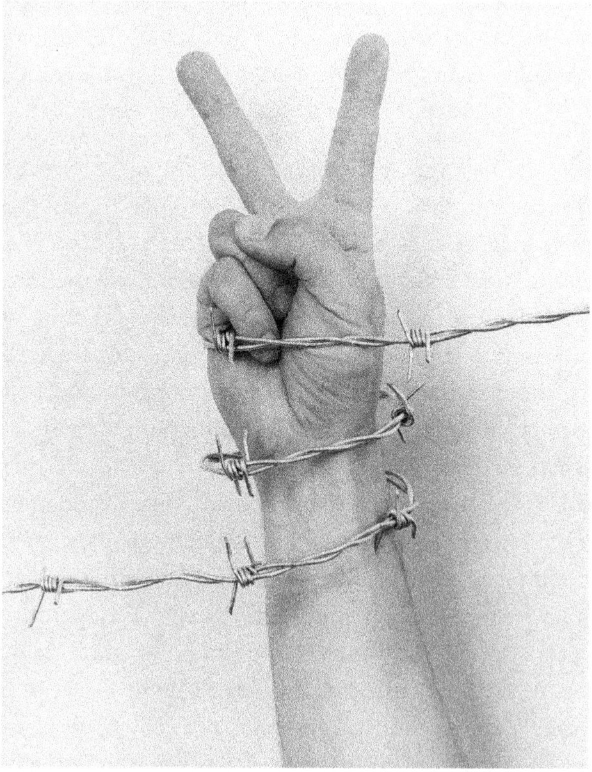

Fig. 3 *Maydays* (1983). Design for publicity.

playing 'in the belly of the beast' (the Royal Shakespeare Company's new venue at the Barbican). While we can understand why this was an argument of some moment at the time, looking at the play from within the context of today's political landscape tends to make other issues stand out as more important. In particular, the attempt to think through the difference between the Left and the Right during a volatile period that saw many people switch allegiances and others simply drop out of politics altogether seems clearly an appropriate task for that time, addressed to a wide audience of varying political stripes. Certain rhetorical questions that appear in the play, such as 'How often do you have to feel betrayed, before you feel despair?' or 'Do you really want this man to run the country?' take on a tangible gravitas from the perspective of thirty years on, in the wake of a contemporary moment that saw the installation of the Lib-Con coalition government of David Cameron and Nick Clegg in 2010.

Edgar has said '*Maydays* is about as grand a narrative play as it's possible to be this side of *Tamburlaine the Great*', and one is almost forced to begin with comments about the overall framework in order not to become swamped in its massive details.[12] It covers the period from 1945 to 1983, ranges over four countries and imagines fifty-three characters. There are a number of structural parallelisms. Each of the three acts contains a political speech that sets the tone for the act. May Day celebrations, commemorations or conferences form fulcrum points for the action in 1945, 1968, 1970, and 1975. A certain number of slogans or sayings are repeated with shifting meanings, such as Trotsky's 'human dust' or Lenin's 'revolutions are festivals of the oppressed and exploited', an excellent illustration of Edgar's 'echo effect' explained in *How Plays Work*.[13] Issues of authoritarianism are seen to belong to both sides of the political spectrum, and Edgar dramatizes both a libertarian right and left tendency, balancing the virtues and liabilities of each.[14]

Or nearly balancing. In the end, as Susan Painter observed in her detailed study of Edgar's plays, he is not neutral on these issues. He criticizes the authoritarian left but he lambastes the authoritarian right, especially those who defected from the left and who transplant their authoritarian training from left-party discipline, using it in the service of a new right ideology, making them – in Edgar's view – worse than traditional Tories. And in his deepest parts, Edgar is himself a libertarian in the sense of a defender of liberty, individual, and community – someone much more committed to fighting against censorship or repression than concerned to maintain order or discipline. His alter ego protagonist, Martin, says, 'I'm not exactly what you'd call a joiner' (p. 218).

We've called Martin Glass the alter ego of David Edgar, yet that is not quite a fair assessment, since Edgar clearly thinks Glass is wrong. Painter says that he is 'the saddest character in the play, and can be read in Sartrean terms as an existentialist tragic hero', but we think there is a case for seeing him as a self-indulgent, undisciplined individualist whose repeatedly revealed sexism is not endearing.[15] Edgar may have based some of Martin on his own life experiences (as he has stated), but that does not mean he wants to establish sympathy for Martin's plight. Rather, he offers a portrait of one sort of defector to the Right – one whose temperament and values do not support working through the confines of tight organizational discipline, and whose anger and frustration with what he sees as betrayal leads him to a revengeful withdrawal from public life altogether. It is, indeed, a childish retreat, supported by the pattern of metaphor throughout the play, which clusters children/childlike/childishness/childhood to signify both a hopeful ideal and a derisive reference to a regressive state.

The true heroic figures in the play are two. Lermontov, the man who begins the play as a young Russian lieutenant, sees that the revolution is going wrong in Hungary, and deliberately allows a young anti-Soviet agitator to escape. Adopting from then on the role of critic of the Soviet system and finally of dissident, Lermontov suffers imprisonment. When finally released to the West, however, he baulks before a streak of British conservatism that seems committed to the same authoritarian ideas that fostered repression in his own society, and resists being co-opted by that right wing movement called, ironically, the Committee in Defense of Liberty.

The second positive figure is Amanda (no last name), Edgar's best woman figure to this point in his *oeuvre* (building on those developed in *Mary Barnes)*, who is shown searching and fighting for a truly humane and meaningful way to live that others might share. She, too, joins the Socialist Vanguard (the fictional Trotskyist party that Martin joins for a time) and leaves when she finds it intractable, but she does not leave political work or become disillusioned. She continues to work in collectives, live in communes, demonstrate and organize, and to teach her daughter Tania the values she believes are important. At the end of the play, Tania joins the young women at Greenham Common with Amanda's approval. In a positive version of the child/childhood complex, she figures a new generation of young people dedicated to trying to make the world a more liveable place for more people. Amanda describes their efforts to Martin (who is threatening legal action to remove the women activists): 'I think in fact that in the end what they are doing, what we all are trying to do, in our many different ways, can only be accounted for by something in the nature of our species which resents, rejects and ultimately will resist a world that is demonstrably and in this case dramatically wrong and mad and unjust and unfair' (p. 324). This is the motivation for political resistance that Edgar validates in the play, but which Martin has lost. The ways people come to lose their political motivation are, in fact, amply represented in the play, and this is one of its links to *Destiny*, which also dramatized the way its characters came to occupy their political positions. In an article describing the path socialist theatre took between 1968 and 1978, Edgar defends the emerging portrayal of psychologically dense characters as designed to 'confront[ing] the gap between the objective crisis of the system and the subjective responses of the human beings within it'.[16] Pointing out sexual politics and race as two subjects requiring representational rather than descriptive terms, he argues that 'this realization that there are subjects with which theatre is uniquely fitted to deal ... has led, I believe, to an increase in plays about various aspects of political consciousness'.[17]

Returning to the play with this aspect of political consciousness in mind, it is perhaps not characterization but dramaturgy and rhetoric which best allow an approach to the core issues being theatricalized. We will look at the play through two prisms, the first, the initial periodization of the British Left offered earlier in the chapter, and the second, tracing critical rhetorical tropes as they condense and contest various significations.

### *Generational continuity and rupture*

The first period of revolutionary activity features much more centrally in *Maydays* than it does in *Continental Divide*, as we explained above (pp. 65–9). The first scene of the play takes place on May Day 1945 with the speech of a 17-year-old member of the Young Communist League (Jeremy Crowther) proclaiming that the victory over fascism is also victory over 'warmongers and capitalists' and that the working class can now build the 'New Jerusalem' (p. 191). This youthful idealism is echoed in Martin Glass's poem, 'Beyond', which he shares with Jeremy Crowther when they meet in 1962. Martin (himself age 17 in 1962) is excited to meet Crowther because he was in the Party and Martin finds that 'really cool'. But Jeremy left the Party after Hungary in 1956 and has lost faith in the Soviet revolution and also in the working class, who, he feels, have become possessed by their possessions – the Hoover Automatic, the Mini Cooper, the television, the gramophone (p. 208). Still sensitive to the idealism of the Spanish Civil War, he feels his generation was born too late and missed the only real revolutionary moment. Throughout the play, Crowther will move further and further to the right, finally becoming a part of the ultra-right pressure group, the Committee in Defence of Liberty. Martin starts the play as a kind of surrogate child of Crowther's – the one who might persevere and 'who'll do it, really get it right. *This* time' (emphasis in text, p. 210).

A second thread of connection to an originary revolutionary moment begins in Scene 2 with Lermontov in Hungary. Here Paloczi, the young student arrested for illegally broadcasting in support of the Hungarian uprising, reminds Lermontov of the May Day in 1947 when Paloczi was 14 (and by doing the maths Edgar provides in the published script, we can work out that Lermontov was 17 in 1947): 'Our liberation, from the landowners and counts. A real revolution, bubbling from below. Oh, very rushed and slapdash, but – still real. And ours' (pp. 197–8). Paloczi argues that the Soviets betrayed the people by dominating them, and that the uprising now is a second chance for peasants and ordinary people to make a real revolution. Lermontov decides to let him go, 'Because – I am of the view – that revolutions should correct their mistakes. If they are not to lose the people's trust. And so – I'm trusting you' (p. 199).

At this stage, Lermontov is more or less in Crowther's position when he left the Party over Hungary, yet the two men will define their paths in opposite directions from this point. While Crowther withdraws into academic life and eventually re-emerges as a right-wing anti-Communist supporting the Committee in Defense of Liberty, Lermontov continually tries to intervene in 'correcting mistakes'. He takes up dissident work, protesting against the Soviet invasion and writing and sending samizdat writings secretly from the camp where he is imprisoned. When he finally comes to the West, he both continues his protests about injustices in his own country and refuses to take part in the reactionary authoritarianism of the right in Britain (which wants to exploit his protests for its own purposes).

The third and final important orientation to the first period of socialism comes from the US, through the character of Weiner, the father of Cathy, who is living in Amanda's commune with her boyfriend Clark (also American). In 1970, with the announcement of the spread of the war to Cambodia, Clark goes to the US and 'is blown up by his own bomb at a US Air Force base in Southern California' (p. 234). Weiner, who is an academic, is attending a conference in the UK and comes to the commune to comfort his daughter. Instead he ends up delivering a long speech (what one might call the play's 1970 May Day speech) in which he bitterly charts his own revolutionary path as the child of immigrant Jewish-Russian parents. Earlier we mentioned that for many in the US, the first stages of revolutionary struggle had been eclipsed by strong anti-communism and by the distance from Europe. Immigrants, of course, carried with them to the US their knowledge of European revolutionary history. Many Jewish immigrants and especially intellectuals participated in the early US labour actions and leftist organizations, including the outlawed Communist Party. Weiner was educated by these 'older men' and followed the 'orders from above' for a time. His account highlights survivors' guilt in his parents' generation, and also a postwar disillusion that saw his generation repudiating the Party and flying solo, but feeling guilt for those fellow travellers who were destroyed by McCarthyism. Then he addresses his children's generation with self-righteous and accusatory venom for attacking his generation's silence and guilt: 'And they kicked away the ladders we had climbed. And even spurned the books we'd read to them. And although there was so much we could remember of ourselves, there was a kind of madness and unreason in their fury that we couldn't recognize' (pp. 236–7). Thus the father who has come to share his daughter's grief ends up attacking her friends, and the recently killed Clark in particular, since he was the son of a rich oil man: 'we noticed you'd got company. The company of spoiled brats, from swanky homes, whose families had never known one day of poverty' (p. 237). The unreason of fury could be felt in the speech of its accuser. This twisted tale stands in for one aspect of the more complicated and diverse history of the Left in the US, but provides a tortuous link to an idealistic vision and a sense of betrayal that has turned in on itself in a particularly vile way in Weiner, making 'the personal is political' seem like an understatement.

All three of these engagements with originary revolutionary moments demonstrate complex subjective responses to belief and disillusion that come out of specific historical circumstances and subject positions. Although Crowther, Glass, and Weiner will travel further to the right than can be explained by their specific earlier experiences, they offer evidence of the initial desire for a radical vision of human collective betterment present in many people who later turn into right-wing ideologues, while Lermontov's actions show that this path is not inevitable.

## *Revolutions are festivals of the oppressed and exploited*

The main focus of *Maydays* is, however, the second period of socialist activity, that of the 1960s and 1970s, from the standpoint of the generation that came of age at that time. Through slogans such as 'it's only rock 'n' roll', the lyrics of 'California Dreaming', puns on Lenin and Lennon, and a put-down of Elton John, the play links the political issues at its core to what was known as the counter culture – the liberatory impulse in most of the political movements of the time that often made demonstrations into (rock) festivals, and sometimes lost sight of the revolutionary goal in the midst of the partying. The saying, 'revolutions are festivals of the oppressed and exploited', attributed to Lenin, begins the play. It is directly invoked again in two more scenes, and indirectly applies to two more, providing the spine of the dramaturgy.

At the very outset, Jeremy Crowther quotes Lenin's epigram in his 1945 May Day address and applies it to working-class celebrations of the victory of the 'Great Anti-Fascist war' (p. 193). This is the most straightforward and literal meaning of the sentence, unambiguous and unequivocal.

In his 1968 May Day address in Act 1, Scene 5, James Grain, leader of the Socialist Vanguard, links the text to the Tet Offensive, the 'de facto resignation of the President of the United States', and the events in the streets of Paris, using the rest of Lenin's quotation to refine and discipline its application: 'Revolutions are festivals of the oppressed and exploited ... At such times the people are capable of performing miracles. But we shall be traitors and betrayers of the revolution, if we do not use the festive energy of the masses to wage a ruthless and self-sacrificing struggle for the direct and decisive path' (p. 214). Grain is portrayed as the disciplined Trotskyist vanguardist who insists on working-class militancy and strict party discipline. After recruiting Martin to the Socialist Vanguard, he later rejects him for refusing to follow the party line and for insufficient commitment to the working class. The notion of harnessing the energy of the festival for a particular programme, present in Grain's version of Lenin, suggests that festivals are anarchic affairs that do not in and of themselves have a purpose or direction, but which can be shaped to a programme.

Paloczi, the young Hungarian militant, has previously made use of this statement in the earlier scene with Lermontov (Act 1, Scene 2). He summons it to explain the revolutionary violence that has accompanied the Hungarian uprising: 'Look. A revolution is a festival. Lenin said that, I was surprised to learn. And the thing about a festival is that it's very tricky to control. We have been drunk this last few weeks. For most of us, exhilaration. But for some, revenge. Mistakes get made' (pp. 198–9). These three applications of Lenin's remarks to specific situations – all in Act 1 – set up the main action of the play as a further commentary on the proposition. In Act 2, Scene 7, it is May Day 1975 and the BBC is reporting parades in the streets of Ho Chi Minh City, where 'the new communist authorities impose severe penalties for looting, prostitution, and "all decadent cultural activities of the American variety"' (p. 270). Martin and Amanda are at a celebratory party attended by a group of characters representing a variety of political tendencies, including Brian, who has left revolutionary politics and joined the Labour Party, and James, who still leads the Socialist Vanguard. Martin, full of foreboding about what he considers the Stalinist new government of the reunited Vietnam, rejects the festival on television and in the living room. In his decisive and somewhat hysterical rejection of revolutionary socialism, he in essence charges the festival with being a delusion: 'You see, I don't think it's just Stalin or even Lenin. I think it is the whole idea.' Flailing drunkenly about with sarcasm and vituperation, he repeats Weiner's accusation and behaviour from earlier in Act 2: he refers to 'the terrible unfocussed fury that we seem to nurture in ourselves, that burns us up, and which we beam about us like a blowtorch, branding everything we touch or see' (p. 276). True as much for Martin as it is for any of his revolutionary friends, Edgar carefully crafts his speech to contain several modicums of truth but overdetermines his behaviour (the drink) and his personal circumstances (he is turning 30) to undercut any notion of this pronouncement as the definitive one.

The last 'festival' of the play is an 'anti-racist rally-cum-rock-festival' in 1978.[18] By this time, Martin has denounced revolutionary socialism in *The Times*, and is not present. The scene shows that festivalization has covered over the fractures of an ineffectual Left; the coalition of many causes perhaps now has none. 'The International Brigade' refers to a band, and in the crèche 'there is a minor riot'. James, who has not been sympathetically portrayed previously (being seen as an ideologue and party bully), is here given a strong voice. He is furious at Martin's defection, and comments on the upcoming election (1979) (audience members sitting in the Barbican already knew very well who had won): 'There is shortly going to be a general election. And in our view the conservatives will win. They will win in part because the working class has been betrayed, not least by those whom we have always said were really on the other side, and who now appear, in their true colours, so to be' (p. 286). There is a modicum of truth in James Grain's charge: one version of how Margaret Thatcher won the 1979 election has to do with ineffective Labour government attempts to regulate wages leading to industrial disputes, wildcat strikes, and severe disruption of public services (e.g., lorry drivers, gravediggers, some hospital workers). This was coupled with internal dissension among the far left and ineffective labour policies within the Communist Party and other revolutionary groups who had turned away from labour activism just as the crisis of industrial action reached its height (the Winter of Discontent of 1978/9.) This scene, then, seemingly unfocused and only there to announce Martin Glass's final break with revolutionary socialism, gives another reading to the Leninist slogan – one that emphasizes that if it is only rock 'n' roll, it is not enough.

Edgar deploys this Lenin citation throughout the play to create a multifaceted image of revolutionary ardour. It captures the volatility of radical mass movements, the risks of too much or too little discipline, the sometimes unpredictable nature of their expressions, and their possibilities for celebration and destruction. May Days are holidays which recognize and celebrate the achievements of 'the people'. As Amanda says at the end of Act 1, 'We must remember, we must absolutely not forget the superhuman things that human beings can and have achieved' (p. 238). However, this invocation of May Days comes at the end of the scene in which we learn of Clark's death in the bombing incident, and hear Weiner's vituperative speech. The last lines in the act are his daughter Cathy's counterpoint: 'It's May Day, Mayday, Mayday' (p. 238). The international distress signal is the flipside of the celebration.

Edgar's insistence on the equivocal nature of revolutionary socialism shows the reason why the critique of the far left, so evident in the play, is not finally a repudiation of left struggle. While the finitude and limitations of human beings have to be factored in to any political equation, there is no justification for considering those who resist 'hooligans, parasites, cranks or crazies' – terms Edgar makes sure are used in the play by both the Right and the Left to describe their enemies – or, indeed, 'human dust'. This term is also taken from Trotsky, first written in 1931 to describe Nazi soldiers, but used by Edgar to indicate the discounting of human beings. James Grain first uses it to describe petit bourgeois supporters of corporate capitalism; Jeremy Crowther uses it to label the demonstrators protesting in support of Central American revolutions, and Martin Glass uses it first to describe his father's attitude to his relatives, and then in his May Day disavowal of revolutionary socialism, when he blurts out: 'I can't believe, I actually refuse to be required by anybody to believe, that anyone is human dust' (p. 277).

Although Edgar has drawn Martin as a bundle of contradictions, and although in this scene we have argued Martin is particularly unconvincing, this proclamation can be taken to be Edgar's as well as Martin's, and is to be judged right and true. It is the bottom line of the play and reflects the playwright's position.

With the careful craftsmanship of this nuanced and complex reading of revolutionary socialism in mind, one can also appreciate the broad strokes of satire that Edgar includes without mistaking them for the main message. For example, the various splinter parties and their newspapers are delightfully sent up in a scene starting with six newspaper sellers flogging their six different revolutionary papers outside a meeting hall. In Act 1, James Grain pitches joining the Socialist Vanguard Party to Martin, insisting that SV is not to be 'confused with the Socialist Alliance, from whom we split, or the Left Opposition, who split from us, or Workers' Struggle, who split from them, or with the League for Revolutionary Socialism, who never split at all'. When Martin asks about the difference, James replies, 'They're wrong and we're right' (p. 218).

In fact, the play goes some way to dramatizing the differences between various groups. Clark chooses to go underground, and becomes violent in the style of the Weathermen; Phil, after Clark's death and Cambodia, adopts the analysis of the Situationists,[19] and is jailed for a bomb attempt by his group on a junior minister, who later turns out to be the leader of the Committee in Defense of Liberty. One scene comprises a squatting action by a group of Libertarians (Edgar gently satirizes them by showing up the ineptitude of the group, who get the time wrong and forget to change the locks, allowing the police to get in ahead of them – 'welcome to the non-stop Revolutionary Cock-up Show' [p. 263]. Brian, as previously mentioned, was a member of SV but leaves and joins the Labour Party, and Amanda moves through various, often unnamed, groups with a through-line of feminism and collective activity in support of peace and justice. Edgar thus offers a reasonably full picture of the different political subject positions embraced by those in the second generation of revolutionary activity.

As Edgar has often done elsewhere, he ends this play on a faint note of hope. The ability of human beings to hold on to the desire and commitment to the struggle to make the world better is an enduring trait, and Edgar believes it is manifest through the grass-roots actions of ordinary people, who care enough to involve themselves in political activity, even when their hopes of success are a long shot. Thus the play ends with the women occupying Greenham Common, while in Russia an academic who Lermontov seemed unable to persuade to get involved in dissident activity agrees to take samizdat documents undercover to the West. For Edgar in 1983, it was not only rock 'n' roll; looking back from 2011, in our opinion, the dramatization still holds.

Theatrically, this play makes explicit the link between public life and performance. The political speeches and the personal monologues that act within the limits of epic realism nevertheless also announce themselves repeatedly as manifestos, proclamations, position papers, and other tracts. Weiner's speech to his daughter and her friends could be considered a political tract, and Lermontov's after-dinner speech is both political tract and also a deeply revelatory personal statement. In each of these situations, actors attempt to persuade others that their explanations are worthy in a form appropriate to the public sphere. Edgar's insight that theatre is uniquely fitted to deal with aspects of political consciousness is illustrated at the metatheatrical level in *Maydays*, perhaps his most theatrical play.

In addition, the metatheatricality continued into the public arena, as *Maydays* became a lightning rod for public debate about the relationship between theatre and politics and how to represent the history of the Left. Looking at the press clippings almost thirty years later, we have been struck by two features: first, the critics respond to each other as well as to the play they have seen, and second, more than in most of the reviews of other Edgar plays, these discuss the issues rather than the production elements or the acting (Anthony Sher played Martin Glass, incidentally, which, given his own history and activism, must have resonated in the characterization). Ron Daniels's direction was widely praised, and the Barbican did not harm the production in any significant fashion (its cavernous space is difficult to fill successfully, and although the play has a broad epic sweep and some large theatrical scenes, it also has a number of two-handers and important monologues). It played to 67 per cent capacity, which was more than respectable.

It was the discussion in the days and weeks following, however, that really marked the production as symbolic of its time and of the state of the British Left. We have already alluded to Peter Jenkins's attack on the play and Edgar's response in Chapter 1 above. What is more notable than Jenkins's view of the play is his position as *political* commentator rather than theatre reviewer. The debate around the play spread beyond the culture pages to engage several commentators with political credentials – James Fenton, political commentator at *The Sunday Times* (who reports being told that Martin Glass was based on himself), and well-known political theorist of the Left, Bernard Crick, writing in the *Times Higher Education Supplement*.[20] Further, the various pundits refer to each other's columns – thus creating the sense of a genuine public event/debate about political matters using a play as its vehicle. Crick defends Edgar against Jenkins, while Paul Allen in the *New Statesman* responds to the *Observer*'s Robert Cushman's derision of *Maydays* as 'not about politics at all, but merely about politicking'.[21] Those critical of the play either find that it is about a radical Left which is irrelevant (rather than a parliamentary Left, which is the centre of politics) or that Edgar's version of the history of that Left is not compelling. Those defending him extol his comprehensive view of a panoramic history and his sense for revolutionary characters, not only 'their nobility of vision, but also of their folly, of the hardness and inhumanity of character they can create, and the ludicrous disproportion between what the broken-down, second-hand duplicator in the squat is churning out, and the sad squat itself'.[22]

His detractors on the Left, and there were a number, criticize two primary aspects of the play – the lack of working-class characters (who would be the proper protagonists of any 'real' Left history), and the galling decision of Edgar to wash the Left's dirty linen in public. John McGrath is his most formidable critic in this regard, and his disagreements with Edgar go beyond this particular occasion. Painter has covered in detail the discussion of whether the play in the Barbican betrays the Left to its middle-class enemy.[23] Another voice of criticism from within the theatre community came from Pam Brighton, Irish director and actor, who was working with Charabanc Theatre Company in Belfast at the time. She starts out with her distaste for the building:

> Going into the building increased my discomfort. I saw from my programme that the season had been subsidised by The Bank of America.
>
> Then came 'Maydays'. It was a play about socialism where not one member of the working class was allowed on stage, a lot of people I could dimly imagine were meant to be my friends were portrayed as cretins, and of course, there were the obligatory nasty Russians.[24]

Brighton's broadside goes on, however, to discuss seriously the gradual diminution of class as an organizing thematic of media and theatre. She finds that the decline of popular, socialist theatre leaves people without alternatives, and she is critical of new arts centres ('all winey and chummy but still . . . emanating a superior style which I expect is more intimidating than the National or the Royal Shakespeare Company'). Even the Drill Hall, where many new feminist, lesbian, and gay plays were first performed, is condemned as 'icily elitist, with its particular brand of feminism'.[25] This piece carries the passion of a socialist still deeply committed to her project and ready to argue with Edgar or any other theatre-makers who do not recognize that 'It is not race or sex that unite the dispossessed, it is class and the way it expresses itself today is as clear as it was 50 years ago'.[26]

We have quoted Brighton at length because, while John McGrath's critique is well documented and well known, there is a fresh and vibrant resistance in Pam Brighton's piece which seems to capture one side of the heady political frisson that marked the production of Edgar's play. The play itself calls out for this kind of engagement, and the discussion within the theatre community about what kind of theatre would be properly political is a central strand of the larger question about what kind of socialist politics would be possible in decade of the eighties.

Twenty years after *Maydays*, Edgar returned to a number of its major themes in *Continental Divide*.

## *Continental Divide*

> One of the things about *Continental Divide* was that it was embarrassing how much David knew versus how little everybody else knew. And he was writing about America! C'mon: he knew more about American politics than about 98% of the people in the rehearsal room.
>
> Tony Taccone (director of *Continental Divide*, Berkeley Repertory Theatre)[27]

> This isn't entertainment. Isn't this the most volatile discussion you had within an Elderhostel? Did you expect me to be objective? I'm in the damn play and I believe in it.
>
> Robyn Rodriguez (actor, *Continental Divide*, Oregon Shakespeare Festival, aftershow discussion)[28]

The umbrella title for the pair of plays – *Continental Divide* – played on words in typical Edgarian fashion, their linkage secured by their concern with one side or the other of a fictionalized election contest in the United States.[29] The plays were commissioned and co-produced by the Oregon Shakespeare Festival (OSF) and the Berkeley Repertory Theatre (BRT), and played at those venues in Oregon and California in 2003, and in Birmingham and London (at the Barbican) in 2004. The individual play titles (*Mothers Against* and *Daughters of the Revolution*) suggest generational change and conflict through familial lines of female lineage. Although in fact the main protagonists are male, the roles of women in the US in the 1960s and the 2000s are well featured in their multiplicity and complexity. If *Maydays* was a play about men with one strong woman character (Amanda), *Continental Divide* provides a gendered landscape of polyvocal dissonance.

The project was ambitious and high-risk from the start: not one but two plays, involving over fifty characters, scheduled to be performed in two US states and then across the Atlantic in the UK. As journalist Chad Jones commented, 'A project of this scope would present a challenge in the healthiest of economies'.[30] *Continental Divide* is built around a gubernatorial contest with wide-ranging issues, adding some major questions about US politics to Edgar's ongoing concerns with the evolution of Left and Right, the persistence of political vision, and patterns of disillusionment and defection. Additionally, it could have been perceived as cheeky of Edgar to attempt to write about the intricacies of a foreign political system as if he were an insider. The largest risk, though, lay in the matter of political theatre itself: could such plays be successful in a time sometimes described as 'post-political' (even in the United Kingdom)? But the United Kingdom had, by 2000, a well-developed cultural tradition receptive to political theatre – could *Continental Divide* find an equivalent context for the plays in the US?

One reason political theatre may have never become a major draw in the United States is that fundamental political principles may seem less in question to US citizens than to many other peoples. Not that there is no political controversy in the US – far from it – but that conflict is likely to be about the *application* of supposedly settled political principles, rather than debate over the core values themselves. Even in very conflicted times, such as the thirties or the sixties, the struggles inside the conventional political system were not so much about the nature of the 'social contract' itself, but rather about who was to be included in it. This tendency, combined with the US electoral and party systems, which favour centrist positions, tends to make US electoral campaigns seem more like personality contests than ideological challenges, and may provide one reason for lower levels of political participation in the US than in the UK. Likewise, it may mean that when people in the US seek 'serious' theatre, they are more apt to look for it in psychological drama exploring the nature of personality, identity and human relationships than in the political sphere, which is usually presented to them in the media as an intense, but low-level, 'horse race'. In a four-part series of articles on political theatre in the US, Chicago journalist Ben Winters confirms our view:

> The politics of American plays has [*sic*] traditionally been more subtle, and revolving around questions of personal identity rather than, say, party affiliation. Playwrights like Tennessee Williams and August Wilson are deeply immersed in the politics of identity, in the relationship of Self to Other, which is as political in its way as a David Rabe piece about Vietnam ... Which means that the politics are under the surface, rather than worn on the sleeve, as you might find them in other countries.[31]

Add to this the practical matter that 'political' plays often involve fairly large casts in order to represent a social body, and that most US theatres cannot easily support large casts (almost none of them are subsidized), and you have a formula for the minimization of political theatre in the United States.[32] Lacking any significant publicly funded support, US theatres must play to their audiences, and rely on their donors, who are generally likely to be moderately conservative upper middle-class people – not the sort who are looking for radically progressive plays for an evening's entertainment. (This is one area where cinema may do better in the US, with such films as *Bulworth*, *The American President*, *Primary Colours*, *Wag the Dog*, and more recently, *Frost/Nixon*, *Head of State*, and *W.*, to mention only films dealing with the Presidency.)

In the run up to *Continental Divide*, recent history has challenged US society in ways that may have made it more open to theatre dealing with political issues. The closely contested presidential election in 2000 between Al Gore (the popular vote winner) and George Bush (the Electoral College winner) had sparked much interest, and this was followed by the complex national response to 9/11. Not only the renewed interest in socio-political issues as a result of current events, but also the widely noted theatricalization of public life had created a self-conscious moment of political and theatrical confluence.

*Continental Divide* was scheduled to be produced just months ahead of an American presidential campaign, and then happened to chance upon the unexpected gubernatorial recall of Gray Davis in California (voted out of office) and the election in his place of movie star Arnold Schwarzenegger.[33] Although Edgar had not portrayed the specific political situation in either the country or the state in question, he benefited from the adjacency of these events, although he feared the reverse: that the theatricality of the actual events would overshadow the dramatized events.[34]

The productions received widespread attention across the country and were reviewed favorably during their Ashland premiere by the British press as well as US critics. Tony Taccone had directed the very successful production of Edgar's *Pentecost* at OSF and at BRT; Edgar had conceived of the *Continental Divide* project with both theatres in mind, as well as the prospect of writing parts for actors including Robyn Rodriguez and Derek Lee Weeden, with whom he had worked on the earlier production. However, Taccone was the critical figure – Edgar's relationship with Taccone goes back to the 1970s, when he came to California for the Eureka Theatre's productions of *Mary Barnes* and *The Jail Diary of Albie Sachs*. Taccone was part of the six-person collective running the theatre, and directed *The Jail Diary*. He has gone on to become one of the major figures in the American Theatre, partly through his association with and development of other important writers' work (Tony Kuschner's *Angels in America* was workshopped at the Eureka and Taccone has continued producing Kuschner plays at BRT). Taccone is an ideal director for Edgar's work because he is intellectually acute and politically engaged (his commitment to political theatre has been consistent and progressive throughout his career). Along with Michael Attenborough and Ron Daniels, Tony Taccone is David Edgar's key artistic interpreter. He values Edgar highly:

> One of the great things about David is that he is really interested in peeling the veil off of information. He is often intrigued by visualizing and expressing facsimiles of processes that are frequently hidden from our public view – the *Continental Divide* debate prep, for instance. He really whets my appetite for

Fig. 4 Artistic director Tony Taccone (*centre*) staged David Edgar's *Continental Divide* at the Tony Award-winning Berkeley Repertory Theatre and the Oregon Shakespeare Festival in 2003 before bringing the show to the Barbican in London.

> learning. I learn a whole lot about how society works. He's got a brilliant analytical mind – he really can take a lot of complex info and synthesize it and put it into a dramatic situation.[35]

Taccone and the cast did a lot of research, viewing documentaries, reading about California and Oregon politics, having experts talk to them (campaign advisors, speech-writers, historians of the American Left – even ecological activists, including a tree-sitter). Edgar was in the rehearsal room a good deal of the time and made modifications to the text all the way to its London production, particularly in the case of *Daughters of the Revolution*, which had the most challenges and problems in development. (See Fig. 4.)

The productions changed substantially between Oregon and California: although critics were positive, audiences were sometimes less positive. Robyn Rodriguez commented on the difficulty of speaking with some of the groups of OSF patrons (in the opening quotation, the Elderhostel group)[36] who were not prepared for the challenge of Edgar's plays.[37] Besides tightening up a sprawling script (over three hours for each play), several characters, including the protagonist of *Daughters of the Revolution*, were recast (as planned from the start) and the narrative line of *Daughters* was tweaked to bring more focus and clarity to the protagonist's central quest. Even Robert Hurwitt of the *San Francisco Chronicle*, Edgar's most sceptical local critic, conceded, 'It's never less than an intriguing exploration of democracy American style by one of England's foremost political playwrights.'[38]

## *Themes dramaturgy politics*[39]

The two plays together portray candidates of the two major political parties, Republican and Democrat, as they vie for the office of governor in a western state – unnamed, but oscillating easily between Oregon and California. Edgar designed the two plays to be neither sequential nor necessarily interlocked: the viewers could see only one, or both in either order. However, since one play, *Mothers Against*, is the Republican play while the other, *Daughters of the Revolution*, is the Democratic play, without considering both together one is left with an incomplete view of the complexity of Edgar's analysis of US politics, political action, and leadership. One of his main ambitions for *Continental Divide* was clearly to provide a 'fair' hearing for both sides: the Republican play has sympathetic characters and the ideological position of those characters is well represented, just as the Democratic play poses its ideological turns with sympathy and its main characters as worthy. Thus it really is necessary to see both plays in order to experience Edgar's central insight that both the libertarian Right and the activist Left have had visionary investments in utopias; both have attracted principled followers; both have had to grapple with lost objectives and changing political circumstances, and both have had to deal with the temptations to the Faustian bargain: 'selling out' some or all of one's vision/principles in order to hope to have an impact on the course of history. (By comparison, both *Destiny* and *Maydays* contain all the relevant ideological positions within a single play – audiences witness the complete set of dialectical encounters within a single event.)

Edgar fashioned the two plays that make up *Continental Divide* within different theatrical styles, slyly mirroring aspects of both groups' politics in the very dramaturgy of the plays. For *Daughters*, he crafted an epic style, owing much to Brecht and to the variations on his work that were familiar to Edgar's generation of British writers.[40] A series of semi-autonomous scenes, linked by the protagonist's quest to find out who betrayed him and his comrades to the FBI, intersects the gubernatorial contest through the connection between the protagonist and the Democratic candidate's campaign manager, who had been members of the same activist group in their youth. The locations jump from campaign office to TV station to forest, where tree-sitters are engaged in a protest against logging, to a community centre where voter registration training takes place. The action travels in time, includes flashbacks, and achieves effects by juxtaposition. About fifty characters appear (if one counts Hecklers and Brunchers), rendered in a combination of sketches and developed types. *Daughters* is, then, a play much like *Maydays* – stylistically epic and deliberately fragmented and multifocal.

For *Mothers Against*, on the other hand, Edgar chose a form more compatible with the US theatre, psychological realism. Here we never leave the domestic interior of a family home turned briefing-room for the gubernatorial debates. A powerful dynasty is at the centre of this social space, where three generations of the Vine family have lived various sorts of public lives. The smaller cast – eight characters – overlaps in only four cases with the characters from *Daughters*, and all are developed with substantial back stories and clear motivations. The action is continuous, and the dynamic is that of a well-made play: a secret is slowly unearthed that leads to its revelation and conclusion.

These seeming stylistic antinomies are somewhat undercut by their similarities. The family dynasty of the Republican play parallels the idea of the 'tribe' in *Daughters*, the term used to designate both the younger generation of tree-sitters and the older generation of sixties activists bound together through affiliation and struggle (and in one case, biology as well). The tightly woven plot of the well-made play in *Mothers* is loosened but by no means banished in the Democratic play: its spine is a detective plot asking 'Whodunnit?' – gradually revealing a secret from the past that creates a *peripateia* of sorts by the end. Thus the two plays are characterized by a dramaturgy of asymmetrical balance. Their form reminds us of Edgar's thematic insistence on similarity as well as difference within the opposing political ideologies under examination.

The plays end somewhat ambiguously with regard to the election itself, although by the time the production reached Berkeley, the outcome was more apparent. This deliberate blurring of the results keeps the play from collapsing into a melodrama or perhaps a suspense thriller: it does not matter entirely who has won, although there are several important consequences, but it matters much more 'how they played the game'. Edgar keeps his audience's eyes on the issues he cares about most by downplaying the question of outcome. This choice and the deliberate non-sequentiality secure some practical theatrical assets as well: each play can be marketed by itself, and, since seeing one play does not provide a satisfactory sense of conclusion by itself, a need/desire for the other is thereby created. Even the balanced sympathy afforded the two political philosophies serves regional market forces where audiences might perceive a more sharply drawn distinction as either doctrinaire or one-sided. In a curious way, the play struggles formally with the quintessential metatheatrical dilemma that also ghosts *Maydays*. As real-life political consultant Mary Hughes, an influence for the character Blair Lowe in *Daughters*, described it to the BRT actress Lorri Holt:

> The dilemma of choosing between what's true and what's purportedly smart is a constant tension in most campaigns, and you resolve it by taking what's real and figuring out the best way to present it. They're not incompatible. The trick is finding a way of saying what is true in a way that the most people can hear. How you present what you say becomes quite important.[41]

If these productions succeed in performing politics so that 'most people can hear', what politics are they performing? For Pam Brighton, *Maydays* made too many concessions, while for Michael Billington, Edgar found the right formula for 'a big public play on a big public theme'.[42] Identifying this question in relation to *Continental Divide* leads us directly into the heart of the plays' own issues. What values are upheld, and what is the price of obtaining a wide hearing – both within the fiction and within the theatre?

One of the great themes of both dramas is the transformation over time of youthful commitments to utopian political visions into more mature if less radical goals. For both the Right and the Left (in the US, at least), the sixties was a period of profound idealism. At least ten characters in the two plays evolve from those early intense, dichotomous, change-the-world stances of youth into a whole spectrum of more complex and nuanced positions in their fifties – characters ranging all the way from an activist still committed to community organizing in the far less encouraging environment of the noughties to an individual whose sole remaining contact with politics now seems to lie in hosting chic fundraisers. Like the varied but related solos in a large jazz ensemble, these diverse performances explore the themes of time, changing circumstances, historical accident, personal experiences, evolving judgments, and competing values as they intersect with youthful starting points. They offer many interesting comparisons with Edgar's similar concerns in *Maydays*, but here the focus is not so much on those who move all the way from far left to far right as it is on the wider distribution of positions that the characters end up inhabiting.

One reason for this difference may lay in the different political cultures in the UK and US. Although the plays involve characters interested in both 'parliamentary' and 'extra-parliamentary' politics, *Maydays* focuses on individuals and groups backing positions that have no chance of winning power through ordinary electoral success, and thus their advocacy of extreme positions is unhampered by any concern for having to deliver on their manifestos. The US play(s), on the other hand, is/are focused around an election contest where some characters, who in past lives participated in direct actions that were both extraparliamentary and illegal, are now within reach of winning office through the ballot box. For the US characters, and in the US context, a central issue is how much must they trim their sails to win, and what does such trimming mean?

Rebecca McKeene, the Democratic gubernatorial candidate, and her campaign manager Blair Lowe, bring to mind the career paths of hundreds of US women, who moved from political activism in the sixties and seventies to the conventional politics of city councils, state legislatures – and by the nineties and noughties, in some cases, the House of Representatives and the Senate – changing the agendas of state and local politics in the process, as the 'gender gap' began to count for something in politics in the US. Ira Kirschenbaum embodies another transmutation characteristic of the period: the radical leftist become neo-conservative; while Claudia Perowne/Ash and Sheldon Vine offer pictures of true believers whose personal circumstances have been changed by the intervening decades, but not their commitments to a sharply dichotomous view of the world. A few individuals are shown as being so trapped by the rigidities of ultra left or right ideological positions – such as Mitchell Vine, the Republican candidate's brother – that they will continue to pursue extreme solutions in the face of gross harm done to ethical principles, human realities, or even to their own selves. However, African-American twin brothers Kwesi Entuli (community activist) and Vincent Baptiste (Republican consultant) offer the most compelling depictions of individuals who remain faithful to their basic value commitments over the period, but who have adapted their ways of expressing those commitments to the changing nature of the actual political situation.

Importantly, the changes in all these characters are presented not merely as the inevitable drift away from the idealism of youth. In fact, Edgar's characters remain more politically committed than the average US citizen over this 35-year period, during which the political process passed from an era where activism and enthusiasm still made a difference to one where the principal activity of political leaders is fundraising for professionalized campaigning. Edgar skilfully signals this concern through Latina characters in each play who would not have been part of actual mainstream sixties politics, both because they were too young and because Latinos were generally not yet full players on the US political stage at that time. They represent changed demographics in US politics, and one, Caryl Marquez, is significantly positioned as a consultant on public opinion and polling.

This wide-ranging scope of possibilities for adaptation and political refashioning in the face of historical change is typical of Edgar's efforts to tell a comprehensive and fair-minded story. These commitments, however, are also the source of some political liabilities.

Although Edgar does not deliberately intend the Republican protagonist to be more attractive than the Democratic one, Sheldon Vine arguably outshines Michael Bern in terms of stature and appeal. In part, this effect is the result of their different placements in the dramaturgy. Sheldon is a candidate who stands by his ethico-political principles in a public test of his willingness to lose in order to stay true to them. Michael is not a candidate at all; thus his personal quest to find the missing piece of his past and concurrently re-evaluate his own political and ethical commitments seems less heroic, less public, and finally less important, even though he ultimately remains as true to his orienting principles as does Vine. In the Ashland production, Mark Murphey as Michael had a difficult time creating a believable veteran of sixties radical politics, in part because the script had not yet provided an urgent enough goal for the character. This aspect was remedied in the BRT production, when Terry Layman, who took over the role, brought a forceful intelligence to the part that helped offset the dramaturgical backseat Michael seems to play. Even so, perhaps the familiar stereotype of the sixties radical as portrayed in popular culture, often rendered comedic nowadays, makes any authentic claim on such a portrait a difficult performance to achieve. Sheldon and Michael deliver parallel speeches about the ideological vision that drives them – identical in fervour, in utopian sentiment, and in persuasive articulation. In performance, however, Sheldon seems to 'win'.

> MICHAEL: [Our place/dream] was for the wretched of the earth. And maybe about making somewhere where they didn't have to be that way. A haven of resistance to all tyrants and all states. It doesn't yet exist, and it may never do so. But I want to live as if it could.
>
> (p. 258)[43]
>
> SHELDON: We moved on to a wider vision: great cities seceding from the state, and states seceding from the union, and within these new utopias the abolition of all taxes, the institution of a voluntary tithe for the public good, the provision of asylum for people fleeing drug enforcement laws and military conscription,

> the creation of a haven in which individual genius could flourish, freed from the fetters of the state . . . I guess, before that phrase got tarnished, a shining city on a hill. (p. 74)[44]

The Democratic candidate, although a foil to Sheldon Vine, is not herself a protagonist and is definitely not inspiring. Rebecca McKeene is a pragmatic politician, drawn to type as a savvy but not especially idealistic candidate, although she once ran a Vietcong flag up a flagpole on the university campus military building. Those days long gone, she now proclaims: 'I hated being in a club where the admission fee was demanding the impossible and defending the intolerable' (p. 269). As a necessary but secondary character in an epic drama, Edgar gives her little interiority in contrast to both Vine and Bern. Although the outcome of the election is downplayed and even rendered ambiguous, Rebecca McKeene does win. The irony is that she wins for the wrong reasons, while Sheldon Vine loses for sticking to his principles, in other words, the right reasons.

This contrast also raises Vine's stature as he emerges as a near tragic hero. The ethical and political wellbeing of the body politic turns on the outcome of the gubernatorial contest. On the other hand, when Michael Bern decides to give up his pending appointment as executive director of a state assembly select committee in order to return to his true vocation, teaching, he has successfully completed his quest and attained self-enlightenment. The price for this choice is direct participation in government: he drops out of the public eye – even if teaching is a form of public service, it is not about governing. Thus he succeeds in affirming his ethico-political principles, but ends in a minor key, personally happy but not part of a vision to change the world (except, perhaps, the worlds of his students).

Even though David Edgar clearly knows the dangers of Sheldon Vine's political ideology, he seems to stack the deck of audience opinion in his favour when compared to either his competitor McKeene or his opposite number as protagonist, Bern. In Berkeley, Edgar and Taccone did counterbalance Vine's appeal by double-casting the versatile Bill Geisslinger as both Vine and Nighthawk in *Daughters*.

Nighthawk takes Vine's vision of the city on the hill into militia territory, showing the extremes of libertarianism as Sheldon Vine's shadow face. 'Citizens' militias guard our families against the enemies beyond our gates. Inside, a free republic of free white citizens, liberated from the chains of federal tyranny' (pp. 256–7). Still, buried in the middle of *Daughters*, in the heart of the forest, Nighthawk seems like a madman, an apparition of extremity, far away from Sheldon Vine's vision of utopian individualism.

That Vine was, in fact, viewed most favourably by audiences is supported by the data: Berkeley audiences were asked by the BRT to hand in their votes for the candidate of their choice, and – despite the fact that the sympathies of audiences in that locale might be presumed to favour the Democrat – Vine won by a margin approaching two to one.[45] In the world he operates in, Vine clearly stands out as an exception – most members of the US political class in the play are portrayed as having more in common with each other (regardless of political position) than they do with the ordinary citizens they supposedly represent. Campaigning (even for Vine) is firstly a matter of raising immense amounts of money, and then using that money to manipulate public opinion (rather than providing any real vision or leadership to the body politic). Even when the candidates and their advisors promote policy positions one might share, their cynicism is corrosive. Because Vine seems to rise above this, at least to some degree, he seems all the better when compared with Bern (see Fig. 5).

The two plays can be viewed in terms of another asymmetrical balance: *Mothers Against* operates as a tragedy while *Daughters of the Revolution* fulfils the genre requirements of comedy. In the first, a tragic hero, Sheldon Vine, loses his battle to heal the community and lead the state to principled greatness. As in antique tragedies, both a family dynasty and the wellbeing of the state hang in the balance. Faced with a decisive choice to take the high ground and stick to his principles or take the expedient path that his campaign manager and campaign chair urge on him, Vine chooses principles, thus willing defeat. In the comedy, all's well that ends well: Michael reconciles himself to political compromise and regains his own vocation to teach, forgoing public life for which he is ill suited and leaving the state in the hands of

Fig. 5 In 2003, Susannah Schulman and Bill Geisslinger starred in the world premiere production of *Continental Divide* at the Berkeley Repertory Theatre before the show transferred to the Barbican in London. This photo depicts Lorianne Weiner and Sheldon Vine from the half of the show known as *Mothers Against*.

the Democratic candidate, a flawed but ultimately acceptable solution. In the closing scene, he and his wife are about to leave for Thailand, where he will be reconciled with his estranged son. Family and state are reconciled, even if the reconciliation is uneasy. In characterizing *Continental Divide* in this fashion, we overemphasize the traces of tragic and comic elements that underpin them. However, these features go some way towards explaining the politics of the performances, which are intertwined with genre considerations.

## *Choosing the right means to the ends*

The election turns on two issues that highlight Edgar's preoccupations with the problems of means and ends. The first is a fictional Proposition 92, Edgar's attempt to embody the trend in US regional politics towards direct popular interventions, something brought forward uncannily in the combination of the actual California recall election and its Proposition

54.[46] Edgar's proposition is a loyalty oath, obviously designed to invoke both the loyalty oaths of the McCarthy era and also the more recent Patriot Act's anti-terrorist excuses for curtailing First Amendment rights. The text of the proposition was printed in the programme for the various productions, a feature that both clarified the text and underscored its status as possible law.[47] The proposition could be expected to be decried by traditional Democrats and supported by traditional Republicans, but libertarian Sheldon Vine is against it because it is 'unconstitutional, unworkable and will criminalize my daughter'(p. 117). Deborah Vine, in fact, is one of the tree-sitters protesting against the destruction of old-growth redwoods, and may be involved in an organization complicit in the second big problem of the campaign: the shooting to death of eco protester Sarah Jane Polowski by a Latino security guard at a lab where she was destroying genetically modified trees by attacking them with a chainsaw. The stand-off between the guard's claims of self-defence and the girl's 21 years and questionable behaviour (is a chainsaw a weapon?) complicates the identity politics issues.

Both candidates would prefer not to take a stand on either issue, but that seems impossible since both are also worried about what their opponent might do, and neither wants to be left in the weaker position, assuming it is clear what that is. In the course of the play, Rebecca McKeene obtains information that Sarah Jane Polowski was shot unarmed at close range, but she still doesn't want to call for an investigation since that will make her look soft on terrorism, a traditional Democratic – and feminine – (voter perceived) weakness. In refusing to pursue an investigation (before the election), she is morally and politically culpable of withholding information that would transform the case. Sheldon Vine does not have access to any special information – except that his daughter might be involved with the group behind the action – but based on his libertarian ideals, he has sympathy with the girl's right to protest and dismay at the government's overreaction. Thus his silence on this matter may be personally motivated because of Deborah, but it also squares with his conscience.

In the case of the proposition, McKeene is afraid that if she comes out opposed to the proposition, she will be accused of ultra-liberal, unpatriotic sentiments, while Vine once again truly believes the proposition is wrong. Thus Michael Bern accuses Rebecca of 'being so obsessed with winning that you end up to the right of the Republican' (p. 268). The Democratic candidate thus appears to be willing to pursue questionable means in order to reach desirable ends (assuming her election is in fact desirable), while the Republican candidate follows his ideological and ethical path, even if it thwarts his own bid for election. Michael Bern himself is at one point even ready to blackmail McKeene in order to ensure she 'does the right thing' – comes out against the proposition and calls for a full investigation of the shooting of Polowski, agreeing to grant amnesty to the witness who can testify to what really happened. He decides he cannot follow through on that path, thus choosing his ethical principles against blackmail but sacrificing justice in the process. In the last scene of the play, Michael says to his wife: 'And wouldn't it be nice to live someplace where you don't have to choose between a moral victory and a real one?' (p. 278).

David Edgar himself might have made this comment while reflecting on most of his recent work. Edgar is exactly the same age as the individuals who are most systematically exploring what their past political commitments mean in their present-day lives. Edgar's plays reflect his own personal evolution from a highly activist theatrical orientation in his youth to a much more complex concern with the political in his mature writing. *Continental Divide* is not simply autobiographical, but it is clear that the plays serve as extended meditations on the political history of the last four decades – Edgar's own, as he has often acknowledged in his commentaries on them. Addressing a large group of OSF regulars about the play and its genesis, Edgar made these connections explicit:

> In the end the plays are a personal vision, based round the history of two sides of the same generation, my generation. The republican candidate Sheldon Vine came from a well-off family, developed maverick opinions and branched off into an unexpected profession, so did I. The central character of *Daughters of the Revolution* is a former 60s activist trying to

> come to terms with the meaning of his youth, who celebrates his 55th birthday at the beginning of the play – by an extraordinary coincidence, I was 55 two days ago. These two characters are not me, because writing doesn't work like that. But the stories are in their different ways, as another character puts it, 'pretty close to home'.[48]

Using these performances as vehicles for exploring the evolution of one's own political positions does not harm the plays, but instead energizes them, giving them a rare vitality: it may not matter who wins the governor's race, but it matters greatly how and why it ends the way it does. The themes intoned by Sheldon Vine in his post-election speech – the issues of deciding not between a wrong and a right, but between two rights; or choosing between security and liberty; or balancing off the common good against personal loyalties; or having to settle for either righteous means or righteous ends, but not both – such themes are endemic challenges for all those who really take politics as seriously as Edgar clearly does.

Edgar's trilogy of plays from the nineties about post-Soviet Europe – *The Shape of the Table* (1992), *Pentecost* (1995), *and The Prisoner's Dilemma* (2002) – record and examine a similar evolution of nineteenth-century ideologies at the end of the twentieth century (as did *Maydays* and *Destiny)*. In the process, these works focus extensively on how the ordinary practices of conventional politics (processes of negotiation and compromise, for example) can produce results which meet a wide range of human needs better than the extreme formulas and drastic measures advocated by either the far right or the far left. *Continental Divide* continues in this path by exploring aspects of everyday domestic politics that are often viewed with cynicism or disdain – campaign tactics, polling, manipulation of public opinion, political money-raising – with a view to understanding whether these practices are in themselves fatally flawed, or can be redeemed by being put in the service of appropriate ends or decent candidates. Like a lot of Edgar's recent work, this analysis of the complex relationships of means and ends central to all politics is exceptionally helpful for any audience willing to learn from these plays.

Furthermore, it seems clear that Edgar has gone to great lengths to present his audiences with plays they can not only enjoy but also learn from. His grasp of US politics is superb – his depiction of the way in which campaigning is now conceived and executed would be remarkably sure-footed and sophisticated for a native, but is more so coming from someone who has not grown up inside the US system (and particularly in that strange corner of the States called California). The ways in which his characters play against conventional stereotypes never allow the audience to lapse into lazy assumptions about either ideology or institutions, and force serious reflection about the possibilities of politics in a style that is knowing but not cynical or dismissive.

In Edgar's efforts to promote political reflection, a combination of generosity to political positions he does not historically support (those on the Right) and the asymmetrical structure of the two plays tends to make the Republican character the more compelling alternative for public leadership, rather than maintaining the balance. It may seem unfair to complain of such efforts at even-handedness and thoughtful presentation, yet they do have some drawbacks. Striving to make clear how a figure like Sheldon Vine can maintain genuine concern with values such as justice in the messy confines of actual events, while holding his libertarian views, risks soft-pedalling the analysis required to arrive at a just solution. Furthermore, narrowing the political horizon of Michael and some other characters to what is ordinary rather than visionary leaves it unclear where the motivation and model for political participation can now originate for those who did not experience the intense political epiphanies of the sixties. The black community organizer, Kwesi Ntuli, offers a partial answer in this respect, as he is unusually faithful to one vision of sixties politics, and continues in a number of small but significant ways to work for a political impact. In a particularly telling moment toward the end of *Daughters*, Edgar has him say:

> So why do I come here? I want activism to be like church. As routine, as regular, as believed, as this . . . You don't have to be a hero. You don't have to be a victim . . . just because our heroes fail

> us, doesn't mean they're wrong. There are no angels. But we will be better people if we imagine that there are. And try to live that way. (pp. 262–3)

Our critique of the politics of *Continental Divide* reveals our own fundamental ambivalence. On one hand, the plays are a tour de force, brilliantly enacting political theatre on every level. The central question of *Continental Divide* concerns the desirability and practicality of pursuing radical political solutions today, or to put it another way, the complexities of pursuing utopian ends when only pragmatic means are available. On the other hand, the structural equivalency between the two political alternatives leaves us unconvinced: the Republican and Democratic alternatives are not equally satisfactory options from our point of view; the Democratic alternative is clearly superior because of its greater egalitarian commitments to social justice. Nevertheless, the plays do ask the most important questions: How radically right or left can you be, and 'win'? What compromises can be accepted and which ones must be rejected? How can one inspire genuine reform of ideas and institutions? These questions, it turns out, are the same for playwrights as they are for politicians. *Continental Divide* is an ingenious, courageous, thought-provoking effort to explore some of the core questions of politics in a theatrical world not routinely supportive of such efforts but deeply immersed in them. Its success suggests that some audiences really do want this kind of challenge.

# 4 Governing memberships

## *Destiny*, *Playing with Fire*, and *Testing the Echo*

> Relations of authority and power cannot completely disappear, and it is important to abandon the myth of a transparent society, reconciled with itself, for that kind of fantasy leads to totalitarianism. A project of radical and plural democracy, on the contrary, requires the existence of multiplicity, of plurality and of conflict, and sees in them the *raison d'être* of politics.
>
> Chantal Mouffe[1]

> The term 'multicultural' has come to define both a society that is particularly diverse, usually as a result of immigration, and the politics necessary to manage such a society. It has come to embody, in other words, both a *description* of a society and a *prescription* for managing it. Multiculturalism is both the problem and the solution – and when the problem and the solution are one and the same we can only be dealing with political snake oil.
>
> Kenan Malik; emphasis in the original[2]

Almost all humans on this planet have organized themselves, or been forcibly organized into, polities of one type or another. Each one of these is different from the others in its origins, history, forms of association, power sharing, protections provided and obligations imposed. Citizenship practices, and other markers, distinguish members of a particular polity from guests, aliens and/or enemies, who are all 'outside' the polity in one way or another. Inevitably, a playwright who investigates politics in his writing must deal in a number of ways with how polities are composed, how membership is arranged, and what happens when these arrangements go awry or break down altogether.

Central to this chapter (and to this overall study) is the discussion Etienne Balibar offers concerning two notions of 'the people' familiar to political scientists: *ethnos*, ' the "people" as an imagined community of membership and filiations, and *dēmos*, the "people" as the collective subject of representation, decision making, and rights'.[3] As part of the imaginative construction of their *ethnos* in nation-states, people find their place in the world with reference to borders and territory as well as via other marks of belonging, such as family and friends, language, and custom; while from *dēmos* come democratic notions of the processes of polity. Perceived as rights, these processes include the right to education, to political expression and assembly, to security and social protections as part of the total understanding of national belonging.

The common conceptualization of an *ethnos* in modern nation-states is that of an historically generated 'community', a (mythical) 'given'; the usual understanding of *dēmos* is that of a contractual association (a rational surrender of some rights in exchange for the better protection of others). The fact that *ethnos* and *dēmos* in any given polity are extensively interrelated but not at all identical provides multiple opportunities for mutual reinforcement between them (when/if they are complementary), but equally chances for conflict and pathology as well. Thus, Balibar argues, the contradiction or chief problematic of social democracy based on nation-states is the problem of exclusions:

> This is why the democratic composition of people in the form of the nation led inevitably to systems of exclusion: the divide between 'majorities' and 'minorities' and, more profoundly still, between populations considered native and those considered foreign, heterogeneous, who are racially or culturally stigmatized ... It is obvious that these divisions were reinforced by the history of colonization and decolonization and that in this time of globalization they become the seed of violent tensions.[4]

While Balibar is talking about Europe as a construction and a collection of nation-states, this conceptualization is also useful for thinking through the consequences of the collapse of the British Empire and the subsequent exclusions relative to its postcolonial subjects. Prior to 1945, being British meant being a full citizen (or 'subject') of the British Empire, not simply an inhabitant of some small islands off the European continent. Even for those who wanted the empire dismantled, there was no obvious alternative understanding of what 'Britain' would signify once the empire had evaporated. For the immediate postwar generation, this was a major conceptual problem, and was a highly contested one. In the place of the empire's organization through citizenship of status and power, there now appeared a blank space or void in the identity space of belonging – belonging to what, and with whom?

Moreover, this same generation had suffered through World War II, gaining an intense shared experience of struggle and victory, but instead of experiencing the promise of peace and plenty, they continued to suffer major economic hardships for a long time afterwards, while the 'losers', for example, Germany, seemed to rebuild their economies quickly and surpass them. In addition to the hole in the centre of the metanarrative of the British Empire and these apparent economic contradictions, a centrifugal force presented by the postwar development of a new Europe (about which they had always been ambivalent when they were an empire) now threatened to suck the remaining marrow out of Britain.

Those who peopled and controlled the new, shrunken Britain of the 1950s–1980s therefore faced a number of problems connected with understanding membership in their own community. In doing so, they certainly began with membership as primary (or 'organic'): you became a subject/citizen by birth, not by swearing allegiance. The arrival of new subjects/citizens from former colonies, admitted by an act of commitment instead of birthright, destabilized the fundamental entitlement of birth in a new and direct way.

In his 2005 introduction to the republication of *Destiny*, 'Thirty Years On', David Edgar writes that the collapse of empire 'hung, silently, like a mighty dark cloud' over 1960s Britain.[5] It seemed to him then that the conditions that led Germans following World War I to turn to fascism were prevalent in Britain in the face of changed circumstances and the dilemmas presented by newly arrived members of the former colonies, arriving as they did in the midst of profound economic restructuring in the United Kingdom:

> The Britain of the sixties was full of the kind of people who turned to the German Nazis – tradesmen, small businessmen and shopkeepers who felt threatened by conglomerate capital above them (in the thirties the owners of department stores, in the sixties supermarket chains) and a newly invigorated and confident working class below. It seemed to me that the loss of the Empire produced a similarly bewildered, angry, vengeful sense of defeat and betrayal as the loss of the First World War had in Germany.
>
> (p. viii)

The island geography of 'the British Isles' also amplified the anxieties being felt at that time, of being overrun by outsiders claiming to be insiders. Certainly from Enoch Powell's 'Rivers of Blood' speech (1968) to Margaret Thatcher's worry that 'this country might be rather swamped by people with a different culture' (1978) ten years later,[6] the symptoms of fascist reaction were plainly visible in British party politics, debates over immigration law, and labour unrest.

Powell's 1968 speech crystallized the early stages of this development. Powell had come from very humble, almost working-class beginnings, gained one of the highest degrees at Cambridge, the youngest professorship in the Commonwealth (age 25), and had an amazing war record (Private to Brigadier in the course of the conflict). He had developed very strong rightist views, and gave a powerful speech in the Commons in 1953, opposing the creation of the Commonwealth, following this up with recurrent attacks on immigration into Britain from former parts of the empire over the years. By 1968 he was Shadow Defence Minister under opposition leader Ted Heath, and, in Birmingham, delivered a powerful protest to the Labour government's Race Relations Bill, which would prohibit racial discrimination in housing, employment, and public accommodations. Quoting and echoing Virgil about the Tiber 'foaming with blood', Powell pointed to the recent race riots in US cities as a warning of what immigration was bringing to Britain as well. Although he was sacked the next day by Heath, and denounced in the press, a Gallup poll taken two weeks later gave Powell's position a 74 per cent approval rating from the general public.[7] It was in the midst of these developments that *Destiny* was conceived and produced.

In 1948 the British Nationality Act had granted British citizenship to citizens of the British Commonwealth, and the first West Indian workers arrived in Britain that same year to begin large-scale Commonwealth immigration. However, this characterization as 'large-scale' was actually relative, and less than it might appear in retrospect. By 1951, 15,000 people had arrived from the West Indies. By 1959, West Indian immigration to the UK was about that much each year. In that same year, only 3,000 immigrants arrived from India and Pakistan. Jumping ahead to 1976, and taking into account the arrival of East African Asians expelled by Idi Amin (see discussion below), there were still only 1.85 million 'non-whites' in the UK population, 3 per cent of the total. And 40 per cent of these had been UK born. Nevertheless, the influx *seemed* momentous and troubling since, as historian Tony Judt observed, 'What made the difference, of course, was that these people were brown or black, and being Commonwealth citizens, had a presumptive right of permanent residence and eventually citizenship in the imperial metropole.'[8]

The contradictions between opportunities for and discrimination against migrants developed through legislation that can be traced from the 1960s. In spite of the availability of jobs and the relatively low numbers of immigrants, the Commonwealth Immigration Act of 1962 limited non-white immigration to the UK through a system of employment vouchers. From 1968, UK citizenship was restricted to persons with at least one British parent, and in 1971 a further act severely restricted the admission of the dependents of immigrants already in Britain (with clear racial consequences). Judt concludes: 'The net effect of these laws was to end non-European immigration into Britain less than twenty years after it had begun.'[9]

Threaded through the same time frame, however, was the first Race Relations Act (1965), which prohibited discrimination in public places and in employment, and provided penalties for incitement to race hatred. A second act in 1968 strengthened the weak first act, extending protections to housing and employment. In 1972, after much controversy and divided opinion, the Conservative government admitted 27,000 Asians expelled from Uganda by Idi Amin. Amin was president, and dictator, of Uganda from 1971 to 1979. In August 1972 he 'declared war' on those whom he claimed were not 'really' Ugandans and were exploiting 'the real Ugandans'. These were Indians who had been brought to Uganda by the British during the early colonial period. They numbered around 80,000 by 1972, and almost all were at least second-generation born in Uganda. They had been very successful as small business people, and now controlled a substantial part of the Uganda economy. They were to be dispossessed (their holdings going to Amin's confederates) and expelled. The 30,000 holding British passports were legally entitled to move en masse to the United Kingdom. The question of whether to accept them was difficult for Ted Heath's government of the time. Thus the ambivalence of the nation towards its new residents shows the difficulty of extending a notion of *ethnos* that would reimagine affiliation and belonging beyond difference.

Through this period, opportunities for employment were still widely available – the English working class was still fully at work. Indeed, initial West Indian immigration was a response to the need for people to work in transportation and municipal service industries. Moreover, by fifteen to twenty years later, the time of the main narrative of *Destiny*, immigrant workers were sufficiently embedded in some levels of the workforce to organize in protest against discrimination – for example, the 1974 strike by Asian workers at Imperial Typewriters in Leicester, struggling against bias that favoured white workers.

While we have been at pains to describe the background of both a public mindset of pre-Commonwealth British 'natives' and of the legislation and regulation pertaining to new immigrants during this period, it is not only because *Destiny* grows out of this history. Edgar faults himself for 'getting it wrong' in *Destiny* with respect to the possible success of a fascist party in mainstream British politics in the late seventies. Yet arguably what he identified were the abiding tensions between inclusion and exclusion in any nation-based social democracy that jeopardizes stable notions of both *ethnos* and *dēmos*. The postcolonial, postwar situation precipitated a near crisis along these lines, and was prophetic of a later moment, explored in Edgar's plays for the noughties – *Playing with Fire* and *Testing the Echo*. What *Destiny* got right was that it predicted the emergence of a populist, sanitized 'left' fascist tendency, represented by the character David Maxwell in the play, but remarkably like Nick Griffin (the current leader of the BNP) today.

We will be attentive to the differences between these periods as much as to the similarities, although the background of British struggles over citizenship, the meaning of nationality itself (Britishness), and the place of law in providing for citizens while protecting various 'outsiders' has become once again a critical matter in the neo-liberal climate of global capital and national contingency. Thus the grouping of the plays in this chapter addresses the continuities of political dilemmas arising from questions of both sovereignty and identity.

Turning, then, to the current predicament concerning immigration policy, the urge to interrogate the idea of Britishness, and the construction of citizenship in the 2000s: the conditions of globalization and its neo-liberalizing transnational processes have cut away more and more of the social supports for an increasingly mobile and deterritorialized 'citizen'. The creation of exceptional zones where people exist without affiliations or security in a state like Agamben's 'bare life' have ratcheted up the democratic deficit experienced by immigrants, refugees, asylum seekers, and illegals, while precarious economic circumstances, the postindustrial permanent state of un- and under-employment, and the anxiety brought forward by the terrorist attacks of 9/11 and 7/7 press notions of *ethnos* toward ever more reactive exclusions.[10] Empirically, the first years of the twenty-first century saw a quadrupling of the annual naturalization of new citizens (compared to the previous ten years), plus a very substantial increase in legitimate foreign residents in the UK because of EU expansion.

In comparativist frame, consider Katrin Sieg's comments on contemporary Germany, which she sets up through the lens of an American critic, Andrea Slane. Sieg points out that while anti-fascist rhetoric has often achieved its effects by posing a binary of fascism and democracy as polar opposites, this is a false dichotomy. Much like Balibar's understanding of exclusion as an internal problem of democracy, Sieg stresses the overlaps between them, quoting Slane on the tensions within nationalism between the universal language of rights and the 'limits placed on the political participation of not only ethnic minorities but women, immigrants, and those without property or education'. While a national community is supposed to bind people together across differences (class, ethnic, gender, etc.), it often falls short of its definitional ideology. Slane concludes: 'Fascism is thus not democracy's opposite per se; it is instead a distortion of this larger nationalist logic, which exposes some of democracy's own deeper historical contradictions by taking them to extremes'.[11]

Looking at *Destiny* (1976), *Playing with Fire* (2005), and *Testing the Echo* (2008), we can see an historical progression offering an analysis of the repressed fascist sentiments of the postimperial condition. In *Destiny*, Edgar was at pains to explain how British subjects (recent survivors of a devastating war against fascism) could turn toward fascism and racism as a result of lost empire and the tensions born of newly arrived commonwealth citizens; in *Playing with Fire*, he looks more closely at the recent failure of government under New Labour to understand and provide state-sponsored policies and programmes for a diverse set of constituencies often perceived to be in irresolvable conflict. For example, by the time of *Playing With Fire* in 2005, neither the native working class nor the immigrants have enough jobs to go around. And by 2008, as *Testing the Echo* underscores, the anxiety of a weak *ethnos* now extends to the fear that the (geographic and political) expansion of the EU may 'flood' the country with even more immigrant workers – although, ironically, these are 'white'. In this most recent play, Edgar also takes up the Islamophobia that has grown since 7/7 and pushes on the definitions and boundaries of belonging by interrogating what it should take to be a citizen/subject, and what possible umbrella of belonging might join the UK's *dēmos* to an *ethnos* now indisputably multicultural and mobile.

## *Destiny*

The play hit town [London] at an ominous moment – the National Front had just won 119,000 votes in London local elections, and over 10 per cent of the votes in Leicester and

> Wolverhampton ... By the spring of 1977 people were eager to know about an organisation that had appeared a joke ... but now appeared more like a threat.
>
> David Edgar[12]

*Destiny* represented a watershed in Edgar's career, not only because it marked the beginning of his long association with the RSC, or because it was his first play in the West End (on stage at the Aldwych), where it became an important national public event.[13] The watershed was more about two critical aspects of his ongoing *oeuvre*. The first had to do with dramaturgy: he had developed a dramatic form that moved beyond agitprop techniques without forsaking political point of view and advocacy, managing to embed social realist techniques of character and situation within a broad epic structure of juxtaposition, historicization, and irony – in short, he had created his own version of the Brechtian form (as would be seen in *Mother Courage* or *Galileo*). The second accomplishment was his ability to address the contemporaneity of the moment with regard to public life in an acute and direct way that intersected with other debates and ferment in the public sphere, contributing directly to public recognition and perception of a crucial time in British politics and culture. In much of his work since, this ability to anticipate the most important issues of the day and stage them in theatrical terms has marked his work. In particular, the plays we discuss in this chapter have been especially tuned to their original production moments, engaging in direct dialogue with other organs of national culture.

Looking back on the play from thirty-five years later, *Destiny* is strikingly both a play for its time and a continuing meditation on the relationship between *ethnos* and *dēmos* with which we began this chapter.[14] At the outset of the second decade of the twenty-first century, the spectre of right-wing anti-immigration sentiments wooing the hearts and minds of ordinary citizens is still visible in British politics. Although the BNP did not do well in the 2010 general and local elections, immigration played a role in the defeat of some Labour candidates and was a major issue in Labour's post-election postmortem.[15] And while it is not likely that the BNP will become a major party anytime soon, the pre-Thatcher threat of right-wing political impact remains stronger compared to the 1970s, and anti-immigration positions have seeped into both Conservative and Labour policies and platforms as well as their articulation through the BNP and UKIP. The larger context of globalization and the recent rightward drift of most European polities show Britain as both the exception and as vulnerable to capitulation. During Gordon Brown's short term in office, Labour positions on immigration exacerbated tensions by linking national security issues to immigrant communities, promising crackdowns on illegal residents, and proposing lessons in Britishness be taught in the schools (we will return to this in relation to *Testing the Echo* below). The new Conservative–Liberal Democratic coalition formed after the inconclusive May 2010 elections jettisoned the Liberals' commitment to amnesty for illegal immigrants, and brought forward further immigration caps.

With regard to *Destiny*, the passage of time puts a somewhat different light on the play. At the time of its first production, the combination of theatrical innovation, the address to a largely middle-class audience on their own terms, and the institutional affiliation to the RSC at Stratford and in the West End, marked a unique theatrical event in the mid seventies; moreover, it also led in establishing the 'state-of-the-nation' play as the recognized vehicle for political writing in the next decade, along with similar accomplishments by fellow writers such as Howard Brenton (*Weapons of Happiness*, 1976), Caryl Churchill (*Cloud 9*, 1976) and David Hare (*Plenty*, 1978). (We have touched upon the debate about this type of play in Chapter 1 above.)

At the time, *Destiny* was a warning against a possible slide to the right that Edgar feared could have resulted in a serious fascist presence in British politics. He has since said he 'overestimated the strength of the National Front' (p. ix), and considers 'conspicuously wrong', in particular, the idea of a possible link between British business and the far right (pp. ix–x). From the standpoint of 2011, the play affords an understanding of the ebb and flow of fascist tendencies within nationalism, especially prescient now, in a time of European xenophobia and fears of terrorism associated with a 'clash of civilizations'. It also continues to capture how individual subjectivity is shaped in relation to ideas of identification and belonging, with special vulnerabilities to extremism in a time of void or absence of the signifier of belonging – in this case, 'Britishness'. Globalization's neo-liberalism engenders more questionable policies, such as outsourcing of jobs to Third World sweatshops and exploitation of illegals, and raises a serious legitimate concern over the welfare of immigrants and Third World workers.

One critical difference between this play and the other two plays in this chapter lies in the stability of its referents or, from another angle, the analysis of its temporal context. It was intended to help audiences understand the effects of the fall of empire and then new immigration on British citizens who occupied a variety of places in the social and class hierarchy of the time. In this sense, it was a 'learning play' for its audiences. Although the play has its own contingencies, discussed below, it is much more settled in its meanings and message than either *Playing with Fire* or *Testing the Echo*, which investigate volatile and shifting situations in which there is neither a clear dramaturgical progression nor a clear political course of action. Almost everything in these latter plays is contingent, and the plays worry their points rather than making them iron-clad. (This may be one reason why *Destiny* was a bigger success than either of the two recent plays – the ambiguities of their representations were less satisfying, according to a number of critics and patrons, than the clear message and analysis of *Destiny*.) We will return to this comparison at the end of the chapter.

*Destiny*'s first scene summarizes and compresses the 'back story', functioning as a prologue to the rest of the play. Set in 1947 on the eve of Indian independence, in a British army barracks in the Punjab, it begins with the voice of Jawaharlal Pandit Nehru proclaiming: 'At the stroke of the midnight hour, when the world sleeps, India will awake to life and freedom' (p. 5). On the back wall of the stage, Edgar calls for a painting of the violent suppression of the Indian Mutiny of 1919 (his use of visual representation, of fine art, as a critical part of his theatrical discourse, is further exploited in *Pentecost*). This short scene introduces four characters, who are historical types: Colonel Chandler, ruling elite, sentimental and 'a little liberal', whose character is shown by his proposal of a drink with his subordinate Sergeant Turner, as well as the Indian Sikh servant Khera, only to order Khera to give his drink to newly arrived Major Rolfe before he can take his first sip (see Fig. 6). This bit of comic business is only one of the humorous ironies of the scene. Khera is quite purposefully slow in his responses, seeming not to grasp what he is asked to do – infuriating Turner but amusing the Colonel, who observes, 'quite a bright little chap, that one' (p. 9).

If Turner is the beleaguered sergeant trying to get things in order for the British withdrawal and the one who most directly deals with the 'natives' (which is why Khera resists him so well), Rolfe is the

Fig. 6 *Destiny* (1976), Royal Shakespeare Company, The Other Place, Stratford-upon-Avon and the Aldwych. (*l to r*) Michael Pennington as Major Rolfe, Ian McDiarmid as Turner, Marc Zuber as Khera, and David Lyon as Colonel Chandler.

born-in-the-bone military man who wants to visit his old garrison once more before he goes home. Turner asks the Colonel if 'they' (the Indians) will be able to come to England to live, and the Colonel replies that Attlee is preparing the legislation, since India is in the Commonwealth. Further, he defends this policy as an obligation. 'We are the mother country, after all.' Rolfe counters: 'I have some reservations' (p. 10). The army men leave Khera to finish packing the trunk, and Khera, alone on the stage, gets the last word. Pouring himself a whisky, he looks at the painting of the Indian Mutiny and then turns to the audience for a toast: '*Civis – Brittanicus – Sum*' (I am a British citizen). A final jibe at the ignorant British, who assume Khera to be ignorant, it also ironizes the end of the British Empire through reference to the Roman Empire (and St Paul's '*Civis Romanum sum*').

These four men become the primary subject positions through which we experience the rise of fascism in the play. The Colonel, the most benign of the English bunch, becomes a Tory MP, 'dignified, worthy. Out of time': The second scene begins with his funeral thirty years after Indian independence (p. 12). His nephew, Peter Crosby, is now standing for his seat in Parliament. While Crosby is similarly mild and patrician, he is part of a new conservative mentality. He is a business type, following the Stock Market and missing the reference to Enoch Powell when Jim Platt, the works manager at the local foundry and chairman of the constituency, cautions, 'bear in mind that we're in Enoch country and you'll be all right' (p. 13). In the same way that his uncle's inclusionary gesture of offering Khera a drink gave way to exclusion in his next breath, Crosby will change from a moderate who appeals to the National Forward Party not to harass immigrants at polling stations to a frightened politician, half sick of himself and his party, who will nevertheless make a statement to the press the night before the election clarifying his position 'against any further coloured immigration' (p. 83).

Sergeant Dennis Turner has returned to become the petit bourgeois shopkeeper who gets squeezed by large business interests. Coming back from India, he has opened an antique shop. Disaffected by what he perceives as a loss of values and increasing threats to his livelihood from both business and labour, he is dispossessed from his shop by a large real estate developer. The man who comes to tell him that is Monty Goodman, who is very obviously Jewish but not a good man. In a double irony, he is both working for a corporation that later may support the neo-fascists, and reinforcing anti-Semitic stereotypes. In the course of the intimidation, Goodman threatens Turner with violence from the Caribbean workers employed on the building project next door. When Turner plaintively asks why the powers Goodman represents would destroy his livelihood, the response (anticipating Gordon Gekko by ten years) is brutal: 'Cos we, we make our money out of money. We covet on a global scale. We got cupidity beyond your wildest dreams of avarice. And you, the little man, the honest trader, know your basic handicap? You're suffering a gross deficiency of greed' (p. 28). Turner eventually becomes the candidate of the fictional far right party in Edgar's text, the National Forward Party.

Major Lewis Rolfe comes back to England and goes into business, but he also stands in the first round for Colonel Chandler's Tory seat against Peter Crosby. He loses, and, feeling bitter, talks to his friend Kershaw, an industrialist who owns the local foundry, about the need for a strong, possibly military-based, class war against workers, unions, and immigrants. When Kershaw demurs, Rolfe appeals to Kershaw not to betray the lower middle class and the NCOs:

> Who, on all counts, have been betrayed. Their property no longer secure. Their social status, now, irrelevant. And in the place of what's important to them, national destiny and hope, we've given them ... You see, Frank, it's not true that we've lost an Empire, haven't found a role. We have a role. As Europe's whipping boy. The one who's far worse off than you are. Kind of – awful warning system of the West. And to play that role, we must become more shoddy, threadbare, second-rate. Not even charming, quite unlovable. And for those – the people that I come from, that despair is a betrayal.
>
> (p. 23)

Thus Rolfe, whose subclass was identified when we were told in the very first scene that he did not go to prep school, represents a particular class interest that invested heavily in patriotism and the idea of a strong military, and in the aftermath of empire and World War II, experiences the erosion of their values and sense of national identity as well as the humiliation of national decline. We might underscore it by saying that 'he takes it personally'. Rolfe has become rich and powerful by the end of the play, one of the businessmen who considers lending financial backing to National Forward after they have taken 23 per cent of the vote.

Khera takes up the offer of British citizenship and comes to England, where he works in Kershaw's foundry and eventually acts as shop steward for the union, which he helped establish. The Asian workers protest against discrimination in wages and promotion, and Khera leads the effort to get the union to support a ban on overtime, and wins. The play shows him in a leadership position as the labour dispute progresses to a lockout and to violent confrontations with the National Forward people, brought in by the management to break the stoppage. He is a fully integrated British citizen – a poster child for a later policy of multiculturalism – but of course he is also subject to discrimination and abuse. His colleague, Prakash Patel, is deported for participating in the strike, since he is technically an illegal immigrant, having fallen through the cracks when the Immigration Act of 1971 closed the borders.

Thus by establishing these four characters as pivotal to the action (Peter Crosby acting as surrogate for his uncle) and also as contrasting social types who react and participate in the political situation in Taddley according to their specific context and experiences, Edgar emphasizes the through line from the fall of empire starting in 1947 to the moment of reactionary racism and incipient fascism in 1976. As Susan Painter points out, Edgar avoids psychologizing his characters, instead giving them socio-political explanations for their choices. She writes: 'He depersonalized the characters on the right by refusing to present aspects of their familial or domestic or sexual lives.'[16] Actually, with the single exception of the Labour candidate (discussed below), Edgar follows through on this tactic with sympathetic characters such as Khera and the socialist-minded working-class Labour supporter Paul as well. For effective epic playwriting, Edgar needed to forge a portrayal of the Right, which, while sympathetic enough to show how they came to occupy the positions they take, would not slip into the 'Hitler had a mother too' psychologism of bourgeois liberalism. When Edgar wrote his magisterial adaptation of Gitta Sereny's biography of Albert Speer, this old sore reappeared again in some reviews as a criticism of representation that tries to delve too deeply into the internal construction of identity in cases of extreme moral disapprobation (see Chapter 5 below).

Thus far we have been looking closely at characterization, usually not the most important aspect of epic dramaturgy, but essential in this case to understanding the lived realities of different strata of the political field. One additional character has a critical role in the overall picture of the political situation: Bob Clifton, the Labour candidate who loses the Taddley seat to Conservative Peter Crosby – maybe, but not decisively, because of National Forward.

In the penultimate scene, following the announcement of the vote count, Clifton congratulates Jim Platt, the Tory party chairman, saying he thinks NF won them the election. Platt responds: 'Only if, took more from you than us, Bob. And who knows where the buggers come from' (p. 86). The ambiguity of whether in the end the NF got more former Labour supporters to vote for them than Tories is critical to Edgar's even-handed criticism of both parties as drifting to the right. He had dramatized the Tory candidate Crosby's final-hour anti-immigration press statement, and in fact the Tory won. However, which way the influence actually shifted is put in question, swinging focus back to the Labour candidate. Clifton is shown supporting Khera and Patel in their insistence on the union enforcing the overtime ban when they appeal to him for support (Clifton tells wife Sandy they organized Asians in the neighbourhood of Thawston to get him nominated, but that he would have supported them anyway). Critically, however, on the night before the election, when Khera and Paul (the working-class socialist managing Clifton's campaign) appeal for Clifton's support to help keep Patel from being deported, Clifton backs off – 'sells out' would be the judgmental appraisal – and refuses on the basis that Patel is illegal in the eyes of the law, and that the law is what Clifton is standing to defend. Challenged by Paul over the relation between law and justice, Clifton says: 'The law's a car, Paul, goes whichever way you steer it' (p. 82).

Unlike the other main characters, Edgar does show Clifton in domestic situations (the only character so dramatized, a move he later considered a 'mistake')[17] and has written a substantial part for Sandy, his wife, who works for the Thawston Community Project. After Clifton comes out in favour of the labour action at the foundry, he gets a brick covered with human excrement thrown through his window and a note threatening the safety of his small daughter. The event comes at the end of an argument or at least an emotional discussion between Bob and Sandy. Peter Crosby had come to their home hoping to convince Clifton to make a joint statement bracketing the race question and leaving it out of the election, something Clifton refuses to do. When he has gone, Bob says something disparaging about the racism of his own constitutency. Sandy tells him not to patronize working-class people he knows nothing about, drawing attention to his class difference from the majority of the people in his district.

Sandy argues that she works 'in the field' and meets 'ordinary people all the time': 'And if you don't think there are real problems in integrating large numbers of people from a totally different cultural background then you need your head examining' (p. 72). She gives him two examples of people who are struggling to adjust to the new multicultural reality. One is a widow who is now the only white person in her street. 'Can't buy an English newspaper. The butcher's gone. The kids smash up her windows. Yes, of course, you'll say, all kids do that, but when the street was white it didn't happen' (p. 72). The second one is an older man of 60, a shop steward who refused to take a cut in bonus rates and got fired and replaced by a Pakistani. She argues that you cannot call these people racist or fascist because they have legitimate grievances, and that their responses are understandable. The brick through the couple's own window interrupts this argument (pp. 71–3).

It seems significant that when Paul and Khera appeal to Bob to make a statement on behalf of Patel (ironically meeting him in a Pakistani restaurant), Sandy engages in the argument against them, backing up Paul's comments on the necessity of following the law. When Khera links the notion of rule of law to the massacre of 1919, Sandy acknowledges the incident but tells him British rule in India ended thirty years back, in effect, accusing him of holding on to the past. When Paul continues to push Bob on the need to try to intervene to keep Patel from being deported, Clifton shows him the note and tells him about the incident of the previous night. Paul accuses him of retreating, so Sandy joins in, 'Ruth's eight months old, Paul' (p. 83).

Here is a difficult set of contradictions, and these scenes are disturbing in a number of ways. Concern for family and the influence of the 'wife' is seen to be part of the reason Bob Clifton does not follow through on his earlier stand. Yet Sandy is drawn as a new breed of strong feminist woman (she chides him for introducing her as his wife rather than by her name and profession at one point), and she does have the experience of working in the Thawston Community Centre to back up her opinions and give substance to her views. On the other hand, she persuades him to act in an essentially self-protective manner, compromising earlier principles. Bob himself knows he has sold out: 'In two days' time we'll know. What profits it a man to lose his party's soul' (p. 84). The Labour candidate is shown backing off of a strong progressive leadership position on immigration issues as he experiences the crucible of risks to his family and his ambitions that speaking out would entail. Of course, he loses anyway, but Edgar is indicting both the Tories and Labour, and calls for the serious struggle around these issues necessary to forge a successful policy on immigration and a renewed sense of belonging that could extend to all citizens.

As David Edgar depicts the vacillation of the major parties, he also shows the growing strength of the fascist side. In 'Thirty Years On', he narrates the development of Britain's recognition that the National Front was a Nazi organization. He points out the tendency of liberal commentators to think claims that the NF was a front were exaggerated, 'a grandiose Leftist fantasy' (p. x). Edgar argues that it was not until 1979 that enough evidence had mounted up to convince the public, as signified by BBC Radio Four's description of the NF electoral outcome as 'the fascist vote' (p. xi). Thus *Destiny* in the mid seventies was engaging in the persuasion of the public in this matter. Painter calls the scene of Hitler's birthday party in 1968, the day Enoch Powell made his 'Rivers of Blood' speech, 'the most shocking scene in the play'.[18] It is completely impossible to miss how brutally racist

Cleaver and Maxwell are on the eve of their attempt to hide their true radical fascism by building a new party (Nation Forward). Anti-Semitic jokes, attacks on communism, praise for Hitler – these are hardcore Nazis. Yet Edgar manages to stage this point clearly while at the same time focusing the majority of the play on the other ordinary British white people who come to join their party.

More striking to us than this scene, with its now familiar trope of Hilter's birthday celebrations, is Act 2, Scene 1, which stages a meeting of the Taddley Patriotic League, chaired by Dennis Turner.[19] This is the event which shows the naivety of the club on the occasion of its decision to join forces with Nation Forward. Their sound equipment does not work, they have to pass around the hat in order to collect enough money to pay the hall rent, and they apparently have trouble publishing enough copies of their newsletter. Maxwell, who we last saw at Hitler's birthday party, is there representing Nation Forward, but he remains silent while members say what they think about becoming part of NF. The scene is brilliant in its orchestration of the way public meetings and grass-roots political processes work, by fits and starts.

The main speakers are as divided in viewpoint and affiliation as they are united in 'patriotism', and with it resentment and open hatred of immigrants. Mrs Howard, a high Tory, misses the sense of values and purpose she associates with the middle classes, and regrets the decline of empire. She notes the 'silent majority' who 'watch their green and pleasant land become more and more like an Asian colony' (p. 41). She mentions people on fixed incomes and complains about the unions. Attwood, who is a union man from the foundry, says he is just as patriotic as she is, although he has voted Labour all his life. Now, however, with 'the many turbans in the canteen', he is worried about jobs for whites. He is explicitly racist: 'And I'll be quite frank about the blacks, I hate 'em. And no-one's doing bugger all about it' (pp. 41–2). Liz, a lower middle-class woman married to a lecturer at the local poly, lives in West Thawston, a heavily immigrant community, and she complains about property values and mortgages. Tony, who is unemployed, points out that Turner's antique business (where Tony used to work) was taken over by a big firm. He suggests that even though they all have differences, they also have a lot in common. Only at this point does Maxwell step in to make his pitch for them to join the party:

> Of course we disagree on many issues. But more, much more, unites us than divides us. It's an old saying, but you can change your class and your creed. But you can't change the blood in your veins ... More seriously we all of us observe a gradual decay, disintegration, in our fortunes and the fortunes of our nation. And perhaps there is a reason – that we have a common enemy.
>
> (p. 42)

The dynamics of the meeting bring together people who might on other occasions refuse to associate. The anger, resentments, and sense of loss of belonging on the part of the group lead them to affiliate with a smooth-talking man with a vision of a larger political cause. This scene is truly horrific because it is wholly credible.

Maxwell suggests Dennis Turner should be the NF candidate in Taddley in the next elections. In his final plot twist, Edgar stages the play's last scene in a bank in the City of London. The discussion between Cleaver, Kershaw, and Rolfe, with Turner in attendance, is about the possible financial backing for NF by business interests. Turner learns that Rolfe owns the Metropolitan Investment Trust, which was the company that forced him out of business. He is truly in bed with the enemy. Gullible, injured, and used, it is hard not to have a moment of sympathy for Turner, although of course he is also the character obsessed with the alleged 'parasitic worms' among immigrant children (which Edgar uses as a running joke against him). Ian McDiarmid, who played Turner in the original production, commented on his approach to the role in terms that connect with the larger issues of belonging around which we have designed this chapter:

> He [Turner] was dispossessed from India onwards and that is a feeling one understands and it was a strong feeling. The play was about what can happen to someone who's dispossessed, who has a void in himself, who doesn't feel fulfilled in any particular direction, who's disappointed by what's on offer, so goes to an area which looks as if it may supply him with what he thinks he

> needs. People looking for an identity, feeling they don't have a personal identity, can grasp hold too easily perhaps of a dogmatic line and consequently be imprisoned by it and transformed by it and made, perhaps, more animal by it.[20]

While *Destiny* remains very much a play of its time, the richness of Edgar's depictions of political processes, and the critique of the failure of main-line parties to come to grips with either the natives' disaffiliation or the new citizens' rights suited the present as well'. Given the current state of play within the UK, but also within the increasingly right-governed EU, this play text is obviously ripe for a completely new major production thirty years on.

## *Playing with Fire* (2005)

> Reading the inquiry reports in the 2001 riot towns, it was clear that the presence or threat of the far right had played a role in triggering all three; but that there were many other contributory factors to the creation of deeply divided, essentially duo-cultural communities in the former textile towns of the north. These included poverty, mutual misunderstanding and suspicion, the increasing hold of religion on Muslim communities, and local and national government policies embarked on from the best of motives, which had unwittingly contributed to rising tensions.
>
> David Edgar [21]

Roughly three decades after *Destiny*, David Edgar returned to its issues in a new play, *Playing with Fire*. Again the focus was on local politics in an economically depressed area far from London, again the rise of the Right was under the dramatist's microscope, again xenophobia and racism figured prominently in the narrative, again the extremely complex interaction of private agendas, incomplete understanding, good intentions, bungled opportunities, and unsuitable processes produced results that no one intended, few foresaw, and all lamented (though for differing reasons). And yet, *Playing With Fire* was very different from *Destiny*, and those differences reflected both changes in the world over the intervening thirty years and changes in Edgar's own understanding of politics.

The generation in its maturity in the early 2000s had never thought of Britain in terms of the British Empire – that was ancient history to them – so they began from a very different starting point. Their self-concept had been formed by the Britain of the late 1970s, as modified by the reign of Margaret Thatcher, the John Major interregnum, and then the ascendancy of New Labour under Tony Blair. Quite a number of conflicting experiences had shaped thinking about the 'United Kingdom' during this period: the Northern Irish question; the nationalism of the Falklands War period; the increasing impact of incremental European integration on British law and policy; multiculturalism; independence/devolution movements in Scotland and Wales; postindustrialization; the end of the cold war and the end of the Soviet Union; the long economic boom beginning in the mid 1990s; the increasing economic disparity that accompanied that boom; September 11th and 7/7/2005; and the worldwide economic recession at the end of the decade. Of all these elements, the single most dominant influence was the long prime-ministership of Margaret Thatcher. As a creator of various changes in British politics and British political culture, and a catalyst and initiator for many others, PM Thatcher used her nearly twelve years in office to transform the British political landscape. To paraphrase historian Tony Judt, Thatcher framed her overall programme as a choice between a 'protectionist, collectivist, egalitarian, regulatory state and open markets, untrammelled competition, privatized resources and a minimum of shared goods and services'.[22] In doing so, she contributed to a revival and reform of the UK economy. However, as Judt goes on to point out,

> As an *economy*, then, Thatcherized Britain was a more efficient place. But as a *society* it suffered meltdown, with catastrophic long-term consequences. By disdaining and dismantling all collectively-held resources, by vociferously insisting upon an individualist ethic that discounted any unquantifiable assets, Margaret Thatcher did serious harm to the fabric of British public life. Citizens were transmuted into shareholders, or 'stakeholders', their relationship to one another and to the collectivity measured in assets and claims rather than in services or obligations.[23]

Thatcher did not merely shrink the notion of a political community – she famously denied that 'society' even existed. This did not mean the decentralization of political authority, however, as she sought to direct all governmental activities tightly from the centre. But it did mean that the notion of a British *ethnos* was certainly emaciated, desiccating the notion of any substantial bonds among individual members or reasons to participate in public decision-making.

When Labour was reinvented as New Labour and won an overwhelming victory in 1997, it did so from a Thatcherite foundation. New Labour accepted the minimalist role of the state she had forged, the highly centralized form of governing she had developed, the extensively privatized economy. If New Labour still carried some residual concern for society, and occasionally still spoke of class, adding in issues of race, gender, and sexuality, it nonetheless sought to address such social concerns indirectly, by attempting to manipulate the privatized economy rather than through direct state action or programmes. The centre of the channel of politics in the UK had shifted significantly to the right.

This is the context for *Playing with Fire*, the drama of the community of Wyverdale, a fictional district of about 250,000 in West Yorkshire. Although the first term New Labour programme has ostensibly returned some local governmental functions to the local councils, it has done so with the expectation that such councils will in turn carry out its wishes, and it uses a number of metrics to assess compliance. The imagined Wyverdale has failed many of these tests, since its white population dominates local politics through its control of an Old Labour local council. Members of the council prevent much, if any, change, and so a trouble shooter is sent out from London to help them shape themselves up, with the threat of more draconian measures if they fail to develop and carry through 'a robust, coherent plan for Wyverdale's recovery. Replete with vision, goals and key priorities' (p. 53).

Although the London specialist shows herself to be managerially savvy, and the local council does eventually accede to many of Whitehall's demands, the changes she thereby brings to Wyverdale result in escalating tensions in the district between majority and minority communities. Into this tinderbox the matches are thrown by chance, and the result is a killing and a riot, with considerable further harm and damage done on all sides.

The second act dramatizes a combination of the judicial inquiry which follows the disaster[24] and a flashback depiction of the events leading up to and culminating in the riot. Police Sergeant Baxter describes the results to the inquiry: 'There's a riot with five million quids' worth of damage and three pubs torched and a sub-post office and a car dealership are trashed and a family burnt out of their restaurant' (p. 96).

Through the testimony of various sectors of the community as well as a more conventional dramatization of events, Edgar explores the ways in which New Labour's approach to politics and especially political change has been seriously inadequate, and its efforts, even when well intentioned, therefore have produced more harm than good. Particularly troubling is the suggestion that, absent a robust understanding of the nature and capacities of a political community, the inevitable outcome of the conflicts and contradictions that generate politics is increasing fragmentation and decay.

So what has gone wrong in Wyverdale? First of all, a number of overarching structural factors guaranteed an extremely difficult road for the envisioned changes. One of these was that Wyverdale as imagined is a classic British postindustrial conurbation: a substantial part of its population are former mill workers, including a large number of Pakistanis and Bangladeshis who had come to England at an earlier time when factory work was still needed. In the present time of the play, much of this older generation is now unemployed (and unemployable), while their British-born children struggle for scarce (low-paying) jobs. Hard economic times have turned both ethnic communities back in on themselves. Into this economically (and sociologically) depressed situation, Whitehall wishes to distribute a few grants to improve some elements in the material lives of certain subsets of Wyverdale. However, the government has no plan to improve the overall situation for all of Wyverdale, so any specific programme to improve some part will inevitably be seen as apparently (or actually) depriving some other part of the city, with consequent ill-feelings and conflict.

This situation in fictional Wyverdale bears close resemblance to the analysis of the post-riot reports Edgar cites in our opening quotation to this section. In 2001 fierce race riots broke out in the city of Bradford and in Oldham and Burnley, whose profiles match many of the characteristics of Wyverdale. The key similarities are the divisions of the community along race and religious lines into two alienated sides, and the violence and threats of neo-fascists on one side and the anger and violence of young Asian men provoked into defending their territory, on the other. Scarce resources meant resentment between the two groups, both of whom perceived the other to be favoured by the government. Few neutral or third spaces existed where members of the communities could have cross-over interactions that might defuse tensions. The inevitable response to the riots was for some to attack the policy of multiculturalism as promoting cultural ghettos in the name of diversity, and for others to argue that notions of Britishness needed to be strengthened and all individuals urged to identify and participate within a common understanding of citizenship. Both of these responses were and are problematic.

In our chapter quotation, political journalist Kenan Malik (himself born in India and brought up in Britain) makes a distinction between multiculturalism as a quality or condition existing in a given society and a policy of multiculturalism in the name of which certain programmes are developed, certain laws passed. Malik recognizes that these are two very different meanings of the term, and that confusion between them creates a wider confusion. As for the state or condition of contemporary Britain, it is a multicultural nation – but only in certain regions, such as London and Birmingham, where racial and cultural diversity is truly 'multi' – where more than two main groups make up the community, and where a number of spaces exist that are 'mixed' (whether neighbourhoods, shopping areas, sports facilities, community or youth centres, or schools). While 'enclaves' of particular cultures, living together, and attending their own schools and churches or mosques may exist, multicultural cities display a wider range of interactional options than so-called duocultural communities. Thus one of the identity issues confounding any notion of 'Britishness' concerns an urban–regional pattern of distinctions between multicultural, duocultural, or in some cases monocultural polities. Their problems and experiences are widely different, and as a result, their value orientations are also far from congruent.

The second deployment of multiculturalism – that of government policy – is rightly open to criticism for its particularity of approach to the nation's communities. While New Labour made multiculturalism state policy, that policy itself did not necessarily turn out to benefit multiculturalism as a practice. When commentators and politicians say multiculturalism has failed, they often do not make it clear that a specific programme of the ruling party (until 2010) has failed, rather than the ongoing project of real people living together, dealing with their differences – to return to Oakeshott – attending to and amending their existing arrangements. New Labour policies are open to these criticisms: inattention to poor white working-class needs or disadvantages when instituting specific programmes designed to benefit immigrant or multiracial groups; promoting certain community leaders or groups as spokespersons for a cultural constituency they may not actually represent; delegating to these leadership groups responsibility for keeping the peace on the streets rather than engaging deeply with the problems themselves; and conceptually creating the silo effect (or separatism) that the policy of multiculturalism should instead contravene. These are the main features of the critique of multiculturalism as a failed policy, although a more reactionary form of criticism simply holds that multiculturalism has failed because no cohesion exists to which all British citizens adhere, a view which inevitably sets up an insider-us and an outsider-them.

Kenan Malik is a more reasoned critic of multiculturalism, albeit an outspoken and absolute one. Writing in the wake of the 7/7 bombings in London by 'home-grown' terrorists from northern cities, he blames a long process of creating a discourse and practices in which culture has become more important than politics:

> Over time, what became subcontracted out . . . was not simply the provision of welfare but political authority too. Rather than appeal to Muslims as British citizens, and attempt to draw them into the mainstream political process, politicians and policy-makers came to see them as people whose primary loyalty was to their faith and who could be politically engaged only by Muslim 'community leaders'. It was a policy that encouraged Muslims to

> view themselves as semi-detached Britons – and that inevitably played into the hands of radical Islamists.[25]

For Malik, multiculturalism shifted the emphasis from politics and democractic processes to cultural differences, creating cultural divisions where there might have been negotiated settlements. For Edgar, this is one important strand of the story, but the other strand is the disparity between economic and social power and powerlessness, marking the communities that rioted and his mythical Wyverdale. Negotiations for shared resources that benefit the entire community, carried out by stakeholders from many subcultures as well as the perceived major divisions, would have been a possible road forwards in these cases, if they had not come too little and too late.

Clearly *Playing with Fire* begins from a different premise than *Destiny*. The threat from the Right is no longer classical fascism or even neo-fascism, but a radical fragmentation and individualization of life that makes the political community meaningless and people feel impotent. Edgar's dramaturgy is now no longer aimed chiefly at helping the audience understand the motives that would drive ordinary English citizens to far right politics (although he sketches in some reasons); instead he is now exploring the numerous factors that might make democratic politics itself, as we have known it, extraordinarily difficult, if not impossible.

The Italian thinker Machiavelli has famously written that 'there is no more delicate matter to take in hand, nor more dangerous to conduct, nor more doubtful in its success, than to set up a new order of things.'[26] And as one of *Playing with Fire*'s main characters, Frank Wilkins, reminds us, 'There is always the risk that even when you manage to achieve change, it often turns out to be change for the worse' (p. 230). Wyverdale's economic situation means that the attempt to introduce any significant change without remedying the overall (dire) employment situation would likely be doomed. But, even if there were a chance, New Labour's approach to politics moved success still further away. *Playing with Fire* seeks to dramatize why this should be the case.

First, the New Labour leadership viewed the problem as essentially managerial rather than political (see Fig. 7). Their trouble shooter, Alex Clifton, did not come to Wyverdale to listen to the local people

Fig. 7 *Playing with Fire* (2005), National Theatre. (*l to r*) Trevor Cooper (Arthur Barraclough), Aaron Neil (Anwar Hafiz), Jonathan McGuinness (Derek Morley), Paul Bhattacharjee (Riaz Rafique), Caroline Strong (Michele Purdy), Emma Fielding (*seated centre* – Alex Clifton), Oliver Ford Davies (Frank Wilkins), Sameena Zehra (Leena Harvey Wells).

and help them fashion solutions which would work for them; she goes there to more or less tell the council what to do, even by bringing in New Labour's favourite type of agent, a consultant, who has all the latest jargon ('performance indicators', 'corporate priorities', 'the three Es – that's Economy, Efficiency, Effectiveness' [p. 42]) – and, incidentally, will sell the council the most advanced services from the private sector. Not only is this top-down approach likely to mislead, but it is compounded in the case of Wyverdale by critical gaps in Clifton's information about the local situation (emphasizing the gap between Whitehall and its provinces). Wyverdale itself embodies the 'whole and its parts' problem in yet another respect: it is not really perceived as a 'city' by its residents. Rightfully, Alex Clifton calls it a 'conurbation' – at least three 'communities' have been forcibly welded together for administrative purposes into a single entity that most Wyverdale residents do not historically identify as their 'community'.

As a result, when conflicts emerge among the various sub-Wyverdale communities, there is no larger allegiance to call upon to help groups work together, and each part tends to go its separate way. The New Labour government's principal response to this dilemma is to try to get Wyverdale to move to a US-style mayoral system of local government, apparently believing that this kind of political engineering will likely produce the desired outcome. In this they are fatally deluded, since the candidate who wins the mayor's position, Frank Wilkins, is someone who the London leadership did not foresee and with whom they would least like to deal: he is the shrewdest local 'pol' there is, but he clearly intends to deploy his political wisdom and skills in pursuit of a populist, conservative, agenda. (We see from his demagogic comments at the Holocaust Memorial event at the close of Act 1 that his agenda, combined with his knowledge of the local scene, can very effectively inflame racism in the community.)

Were these two impediments – the overall socio-economic context and New Labour's stunted view of top-down politics – the only challenges Wyverdale faced, the dice would already be loaded against positive change. However, Edgar deftly develops a third level of impedimenta: actual political change must be carried out by real living and breathing human beings, with their infinite variety of perspectives, abilities, histories, personal agendas, sensitivities to slights, capacities for risk-taking, and religiously-based cultural conflicts. The Old Labour types on Wyverdale Council may be 'dinosaurs' (p. 28), but some of them are very canny students of politics, and understand far better than the New Labour hotshots what moves people, what can work and what will not, and what the likely consequences of an action might be. In the inquiry scenes, some ordinary local residents turn out to be far better than their leaders at acknowledging failings by their own sides and offering to compromise over some of the differences between communities. Thus Edgar makes a case for local knowledges, and the ability of ordinary citizens to participate in their own governance.

However, the New Labour consultant Alex Clifton, arguably the 'change agent' in this situation, undermines her own credibility by developing a romantic relationship with one of the parties she is supposed to be shaping up (the Bangladeshi councillor Riaz Rafique). This ill-advised liaison compromises her ability to promote him as a candidate for mayor, and repeats a similar episode in her past (although based on a different kind of mistake), thus jeopardizing the gains she is trying to achieve with her brief. The question of adequate political leadership is left hanging, although by the end Alex has learned some hard lessons and recommits herself to further efforts.

The play could have been subtitled 'The Education of Alex Clifton', and played as a *Bildungsroman*. When we first meet her in the opening scenes, she is the protégé of a New Labour junior minister who holds out the promise of a major career advancement if she is successful in Wyverdale. When we last see her in the final scene, she has abandoned her Whitehall mentor and job to stay in Wyverdale and try to repair some of the damage at least partly brought about by her actions – especially to challenge and defeat the programmes of the new mayor, Frank Wilkins. In between, she has actually accomplished most of the goals she was set (although many of them eventually turn sour): the Cabinet has added a minority group member, grants have been applied for and won, a 'mayoral' system has been put in place, and a number of other reforms implemented. Alex has used a variety of tactics, from threats to alliance-building to rational persuasion to accomplish these goals. However, her own lack of enough experience and local knowledge and her reliance on a top-down New Labour ideology of spin compromises her accomplishments and leaves her blind-sided by the eruption of the municipal riot in Act 2.

As an example of the kinds of actions which have caught out Alex, the most extensive and ironic must surely be her intervention in the problems with prostitutes operating in a section of the district called Broughton Moor, where the Pakistani/Bangladeshi community is situated. The predominantly Muslim neighbourhood of Broughton Moor would like to get rid of the (white) prostitutes and their kerb-crawling johns altogether. The white Morrison Estate would equally not want the sex workers to impinge on them. Alex shows her mettle by proceeding to gather information on scene, directly confronts some of the participants, and listens carefully to her local informants. She has some suggestions to improve matters – 'block the cruising circuit, make a few streets no-through roads' (p. 35) – but adds an unsolicited objective of her own to the list: to improve the lives of the prostitutes, in the hope of getting them 'off the trade'. So she proposes a drop-in centre, which could assist the women with health issues, literacy instruction, and job training. Alex seems unaware or unconcerned about how negatively such a shelter is likely to be viewed by local residents, since they see it as only increasing the likelihood of the streetwalkers remaining on their streets. The final irony is that a week before the riots, posters went up on the walls of the centre condemning the 'murder' of Darren Purdy, who was killed in a knife fight with some young Asians, calling him an 'English Martyr' (p. 96), and during the riot the crowd attacks the centre.

Meanwhile, in the white district of Thawston, the only Bangladeshi restaurant in the neighbourhood, a start-up financed by the council, is burned down by the residents. Police Superintendent Ricks sums up the rioting: 'So at present, it is Asians going for white stores in Broughton Moor and whites selecting Asian targets in Thawston' (p. 129). This is hardly the outcome Alex had expected.

Other policies she has urged on the council are met with similar downsides: a number of measures which recognized and benefited the 'minority' population group could only be achieved by cutting back on general service programmes (libraries, public swimming pools, and rubbish collection), or by making redundant workers who had long held public service jobs (when these were put out to bid). Again, Alex does not seem to be aware of the price these reforms will cost in further estranging the local white community, in adding to the overall economic difficulties and social tensions in Wyverdale, and in alienating individuals such as Frank Wilkins, who becomes a formidable enemy when Alex's attempt to promote Riaz leads the council to force Frank to resign as Cabinet Member for Education in order to name Riaz to the post.

Beyond Alex as an individual, however, Edgar uses the second act to stage how neat cause and effect do not apply or break down when trying to understand the synergies of polarized communities. There is not, neither in the inquiry nor in the scenes that follow, a clear and coherent chain of events that explains the riot. Buried in the second act, there is a private conversation between an uncle and his nephew, who has been involved in the riot events, and afterwards Anwar (the uncle and eventually a candidate for mayor against Wilkins) addresses the group of councillors and Alex:

> You know, it is sometimes hard to know quite how things start . . . Maybe it is a councillor who is deceived and makes a speech and a hothead takes his microphone. Or maybe it is a banned march or new roofs or a hang-out place for prostitutes. Or a translation unit or the need for a translation unit. Or perhaps it is a man who comes out of a pub in his local-team regalia. And perhaps he calls out 'Paki, make my day.' And 'We know you, Paki, and why not fuck off back to where you didn't come from?' And perhaps the Paki takes him on. With predictable and immediate results. That would be a night's work, would it not? (p. 128)

All of the suggested instigating possibilities have a direct link to the action of the play as we have seen it, and the speech insists that although one of them (most likely his nephew in the scenario with the football hooligan) strikes the actual 'match', it could just as easily have been one of the others, or indeed all of them together overdetermining that somewhere, randomly, a breakdown in civility leading to violence will occur. The speech sums up most of the reasons we have been describing for the failure of effective multicultural policies and politics.

The play ends pessimistically, with Frank elected mayor and all parties within the community more estranged and entrenched in embattled positions than they were before New Labour came to the district to 'sort them out'. Alex, stubbornly refusing to give up, decides to stay in Wyverdale and fight Frank, but this is a minor key matter, one of Edgar's typical codas that figures how people can keep on keeping on in the face of serious setbacks. The overall effect, however, is a demoralized sense that democracy has failed in Wyverdale, and that the kind of 'attending to arrangements' that Oakeshott had in mind has been completely swamped by forces too complex and too ferocious for the fallible humans attending to their arrangements to work out.

We find *Playing with Fire* one of the most insightful and important plays of Edgar's canon, but in this judgment we are in scant company. The journalistic critics savaged the play, although it drew good audiences.[27] Within the academic community, theatre scholar Alan Read singled the play out for exceptional derision:

> I am wondering why this play is so resolutely recalcitrant when it comes to anything we might describe as 'political'. The more it seeks relations with the world, the more singular and isolated from that world it seems ... It is not political in any sense, which is marginally, other than it is about politics. Its subject is politics while this subject ... appears to be escaping its politics.[28]

Read's comments are a bit of an *ad hominem*, inasmuch as he launches this broadside but does not discuss or explain his judgment (having previously declared that explanations are suspect and, quoting Bruno Latour, are an expression of power while descriptions are better because they 'recompose potential contents'); he fails, however, to offer much redescription himself.[29] Nevertheless, Read must be taken seriously because he is a leading representative of those theatre scholars who are committed to the critique of discursive, 'traditional' theatre experiences. In conclusion to this part of the chapter, we take a look at our own experiences of *Playing with Fire*, as well as those of some of the other critics, to try to understand what went wrong with the reception of this play. While we are still quite sure it is an important work, we will reconsider some of our own judgments.

Beginning with a summary of the main criticisms of the play, we have found three recurring themes in the newspaper journalism: first, that although well researched and fair-minded, the play is too 'tendentious' (Billington), 'not engaging' (Bassett), 'muddled by extraneous detail' (Shenton), 'the characters are bland and, unusually for Edgar, the ideas little better' (Edwards).[30] These comments seem to be a familiar collection of the sorts of responses Edgar has received during his entire career from spectators who do not want to get (and stay) involved in complex intellectual issues at the theatre. The difficulty with dismissing them, however, is the frequency of this formulation or something very close to it, such as Paul Taylor complaining that 'Edgar can't make us care about their relationship [Alex and Riaz], and he writes in a manner that suggests that his hobby is to sit on committees'.[31] While we do not 'care about their relationship' – because it is inappropriate and gets in the way of critical political action – we have to acknowledge that the evidence stacks up against the involvement of other spectators in the play.

The second theme that seemed to dog the production is that it was confusing for audience members to follow. A number of reviewers admitted getting lost in the second act. For Jane Edwards, it 'grows increasingly tedious'; for Billington, 'it loses me' and 'it doesn't quite add up'.[32] The most forthright comment of this sort was Georgina Brown's: 'I got rather lost here and, at the end, was confused as to what might have been done or not done to avoid future uprisings. I wanted fingers to be pointed, but Edgar remains scrupulously – maddeningly – non-committal'.[33] This comment was echoed in part by Sheridan Morley, who found Edgar's 'refusal to take sides renders him like the judge at his own tribunal, impressive but distant, denying us the chance to care too deeply about any of his characters'.[34] We pointed out earlier that the shift in racial politics in Britain since *Destiny* and Edgar's own changing political assessments had changed the kind of play he writes, moving away from the explanatory and perhaps even exhortatory *Destiny*, sure of its diagnosis and its cure, in favour of a more sophisticated but unresolved description of political affairs that needs to be dramatized in all its polyvocality in order to be grasped as the conundrum it currently is. (In response to Alan Read, we are saying the play does not provide the kind of smug explanation he eschews, but rather the very kind of redescription that could 'recompose essential contents', but – never mind – he clearly did not think so.) The point here is to concede that for some theatregoers the absence of diagnosis and remedy may be disappointing, or even disturbing, since the unresolved dilemmas confront us all. It is not possible to walk out of the theatre with a light heart after this play unless one is very, very obtuse or thick-skinned. And that does seem to be part of Edgar's point.

Lest this discussion turn into a defensive set of arguments in favour of the play, we will finish with a description of our performance experiences. The play had a workshop period in the Studio at the National Theatre, and we were invited to the final reading that came out of that work (2005). Relaxed but focused, the cast, many of whom ended up in the final production, rendered the play alive and pulsing with energy and emotion – so much so that it seemed very close to tragedy. We felt for all the characters, not just the ones whose views we shared. It was the communal defeat, often self-inflicted, that was painful. Afterwards, the actors and director (and David Edgar) sat around the tables where the reading had taken place and discussed almost line by line the progress of their work on the script. These British actors were intelligent and engaged, not afraid to join in debate and discussion about their characters, the main actions, the relation between the scenes and 'real life'. Emma Fielding and Oliver Ford Davies were particularly acute in their observations and questions. Watching Edgar take notes and mostly listen, we also recalled Tony Taccone's comments about working with Edgar, 'He is probably the best writer I've ever worked with for respecting what I do. He understands and has respect for himself as a writer and for other people and what they do.'[35] Michael Attenborough, too, seemed more invested in learning from the experience than imposing his vision or influencing the actors' views of the play. We left the workshop being certain the play would be a success with audiences.

This workshop performance turned out to be, however, the most satisfying of the three we attended. The second performance was during the main run of the play at the Olivier Theatre at the National, and we went on a night when there was also a public discussion after the play. We were disappointed in the performance that evening: it seemed too slick and fast-paced, and Fielding's Alex seemed harsh and unsympathetic, even as she grew in self-knowledge as the play progressed. At the time, we thought it might be because the more intimate and emotional experience we had had at the workshop prevented us from appreciating the play fully in its new setting. During the aftershow discussion audience members who spoke were often cranky and irritated. They questioned the play's premise (New Labour critique), the complicated plot, and several Asian audience members complained about stereotyping. While some comments were positive and appreciative, the group that evening fairly well matched the newspaper reviews.

It is not 'new news' that different venues, production conditions, and moments of production affect reception and indeed production itself.

However, it helped us to understand a little better why the play was not as well received as we had expected. Looking back through the reviews, we now saw comments about performances and staging that echoed our own responses. Susannah Clapp found the production 'too slow and too perky', and felt the 'strong cast' broke 'the habits of their acting careers, becoming mouthy and shouty'.[36] Kate Bassett found 'the snappy delivery of lines is meant to create an atmosphere of thrusting urgency, but this trick rapidly becomes tiresome', and 'Fielding's pushy Alex is intensely irritating, vocally monotonous, and self-consciously arch'.[37] Georgina Brown also described Fielding as 'irritating' (we wonder if the actor 'takes the hit' for displaced irritation at the play or its situation itself?), and mentions Attenborough's fast-paced production with disapproval.[38] Thus gradually we began to understand the multiple features of both play and productions that provoked resistance in the public that went to see it.

David Edgar has had a remarkable number of successes as a playwright, but unfortunately, *Playing with Fire* had not turned out to be one of them. The gamble of presenting a confusing situation without offering a resolution did not pay off. And of course, as theatre historian Jim Davis comments, 'it is possible Edgar misjudges the degree of subtlety or complexity that spectators can take in at one sitting'.[39] Perhaps a revival will one day give a second chance to this rich and densely packed creation. Certainly the problems it dramatizes will continue to be urgent during the Lib-Con years; it can only be hoped that they do not seriously worsen.

## *Testing the Echo* (2008)

> To be associated in terms of the recognition of liberal democratic principles: this is the meaning of citizenship that I want to put forward. It implies seeing citizenship not as a legal status but as a form of identification, a type of political identity: something to be constructed, not empirically given.
>
> Chantal Mouffe[40]

> There was widespread recognition among blacks and Asians that talk about Britishness was a means not of extending citizenship

> to all Britons, whatever their colour or creed, but of denying equal rights to certain groups.
>
> Kenan Malik[41]

Closely related to Edgar's concerns with multicultural policy and its failings, as dramatized in *Playing with Fire*, is a concomitant concern with the way 'Britishness' became a key New Labour idea, especially under Gordon Brown. After September 11th and the 7/7 bombings, the separatism of cultural communities, especially religious communities, seemed to many people to be the 'seedbed' of terrorism. People were fragmented, lacking a sense of belonging to Britain, so the argument went, and as long as they had no allegiance or identification with Britain, they were susceptible to attempts to betray it. Edgar recognized that people become British citizens for many reasons, and that affiliation (*ethnos*) is shaped through many pathways and relationships of kith and kin. Three years after *Playing with Fire*, Edgar wrote *Testing the Echo* to explore the various meanings of Britishness, not just as an ideology but as a lived reality among a diverse group of people preparing to take their citizenship tests.

At the September Labour Party Conference in 2007, just three months after his election as party leader (making him also Prime Minister), Gordon Brown made a speech announcing a new policy initiative on Britishness, though in fact he had been talking about it for some time. As early as 2005, when he was still Chancellor, BBC's *Newsnight* television programme broadcast a long item on Brown's ideas about Britishness. In the words of political editor Martha Kearney: 'This isn't simply a question of national identity. It becomes increasingly apparent that these ideas are underpinning an entire political philosophy.'[42] In January 2006, Brown, himself a Scot, called for a new national holiday to celebrate Britishness and likened it to July 4th in the US. As time went on, Brown's earnest comments on patriotism and the virtues of the British flag nestled side by side with inclusive comments about multiculturalism being the fabric of British society, and about inclusion and identification being his goals. In March 2008 (as *Testing the Echo* was touring around the country), Lord Goldsmith issued a report, commissioned by Brown, on citizenship. Goldsmith's recommendations included establishing a new national public holiday, council tax discounts for volunteer work, language loans for new immigrants to learn English, a type of community service to enhance 'citizen education' and special 'coming of age' ceremonies for school leavers to mark 'the moment they move from being a student of citizenship to being a real citizen in themselves'.[43]

But some of Brown's other initiatives showed a rapid change towards a more chauvinistic conception of Britishness. This was apparent in early spring 2008 in his strong support for the 42-day detention bill. This bill would have allowed suspects to be held without charge for forty-two as opposed to twenty-eight days. The PM said the bill was necessary in order to achieve national security in a climate of terrorism. It was part of his attempt to show he was 'tough' on security matters. However, concern for the infringement of civil rights caused consternation about this policy, especially among groups who felt especially targeted (e.g., Muslims, immigrants, and asylum applicants). Human rights and civil liberties groups criticized the bill, and fierce public debate accompanied the proposal. The bill was somewhat supported by public opinion, but not by some of Brown's own party, and not even by agencies such as MI5 – the British equivalent of the CIA – who announced that they had not asked for such restrictions. It was barely approved in the Commons, and overwhelmingly defeated in the House of Lords in October 2008. In the run up to the June 2010 general election, Brown also began to talk about tightening immigration loopholes in the points-based system instituted by Labour, stating: 'The system we have introduced gives us the ability to secure the skills we need and to secure our borders against those who are not welcome here.'[44] The shift from the language of hospitality and communality to exclusion and hostility was complete.

*Testing the Echo* took up the question of citizenship and the meaning of Britishness in the face of this hardening climate. Edgar's play was commissioned by Max Stafford-Clark for the Out of Joint Theatre Company, and was based on interviews conducted with people who were studying to take their citizenship test or enrolled in citizenship classes. It also includes quoted versions of several texts produced to describe Britishness or to give a 'potted' version of British history to newcomers. Eight actors play multiple roles, cast across race and ethnicity, to represent a cross section of people who might be seeking citizenship: a teacher of English for speakers of other languages (ESOL) and her family, and some 'native' co-workers of a candidate for citizenship. Edgar dramatizes the different reasons people might seek citizenship, and spectators come to understand that identifying with a community of citizens is dependent on mutual recognition and participation in valued activity. At the swearing-in ceremony towards the end of the play, the candidates who come together act as a social group to prevent the interruption of the ceremony and insure one of the group members is able to complete her swearing-in, thus embodying Chantal Mouffe's concept of citizenship for radical democracy.

For the audience, the opening scene of *Testing the Echo* might make it seem like they have turned up for the wrong play or at least one that does not match its adverts: the action taking place in front of them does not seem to be about 'Britishness' (except negatively), or becoming a citizen (except derivatively), or – for that matter – about a voluntarily chosen activity.[45] Instead, the opening lines are in Arabic, and it quickly becomes clear that the speaker is forcibly intervening with a substance abuser (who speaks 'native' English), beginning the process of forcing him to come off drugs, 'cold turkey'. Since the play will return to this activity between these two men a number of times, and its outcome will directly affect the outcome of the narrative, it is vital to see how it can be an image (or counter-image) for the process of becoming a citizen.

Jamal, the one who initially speaks in Arabic, has undertaken to get Mahmood off drugs, a role (we later learn) he has apparently played before for others. Forcibly intervening in another's life seems to require exceptional motivation and legitimation – we understand in time that Jamal acts as an agent for others – at least for Mahmood's family, perhaps also for the woman who loves Mahmood. The play's opening signals this simplest kind of membership in the smallest kind of human community of kith and kin. However, Jamal also acts out of another motivation; he seeks not so much to get Mahmood to leave the drugs world as for him to *return* to his 'real' world, as a member of the *ummah*, the community of all believers. Jamal calls to him in Arabic, the language of the *Qur'an*, because Mahmood needs to abandon the false gods of drugs and return to the true God. There he will find others, who will welcome him, protect him, help him live by the law of God. The *ummah* offers him a complete and entire way of life, no matter what the particular social or political order of the time might be. Jamal says that if Mahmood begins to return to this better community, then he will be 'no more just an echo of a shit English person or a shit English life'.[46]

Jamal seems quite rigid at first in his handling of Mahmood, provoking association to violent and controlling images associated with Islamist groups, but then we see him begin to negotiate with Mahmood, as the latter makes clear he knows he needs to recover himself, and will make the difficult and painful effort to do so. But he wants some exceptions to Jamal's tough treatment – particularly, he wants to be visited by his English girlfriend and to be brought a book. Jamal at first is opposed, thinking this is a trick to access some drugs. When Mahmood pleads that his request relates to his affection for his girlfriend and to a duty he owes his father, Jamal accedes to family love, and will allow her to visit – briefly – and bring the book.

This opening scene is followed abruptly by one in which the actors in the play, out of costume and speaking in their own names, bark out in rapid fire a series of questions from various nations' citizenship tests. Then, with the third scene, it would seem the actual narrative begins with the already mentioned British citizenship ceremony. Yet this event is interrupted midstream by the sudden intervention of a man of Pakistani background, whose aims are unclear, except that he is searching for someone, and seems to think that something else besides the ceremony is taking place. At this point, the interrupted ceremony breaks off and is not resumed until the very end of the play, so that it feels like pausing the digital recorder while we return to recover the back stories that led up to this point. Much more than this is accomplished during this pause, however: most importantly, solutions to the problem of the apparent clash between the demands of political unity and cultural diversity are staged and probed for possible resolution.

The juxtaposition of these opening elements is the backbone of *Testing the Echo*: on the one hand, returning one's allegiance to God and resuming one's place in the worldwide community of all believers; and on the other, committing one's allegiance to the British political community and assuming a place as a British citizen/subject. Jamal's dismissal of being English is echoed and mirrored a number of scenes later by a character at a middle-class English dinner party, who dismisses being at once Muslim and British – both sides, it seems, initially believe that you cannot be both truly British and truly Muslim (pp. 79–81). The character of Emma, the ESOL teacher, becomes engaged in severe classroom conflict over the tensions produced by some seeming incompatibilities of being British and being Muslim. From the initial emphasis on this stark apparent contradiction, Edgar weaves an extraordinary counterpoint of inquiries into how exclusive these two kinds of community memberships really are, anchored by the success of Mahmood's 'treatment', his return to Islam and the developing rapport between him and Jamal. This process leads to the last scene of the play, when the interrupted citizenship ceremony is resumed, and he and Jamal intervene with the Pakistani interrupter, enabling the ceremony to be completed.

The play does not suggest that there is any guarantee that membership in the *ummah* and British citizenship will always, in fact, be compatible. However, it does argue that they need not be contradictory, that each has its value in its own proper sphere, and that, under the right conditions, they can be complementary to one another. It also examines many of the ways in which such a harmonious outcome can go awry, and the demands of religious belief or citizenship can seem to be – or actually be – hostile to one another. Edgar stages the ways in which 'being British' is seen today not so much as passing a civics test, as being a participant in a way of life (which includes British history and government, but does not make them primary). This British way of life, with its core values as well as its mundane characteristics, is directly and indirectly played off against Islam as a way of life to explore the many occasions in which the two can be partners, enemies, or simply irrelevant to one another.

The evolution of the relationship between Jamal and Mahmood is thus central to the play, and from the hostile beginning at the opening, their relationship gradually develops a more even-handed character. The scenes involving the two are kaleidoscopically intercut with (sometimes very brief) scenes of the several other developing stories, so that after Scene 1, we only next encounter Jamal and Mahmood in Scene 22, when Mahmood's girlfriend Bernie appears (Jamal labelling her *kufr* or 'foreign', meaning English) and after some confrontational interaction with Jamal, is allowed a few minutes' visiting time with Mahmood. Although he is clearly suffering the physical consequences of drug withdrawal, he is also keen to get her to help him study the book she has brought at his request: *Life in the UK – A Journey to Citizenship*, the primer for the citizenship test that Mahmood must pass to fulfil his father's fondest desire – that he gain British citizenship. So, while Mahmood is genuinely devoting himself to prayer and reimmersion in his membership in the world of Islam, he is simultaneously seeking to become British. The only problem with this scheme is that his girlfriend, apparently a British citizen by birth, ironically cannot help him in his task, because it turns out that she cannot read – it is impossible, of course, to become a naturalized British citizen without being able to read, but you could easily be a citizen by birth and be illiterate.

Because of Bernie's limitation, by Scene 30 Mahmood coaxes Jamal into helping him prepare for the test by asking him questions out of the book. Jamal has now moved from forcibly assisting Mahmood to rejoin the *ummah* to reluctantly also helping him to qualify for joining Britain. Mahmood makes it clear that he understands from his father that such joining is not simply signing a constitutional social contract of rights and duties, but is more fully a membership in a way of life. After getting Jamal to ask him a series of questions on British life, Mahmood responds:

> MAHMOOD: Ask me another.
> JAMAL: Why are you doing this?
> MAHMOOD: It's for my dad.
> JAMAL: I thought your dad went back to Pakistan.
> MAHMOOD: That's why.
> JAMAL: That's *why?*
> (*Slight pause.*)
> MAHMOOD: He says if I'm a British citizen then when he dies my cousins out in Pakistan can't have me thrown in jail when I go

> back to claim the house. I guess for you that all sounds pretty fucking crazy.

This speech is followed immediately by Mahmood's soliloquy to the audience:

> MAHMOOD: He allus said as how you couldn't understand the British till you'd borrowed cups of sugar over garden fences or took holidays in Morecambe. He took me to the place near Keighley where there's this little house where three sisters all wrote books in tiny books, and the garden leads into a cemetery. He told me the difference 'tween church and chapel. How dukes are up from earls and earls are up from marquises. And how the British ruled the waves and minded their own business and was gonna fight the Germans on the beaches and the landing grounds in their finest hour. (*to* JAMAL) I guess for you that all sounds pretty fucking crazy.
>
> (pp. 46–7)

By the next time we encounter these two men, in Scene 67, roles have become significantly reversed, as Mahmood is now interrogating Jamal, framing the questions as something like multiple choice questions, but now posing alternative instructions from the Qur'an for Muslim life and practice. Mahmood particularly juxtaposes for Jamal what seem to be injunctions to violence with commands to protect the innocent at all costs, and quotations which emphasize religious belief as freely chosen with those pointing up the coercive nature of religion. The contradictions embodied in these questions leave Jamal without any immediate answers.

However, Mahmood has thanked him very generously for 'saving his life' by getting him off drugs and returning him to Islam. Jamal has also clearly helped Mahmood pass his British citizenship test, so Mahmood invites Jamal to join him at the citizenship ceremony. Jamal's agreement to come, and his actions there are perhaps his answer to the questions Mahmood poses, for now he directly intervenes to 'protect the innocent' and permit all the participants – and especially Tetyana (see below) – to finish the ceremony and become citizen members of what he has earlier derided as a 'shit English life'.

The other participants in this ceremony come mostly from Emma's ESOL class. Despite the fact that it is a 'language' class, its appearance in the play begins with an extremely powerful activity/image which will be interwoven with the Jamal/Mahmood imagery as the work progresses: at the outset, Emma has divided up the class into groups and is leading them in an understanding of the concept of (musical or linguistic) stress by having them clap in different rhythms, but rhythms aligned to each other. This image, of the production of music out of a number of different musical accents or rhythms – either harmonically, like 'western' music, or 'additively', like some south Asian or African rhythmic structures – is a powerful complement to the one with which we have begun (the 'contradictions' for Mahmood between being British and being Muslim).

As students of politics beginning with Aristotle have observed, the choice for political communities is not really between complete cultural homogeneity and civil war; rather, all polities – even small ones – inevitably contain many kinds of heterogeneity. It is how the heterogeneities are aligned that is critical. As in music, where harmonies, or polyphonies, or complex rhythms and counter-rhythms all depend for their value on intricate interrelationships of *different* notes or beats, so too in politics: it is not the presence of differences in the community, but how the differences are related to each other that determines whether the differences will be helpful or harmful to community life. Unity is actually typically better if it is *not* uniformity.

If Jamal and Mahmood model dialogue/negotiation as a way of handling difference, then the ESOL class starts with exploiting the promise of the dynamic interaction of diverse elements. Obviously, these two are not mutually exclusive strategies, and so if a central proposal of the play is that it is possible (and even beneficial) to be *both* British *and* Muslim, then various combinations of the dialectical and the harmonic approaches to difference seem to offer the best hope of achieving this.

Another kind of unity from diversity – that of the marketplace – is brought to light in the dinner party scenes, in which the four participants (one of whom is the ESOL teacher Emma) complain about the efforts of market researchers (and, perhaps, sociologists) to classify them into groups or 'tribes' according to their shared consumption patterns, rather than any consciously chosen membership. They agree that they belong to such groups, but actually also to a multiplicity of them, dramatizing a principal feature of democratic theory and practice – the existence of cross-cutting interests and filiations in society: someone with whom one shares an interest on environmental issues may be someone one opposes on criminal justice issues, so that citizens have the experience of being in the majority one day and the minority the next. This should strengthen the tendency to be moderate in the advocacy of majority power in order that members of yesterday's majority can receive moderation when they are in the minority today, or else citizens can begin to see most decision-making as negotiating an outcome out of numerous partial interests. The centrifugal effects of difference in society are thus tempered by the cross-cutting effects of interest patterns, at least in societies which do not have one single cohesive dominant group.

But the dinner party participants do not consciously pursue such theory. Instead, three of them attempt in various ways to answer the arguments of Emma's sister Pauline, who moves directly to the position that being a Muslim is incompatible with being British. At some points as the debate goes forward in this scene, Emma is simultaneously embroiled in an overlapping scene with one of her more demanding Muslim students, a clash where she is defending being British ('tolerant', 'playing fair', etc.) to the student at the same time she is defending being Muslim to Pauline. The core of this defence is that citizenship in any modern secular European-style state is incompatible with a fundamentalist practice of any of the monotheistic religions. This contradiction is never fully resolved within the play, leaving us to think that perhaps civic peace in modern nation-states depends upon the lukewarm practice of religion by large numbers of the faithful, since full 'separation of church and state' is not an acceptable compromise for the truly devout (of any major faith tradition).

An additional idea important to the play and developed through the dinner party scene is the notion that 'society' is a large umbrella term, capable of including within it a number of 'communities'. At first glance this seems to be another answer to such problems as, 'Can one be both a good Muslim and a good British citizen?' But such formulations do not explain how these two concepts are interrelated: if 'community' means the religious community of a devout fundamentalist Christian, Muslim or Jew, 'community' will then have become so all-encompassing a term for the member that it will allow no room for any larger, more all-inclusive conceptualization – instead, his religious community will be coterminous with 'society'.

Many of the reasons for seeking British citizenship have to do with situations the applicant is fleeing, avoiding, or gaining leverage for, rather than a positive attraction to Britain as a society and polity. These reasons provoke the fundamental question about political communities: what do the citizens expect from them? If the purpose of the polity is limited to the purposes for which it is originally created, then the state should be a minimalist state, enabling economic wellbeing to be secured through the private market, and personal security to be guaranteed against both domestic and foreign threats. But if polities show that, once the community has been formed for the sake of bare life, its potentialities for promoting the good life for its members now come into view, then citizens are likely to adopt a much more expansive concept of the role of the state in the furtherance of the general welfare. Many very rewarding personal friendships began as mundane situations of work-sharing, classroom seating arrangements, or cooperating with neighbours. Had the individuals not spent time together for such quotidian reasons, they would never have become sufficiently familiar with one another for friendships to flower – yet such friendships, when they succeed, will take them far beyond the reasons for which they first met and interacted. So, also, this seems to be the argument about reasons for joining a new political community – the applicants' motivations mostly seem to be very specific and mostly 'reactive'. For them to become fully participant members of their new society, they will have to gain reasons to join in more positively and extensively.

*Testing the Echo* also explores the problem of the community's narrative. At first glance, it seems that one feature common to all communities (and thus requirable of all citizens) is a knowledge of the community's story, its common historical narrative. But as the play's use of bits and pieces from the British story show (told through their various iterations), even the simplest version of this history is controversial and contested, and so it is not immediately obvious what story should be expected to be learned by newcomers. Nor is it ever clear that this is a useful strategy.

We are shown all this through one of the play's central narratives: the interruption of the citizenship ceremony. The reason that this happened, we learn, is that one of the participants is a Ukrainian woman named Tetyana Mikhailovna Ismael. Her husband, a man of Pakistani background, has been using her *sans papiers* immigration status as a weapon to keep her in a marriage she (mostly) wants to leave (actually, what she does not know is that this is not true – she cannot be deported just because she might have left the marriage). Citizenship would allow her to act on a more equal and independent footing. So, she secretly prepares for the citizenship exam. But the process of preparing has brought her closer to her stepdaughter, 11-year-old Muna, whose affection and relationship has thereby become a reason for remaining in the marriage. Once again, we consider a case with a complex set of motives for seeking citizenship.

In the final scenes, we see Aziz (her husband) break into the already underway new citizens' ceremony in order to find Tetyana (and, she fears, prevent her from becoming a citizen), only to be thwarted by Mahmood and Jamal, who enable the ceremony to be completed. However, then we find that Aziz has actually tracked Tetyana down in order to tell her that he had lied to her – he actually has no hold over her based on her immigration status. Even more importantly, he now wants to tell her that both Muna and he need her and want her to stay married. She turns out to be open to that, but wants a renegotiation of some central aspects of the relationship, including her right to remain in her orthodox religion. Once again the play has moved between a tiny community, the family, to the larger ones of nation and religion, and drawn its lessons – and paradoxes – from the nature of each and their collisions with one another.

We get another, related, 'take' on these same issues with Emma, the ESOL teacher. No one in the whole play is more in the middle of all the conflicting pushes and pulls of affiliation than Emma. Because one route to citizenship is the ESOL class, Emma must routinely defend some of the more inane features of English language and popular culture to immigrants, while defending Muslims to middle-class Brits like herself, all the while being set up for a fall by one of her more assertive Muslim students. This experience increases her uncertainty about whether she wants to continue ESOL work at all. She performs equably, insightfully, even heroically in these multiple and conflicting roles, although the metaphor of 'stress' (in music or language) that she used for positive purposes at the beginning of the play becomes a reality of 'stress' that may be more than she can cope with at the end. All the unresolved conflicts in her situation, though, seem to be the unresolved conflicts in the nation at large – presented for the audience to apprehend and digest, testing all the echoes of community and conflict inherent in a multicultural society.

Although Emma's story, then, seems ultimately negative, Mahmood's seems to offer a positive, if limited, outcome, and – in a different direction – Tetyana's as well. Perhaps the most hopeful story, though, is a seemingly minor one, which at first appears to be in the play for comic relief: the Korean Chong Myung Yoon and his workmates. Like Tetyana, Chong is studying 'Britishness' out of a book so he can pass the exam for citizenship, and at first his co-workers give him no end of trouble about this undertaking. In fact, these working-class mates seem like just the kind of people usually stereotyped as xenophobic and anti-immigrant bullies. But, as the play goes on, their harsh teasing of Chong gradually transforms into assisting him – personal friendship apparently trumping xenophobic tendencies – and Chong turns out to have already mastered the right kind of information (knowledge of English football history) to legitimate him in their eyes. By contrast, the educated middle-class people at the dinner party with Emma seem more hostile to foreigners than these working-class men and women. This story, then, among other results, dramatizes one of the central positions of the play, that every community needs more than just a 'social contract'. Along with that contractual framework goes the lived experience of common endeavours, common language, and evolving personal filiations. Chong is already an accepted member of his group's small work community, and his success in gaining citizenship is thereby celebrated by that group.

The play is dedicated to Max Stafford-Clark, with whom Edgar had hoped to work closely during this project. Unfortunately, Stafford-Clark's unexpected serious illness made this collaboration impossible. Edgar worked with the Out of Joint interview method, and the cast spoke to Birmingham Respect councillor Salma Yaqoob and Bernard Crick, who wrote the history section of the *Life in the UK* handbook, among others. Edgar considers the style of the play a departure from his usual narrative strategies, with its fragmented and non-realistic scenes held together through thematic or associative features. Matthew Dunster directed the show, which toured to eleven regional venues in 2008, from Edinburgh to Guildford, and also to the Royal Theatre of the Hague. We saw performances at the Salisbury Playhouse, Warwick Arts Centre, the Tricycle Theatre (London), and Birmingham Repertory Theatre (see Fig. 8).

The experience of watching the play in different venues and over the entire run of the show highlighted a number of features for us, as multiple viewings of *Pentecost* had also done. The play was served best in the most intimate and interactive setting – the Tricycle – where the audience wraps around the stage in such a way that members see each other as easily as the stage action. The Tricycle, of course, also carries certain values by virtue of its history and status as a premier political theatre: here, at least, one does not worry as much about whether the audience will be interested enough to pay close attention. The show was very successful in this location.

On the other hand, when the show opened in Salisbury, it was rather rough and had not 'bedded down' yet (as theatre people sometimes put it). The intimacy of the stage there – and the goodwill of the local patrons – underscored some of the shortcomings, because they were so 'up close and personal'. For example, the rhythm and timing needed to manage the intercut dialogue of the dinner party scene with the teacher–student exchange is hair-triggered, like much of Caryl Churchill's work, whose slash notation Edgar adapts for the grammar of his own piece. The insufficiently polished rendition of this scene threw off the rhythm of its polyphony so that it was difficult to hear/understand the fast-paced

Fig. 8 *Testing the Echo* (2008), Out of Joint on tour. Design for publicity.

dialogue, which is, as in all Edgar plays, essential to its rhetorical success. We were confirmed in our perception that Edgar's plays need vocal work of an exceptionally high standard as a key feature of production.

The Warwick Arts Centre is a cavernous space, and it worked fine for the comic tableau scenes, such as the British history satires and the citizenship test questions, but did not serve well the intimate scenes between Tetyana and Muna, where the child's affection for

Tetyana and fears about losing her presence subtly begin to affect Tetyana's attitude towards her situation. Heart-warming performances by Farzana Dua Elahe as Muna and Kirsty Bushell as Tetyana were most effective in other spaces. By the time the show closed at BRT, it was extremely well polished and precision-timed, and the thrust stage suited the piece well. Although a larger venue than either the Tricycle or Salisbury Playhouse, it can be an inviting space – and a regular audience welcoming a local well-known friend such as Edgar gave the performances an additional boost.

The play received a positive reception, for the most part, certainly warmer than *Playing with Fire*, judging not only from reviews but also from the feel of the audiences around the country with whom we watched the performances. (It was seen by over 14,000 people on its tour.)[47] Best, perhaps, was Ian Shuttleworth's appraisal, which sums up the chapter's multiple views of Edgar rather well:

> It was while watching Matthew Dunster's excellent, pacy ensemble staging for Out of Joint that I realized why I so like David Edgar's writing. Edgar has fallen some way out of fashion in recent years: respected, even revered, but not feted in an immediate way. That is because his kind of liberalism has also become *passé*: a kind that is not afraid to talk turkey rather than waffling in buzz-phrases. When Edgar examines a topic, he asks questions that are not rhetorical nor ends in themselves: he actually wants answers. He recognizes this process must also include an honest examination of our own standpoint . . . Myths can embody collective human truths, and it is these Edgar constantly delves for – not in an airy way but with his sleeves rolled up, digging vigorously in our social and cultural soil.[48]

Well, we might quibble with the characterization of Edgar as 'liberal', but still . . . the image of Edgar digging in social and cultural soil does him justice. *Testing the Echo* stages embodied experiences of belonging in a time of great uncertainty about governing memberships. Better than a debate or essay, the play demands that we feel what it is like to be in another's shoes.

# 5 'A legend in your own time'

## *The Jail Diary of Albie Sachs, Mary Barnes,* and *Albert Speer*

In a lot of ways, I find the process of adaptations is very like the normal process of play-making.

David Edgar[1]

David Edgar is a skilled adapter, and is perhaps best admired for that talent. *Nicholas Nickleby*, his biggest 'hit', is probably also his best-known adaptation, but the plays we discuss in this chapter are also adaptations, and he has adapted or translated a number of classical dramas as well, such as recent versions of Ibsen's *The Master Builder* and Brecht's *Galileo.* In 2010 his highly successful adaption of *Arthur & George*, the prize-winning novel by Julian Barnes, was co-produced by Birmingham Repertory Theatre and Nottingham Playhouse.

In fact the subject of adaptation is a bit of a sore point with Edgar, who feels the dismissal of the artistry of adaptation by certain scholars and critics (for example, Michael Billington) is unfair and unreasonable.[2] David Hare has also taken the critical establishment to task for finding the Tricycle's tribunal play about the Stephen Lawrence inquiry, *The Colour of Justice*, created by Richard Norton-Taylor, not suitable for the Best Play Award of 1999, because they would not see editing as creative writing.[3] The focus of our chapter on Edgar's adaptations takes for granted that these are legitimate new plays in their own right, but we also seek to understand 'the relationship between the original work and my [Edgar's] perception of it'.[4] We are also interested in the matters of aesthetic craft that shape the dramaturgy, and finally of course are committed to the political inquiry of the entire volume – what do the human exemplars here portrayed communicate via Edgar about themselves as political animals and intersubjective beings embedded in particular socii?

It is no coincidence that adaptation gets linked with documentary writing in the hierarchy of creative writing ventures. Both involve creatively reshaping other documents – what John Grierson, one of the early theorists of documentary, described in the 1930s as 'pass[ing] from the plain (or fancy) descriptions of natural material, to arrangement, rearrangement, and creative shapings of it'.[5]

*The Jail Diary of Albie Sachs* (1978) is probably the closest David Edgar has come to writing verbatim theatre, insofar as it is based on the autobiography of the same name, and largely although not entirely confines itself to material present within that memoir. Thus Albie Sach's verbatim account of his imprisonment is the source of the play. We use the term a little loosely here, however, because Edgar does write fictional bookends – a hypothetical speech that Sachs gives just before his imprisonment begins the play, and a final fictional scene (although one based on an actual incident), placed after Sachs's second period of detention and just before his departure for Britain, which sums up the play. Yet the playscript follows the published diary very closely, and surely some of the same truth claims which give authority to verbatim theatre feature here: these events really happened; the words that are spoken are the words of the protagonist; this text is an historical document.

Elsewhere Reinelt has argued that documentaries make a promise: 'to provide access or connection to reality through the facticity of documents, but not without creative mediation, and individual and communal spectatorial desire'.[6] In the case of *The Jail Diary*, Edgar is a creative mediator well aware of the individual appeal of his subject, and also of the socio-political context which generated desire for a new South Africa, a project finally realized thirty years after Sachs was held in solitary confinement under the infamous Ninety-Day Law that allowed the South African government to imprison him (or anyone) without formal charges for consecutive three-month periods.

The other possible problem involved in considering this play as a form of verbatim theatre is that Edgar has distanced himself from this form in his writings about the theatre. In talks to academic conferences at the universities of Reading in 2004 and Birmingham in 2007, Edgar characterized verbatim theatre as existing in an historical relationship to fact-based theatre of the fifties and sixties (citing Kipphart and Weiss), which he considers 'a kind of abdication'.[7] Instead of putting forth an argument or interpretation of reality in dramatic form, Edgar charges this type of theatre with only presenting documents and allowing the audience to do all the interpretive work. While he is careful not to simply extend this critique to contemporary verbatim theatre, he comes quite close to it: 'I wonder if . . . there isn't an element of, if not abdication, then a desire to present a rather wider configuration of dots for the audience to try and join up'.[8] In contrast to this form, Edgar prefers 'faction', a form of fact-based theatre in which 'a number of actual phenomena are conflated and fictionalized in order to present a thesis about their underlying characteristics'.[9] The advantage of this approach is that it does not make any truth claims about details, but asks the audience to see the analogy between the fiction and the factual historical cases and to agree (or not) that the thesis of the play applies to the reality at hand. Edgar cites his eastern European trilogy and *Playing with Fire* as examples, and we discuss this in Chapter 6 below.[10]

However, in the late 1970s Edgar was working much closer to a more directly fact-based theatre in plays about Albie Sachs and Mary Barnes. Both plays derived a good part of their power from direct links to the real personages on whom they were based. Arguably, no fictional analogue could have been as compelling as the real thing. The plays make that documentary promise – to provide access, creatively mediated, to real objects of desire. They deliver in various ways, but in the case of *The Jail Diary*, the autobiographical voice of Sachs in direct address to the audience constituted the main vehicle of delivery.

Albie Sachs is a maybe hero and joins Eddie (the character name for Laingian psychiatrist Joe Berke in *Mary Barnes*) in giving Edgar the opportunity to probe the limits of human finitude, the relationship between individual acts and communal systems, and the personalities of mythic leaders or characters. Like his mentor, R. D. Laing, Berke is a charismatic figure, and his attempts to help establish a therapeutic community so radical it could accommodate Mary Barnes's impossible behaviour is the central focus of the play. Like Albie Sachs, Joe Berke (or Eddie, as he is called in the play) has vision and personal conviction that inspires people to follow him; like Sachs, he is severely tested by the limits of his ability to be a 'good man' in relation to a corrupt system and the needs of a specific community.

Some years later (2000), Edgar wrote a third play about a high-profile individual. Albert Speer is the third figure, perhaps an anti-hero, whose memoirs, from prison, raise some similar issues about the nature of detention and isolation that are raised in *The Jail Diary of Albie Sachs*. But, more importantly, they continue the exploration of the relationship between individual action and political responsibility, self-knowledge and self-representation central to the earlier two plays. In *Albert Speer*, of course, Edgar adapts Gitta Sereny's biography, so the connection to self-representation is indirect. Albert Speer interests Edgar as a means of examining how the evils of the Nazi regime came to be accepted or overlooked by Speer in his pursuit of architectural (read artistic) greatness. Speer claimed he did not know about the death camps, but if that is false and he did know, did he know at a conscious level?

In all three of these cases, Edgar combines facts and documents with the shaping putty of fiction. Mostly, these plays can be seen as 'dramadocs' (or 'docudramas', as US parlance has it.) Of course they could also be seen, especially from the distance of the present, as history plays, but the epistemological investment in documents and facts overrides this category, involving the plays in various substantial truth claims. In particular, the plays put forward fact-based views of their protagonists.

The combination of fiction and fact that fashions the plays derives some of its power from the actual exemplars who are portrayed as public figures. The plays probe a political problematic equal in importance to others we are investigating in this study: the question of exemplary individuals in relation to their role in history, and the even more basic question of the relationship between individuals and society. The public figures for whom the plays are named provide particular human foci for this investigation.

The issue of individuals and society, as well as those surrounding exemplary individuals, are not new problems, and a quick review of previous thinking about them may be useful. In Greek, Roman, and medieval[11] political theory, starting with Plato and Aristotle, inquiry began with the assumption of a correlation between citizens and their regime: a 'good' regime required 'good' citizens and 'bad' citizens produced a bad regime (and vice versa). One major corollary of these axioms was that it did not seem possible to be a 'good' person in a bad regime.

The problem, then, was how to produce both good persons and good regimes. Over time, much investigation centred on the promise of legal systems for directing both individuals and regimes towards the good, and this concern unites the divergent thinkers of the Middle Ages. But modern theorists, beginning with Machiavelli, Hobbes, and Locke, began to develop a different solution. They argued that pursuit of 'the Good Society' was always doomed to failure, and usually was counterproductive: in reality, dystopias were much more commonly the outcome than utopias. Instead of aiming for the heavenly city on earth, they argued, it would be better to develop a society that was peaceful and fair in its structure, and which allowed individuals to pursue their own moral success or failure – and that, therefore, did not require saints as citizens. Modern constitutionalism is one form of this approach; libertarianism (with its base often in a market model of society) is another.

As the nineteenth century developed, the rise and spread of constitutional regimes in Europe seemed to promise that this approach would develop societies that at least reduced the use of force, replaced arbitrary action with the rule of law, rewarded talent with appropriate responsibility, and allowed citizens to participate in public decision-making – or to opt out of it altogether. Citizens did not need to be 'good'; they only needed to follow the rules. Politics had become an engineering problem. And one could follow one's own moral agenda, and be a good person, even in a bad regime.

Then came the political crises generated during and after World War I, and the subsequent rise of totalitarian regimes. These new regimes had found ways to focus the enormous power of the modern state to overwhelm all opposition, and in the process make everyone living in the society complicit in its crimes. They usually did so under the colour of constitutions and laws. And they committed horrifying crimes.

During and after the Second World War, the acute anxiety about how it was possible for many Germans – as individuals and as members of judicial, religious, professorial, and other institutions – to be complicit with a totalitarian regime like the Nazi system, and with the events of the Holocaust, provided the most graphic example of this problem. In more recent times the post-structuralist critique of thinkers such as Foucault and Althusser examined the limits of the autonomy of individual subjectivity in relation to repressive disciplinary regimes such as prisons and asylums or the political systematics of state apparati. From this point of view, it may not be 'wrong' to ask why someone did not oppose the Nazis; instead, it may be absurd – there was no basis for such opposition.

Another view of this problematic assumes opposition may be possible, but asks whether in a given circumstance it is better to work for reform within a system or break with it entirely through revolutionary actions. Should all the German judges have resigned in the face of Nazi corruption of the legal system, or should they have continued to try to achieve what protections remained for the innocent? Revolutionary defiance often looks good but accomplishes little; change may come more through the efforts of reformers than rebels.

In this chapter, the three plays taken together show Edgar working through these issues by dramatizing three historical contexts and the actions of three concrete individuals in response to the ethico-political challenges of their predicaments. We move from the play closest to verbatim theatre (*The Jail Diary*) to a play less closely linked to the source text (*Mary Barnes*), to a play which through adaptation of a contemporary biography, enters the multivocal debates about the interpretation of originary memoirs (*Albert Speer*). These matters of form have a direct bearing on the answers that can be formulated to the overarching political problematic because they carry a truth claim about reality through their quasi-documentary status. Edgar has written in his introduction to the plays *(Plays: One)* that he was working within and learning to perfect social realism modelled after Lukács; however, arguably it is not the aesthetics of social realism that is critical here (indeed, the plays concatenate realist and epic dramaturgical forms), but rather the epistemology of Lukács's theories – a realist philosophy based on observation, evidence, documentation, 'objectivity'.

## *The Jail Diary of Albie Sachs*

In 1963 a young South African advocate was imprisoned for his activities in opposition to apartheid. Under the newly established Ninety-Day Law, he could be held without formal charges and interrogated for up to ninety days; then he could be rearrested and held for another three months (*ad infinitum*). Black South African activists had been detained and imprisoned repeatedly in this manner, and some, like ANC leader Nelson Mandela, had been convicted and imprisoned for life on Robben Island. Sachs had defended a number of these political activists, and succeeded in keeping some of them out of jail. Now he, a Jewish white man, was undergoing interrogation and detention in a moment when the state was increasing its surveillance and persecution of all 'freedom fighters' who defied the national system of apartheid.

The play recalls the period of South African history under apartheid in the early 1960s. Since 1994, when South Africa held its first true democratic elections and apartheid ended, the 'New South Africa' has been trying to deal with its violent past and struggling to build a new multicultural society. The focus on the Truth and Reconciliation Commission and the more recent challenges to democratic government in the new era have made the earlier days of the struggle against apartheid recede a bit in the memory of those who were not there, so a brief recap of the main events of that decade may be helpful.

The 1960s saw the banning of the African National Congress and the Pan African Congress, the main oppositional organizations representing South African blacks in the strictly segregated society that used its infamous 'pass laws' to allow blacks into the cities only to work for a limited amount of time; they were otherwise to return to their 'tribal' 'homelands', impoverished areas away from the white developments. During their employment, black workers were to live in townships, which had no basic services such as banks, supermarkets, or retail shops, and where overcrowded housing consisted of tenement blocks and shacks. If caught without a passbook, people were arrested, and in the first years after the pass code became law (1952) arrests were averaging 2,000 a day.[12] When people were returned to their 'tribal homelands', the situation was worse. Allister Sparks, prize-winning South African journalist, describes the situation in his study of life under apartheid:

> The reserve areas, supposedly havens of traditional African life based on subsistence farming, became overpopulated dust bowls disfigured by large 'resettlement camps' where hundreds of thousands of uprooted people were dumped. Outside South Africa's cities huge complexes arose where hundreds of thousands of other blacks lived – with no business centres, no downtowns, no highrises, just endless sprawls of little gray, drab, uniform, matchbox houses, these were not so much townships as gigantic barracks to accommodate an army of workers.[13]

The systematic exclusion and persecution of black people worsened through this period (forced removals destroyed their makeshift townships and displaced thousands to make way for 'urban renewal' for whites). Blacks could not own property, they had segregated and inferior health care and education (which excluded women), and they did not have the right to strike or, of course, to vote. Any white person could stop them on the street and demand their passbook.

In 1960 the Sharpeville Massacre saw the police open fire on an unarmed and peaceful group of demonstrators, leaving 69 people dead and 180 wounded. This event is generally regarded as a turning point in the struggle, when the black political parties and trade unions were outlawed, and they shifted towards violent resistance. As a result of some acts of sabotage, the government instigated a set of security measures under a State of Emergency that made South Africa a police state. In 1976 the Soweto Uprising formed another watershed. On this occasion, a peaceful student protest against being instructed in Afrikaans ended in rioting after the police opened fire into the crowd. Twenty-three, including some teenagers, died in the first day, and by the end of the year around 600 people had died, most of them black.

These two massacres, Sharpeville and Soweto, almost bookend the period between 1960, when Sachs was practising law, representing mostly black clients facing the death penalty or imprisonment for their political opposition to apartheid, and 1978, when the play version of *The Jail Diary of Albie Sachs* was first produced. When Sachs was first arrested and imprisoned under the Ninety-Day Law in 1963, he was one of the first white persons to be so detained. An idealistic and non-violent person, this experience shook him thoroughly. He describes the experience and his reactions in the diary.

In his jail diary, Sachs reflects on his own ability to remain committed to resisting his interrogators and his understanding of what constitutes 'honour' and 'dignity' in terms of his treatment and his self-image. He also foregrounds the nature of the prison system he encounters and its imbrication within the apartheid regime, the corruption of the legal system (the supposed last defence against tyranny), and how his race and class privileges influenced his behaviour and treatment. The isolation of being in solitary confinement for a long period of time (168 days) is represented through the diary, even as the voice of Sachs turns outwards to communicate with an imagined community outside the prison. Sachs even explicitly imagines himself writing for a theatrical performance. This 'solo performance' is both memoir and play.[14]

'So this is what it's like.' The first line of the memoir sets out the performative task. The diary will recount what has happened in order to demonstrate what it is like to be a person like Sachs, in solitary confinement under the Ninety-Day Law, in 1963. Edgar uses the phrase to make a similar claim for his play – and to weight it towards a social rather than an individual focus. He does this by beginning the play with an imagined speech delivered by Albie Sachs to an audience at a meeting. Sachs ironically and mockingly thanks the Minister of Justice, Balthazar (John) Vorster (later, Prime Minister, 1966–78) who is responsible for the Ninety Day Detention Act which is now being used against whites as well as blacks for the first time in an escalation of attempts to repress the opposition against apartheid. The fictional Albie Sachs of the play tells his audience that this law makes it clear how scared the government is in the face of their opposition:

And that's not bad. It's good, that they're so scared, they're scared enough to use it on the whites, on us, because it makes *us* choose what side we're on, it tells us, and we didn't know, it tells us what it's like. So thank you, Dr Vorster. You have told us what it's like.

(*Pause. The speech is over. He turns upstage, looks at the cell.*)

So this is what it's like.

(pp. 3–4)[15]

Thus the audience addressed is a white audience, and the message is a challenge to choose sides and be aware of the import of the law. In an analogous move, the play is addressing British whites in the late 1970s who could be politicized by understanding the nature of the repression in South Africa through the paradigmatic treatment and experiences of Albie Sachs. In the following scene, Sachs repeats the phrase to himself shortly after seeing his cell. His private journey of discovery of what it is like begins with his own detention.

The epistemological claims for the theatre piece are here asserted: Sachs will document through his memoir 'what it is like' to be detained in a cell, but also how whites are implicated in the apartheid system and must choose their side. Because it really happened to a credible personage, we should believe it. Edgar will demonstrate through dramatic mimesis how Sachs speaks his truth to us. The first-person narration of the memoir is preserved through much of the play, the character repeatedly speaking directly to the audience. However, the memoir is also dramatized in scenes involving other characters – the jailers and interrogators that we know in the diary only through Sachs's accounts of them. In the play, the illusion of separate characters is sometimes foremost since the bodies of the actors act as surrogates for the constructs of the memoir. On the other hand, they are represented as types in Lukács's sense – composite characters who stand in for historically grounded paradigmatic figures. Thus the representational scheme is complex – verbatim in the case of Sachs, and with the other characters insofar as they have been quoted 'verbatim' by Sachs, but second order in the sense of being represented as autonomous characters in dramatic scenes created by Edgar.

Apart from this set of choices concerning narration versus dramatization, Edgar's creative mediation is also clear in the shaping of particular sequences. In the memoir, Sachs recounts his battles with fleas and his attempts to get his flea-infested blanket changed in an account ranging over two chapters, from his personal encounter with the creatures ('You bastard!' ,when the flea escapes him),[16] to a series of complaints sent up the prison hierarchical chain. This topic is interwoven with other activities of his prison life, including some Bible reading – the only book he is allowed – exercising to keep fit, and warding off boredom by cleaning his comb with a fishbone, or playing draughts using a check towel as a board, and toilet paper and orange peel for markers. In Edgar's adaptation, the specific items of comb, fishbone, towel, orange peel and so on are retained, but these details are contained within the fifth scene structured as his fifteenth day, from the time he wakes to the end of the day when he sings and whistles with an anonymous, unseen prisoner. Then the sixth scene is devoted almost completely to the effort to get the blanket problem solved, and is mostly narrated rather than enacted.

It begins with Sachs waking, trying to catch a flea and explaining the blood on his vest to the audience: 'Not the brutality of the apartheid state. The violence of probably unsegregated fleas. Who have become intolerable' (p. 23). The Constable comes in and Sachs asks for clean blankets because of the fleas. The Constable says he cannot do anything, and that Sachs will need to see the Sergeant. From his exit, Sachs picks up the story and delivers a long monologue structured as a story-based joke with several repetitions and a punchline. He recounts speaking to the Sergeant, then the Station Commander, followed by the Captain, the Magistrate, and finally the Major. In each case, there is a long rationale for why the particular person cannot help with the problem. The punchline is that once Sachs gets to the Major, who is at least open to hearing his complaint, he has in fact forgotten it. The absurdity of the situation and the great efforts needed to pursue such a mundane relief combine to give the shape of the scene its thrust.

Edgar has theatricalized the material, changing it not in substance – mostly – but in shape. The weak qualifier 'mostly' is necessary because one change is arguably significant. In Edgar's play, the forgetting occurs in the last instance, with the implication being that after jumping through so many hoops, Sachs is exhausted by the efforts, and simply forgets his purpose. This is also funny. However, in the memoir, Sachs reports the forgetting at a much earlier stage – it is a symptom of his inability to hold focus on things in his mind as a result of the isolation and disorientation in his situation. Already with the Sergeant, Sachs forgets to ask about the blankets and writes, 'I forgot to ask him. I keep on forgetting the simplest things. I must, I must, I must remember tomorrow.'[17] He comments on his efforts not to forget when he speaks to the Station Commander. At the end, at the level of the Major, he forgets again, as Edgar depicts this in the play. The discrepancy between the memoir and the play is not large – after all, Sachs tells the story and plays all the parts quoting the officials in the memoir just as Edgar has it in the play. But Edgar's treatment of the act of forgetting sharpens the theatrical effect of the scene written for the stage and gives up for the moment the focus on the effects of such imprisonment on concentration and memory. It emphasizes the Kafkaesque nature of the social relations between Sachs and his oppressors, and places attention on the governmental structures and the penal system in particular, rather than on the psychology of Sachs himself.

Edgar does emphasize the isolation of prison confinement and its effects on Sachs. This is one of the most important of Sachs's themes in the *Diary*, and Edgar selects multiple instances of his concerns for use in the play. Sachs continually makes the point to his jailers that he considers prolonged isolation cruel and uncivilized; Edgar includes this in several places. He also includes Sachs's description of his response to learning about the assassination of John F. Kennedy. The scene is Christmas Day (more than a month after the assassination) and Sachs is the only prisoner left as the others are all out on bail. He is alone and in direct address mode for the entire scene. He meditates on his situation:

> I cannot understand the cruelty. I do believe, still, just, that men are basically good and fine and splendid.
> But I cannot understand the pain. It's not an attitude, a state of mind, it is a matter of one's circumstances. It is real. I think of medieval monks, who volunteered to suffer silent isolation. There's no glory there. There is no glory, in a suffering which drives out love.

> Self-sacrifice with love may well be fine. But self-denial coupled with individual pain, that is absurd.
> The pain I feel is not ennobling.
> It is useless.
> It's destroying me.
>
> (p. 43)

Sachs then recounts trying to see newspaper headlines, making out K-E-N, and thinking it was something about Kenya. Three days later he heard that John F. Kennedy had been killed. 'And all I thought of was,' he tells us, 'if there is war, maybe I'll be shot.' He recounts several other self-centred thoughts he has had and concludes by asking where freedom fighters tortured in Algeria or the resisters to the Nazis got their stamina. 'All those bloody heroes. Where did those bloody heroes find their will. And here's me, in my concrete cube, sat nursing my own useless pain'(p. 44). In the *Diary*, Sachs is even more explicit about this Kennedy incident, writing: 'Now comes the part of the story of which I am particularly ashamed. Of all the things they have done to me, this is the worst: they have made me think of everything that happens in the world in terms of how it affects me.'[18]

The *Diary* contains a number of passages reflecting on Sachs's inner states – they are concentrated in five chapters spread throughout the book, each one titled 'Reflections'. They return to the issue of the effects of isolation, the fear of losing the strength to resist, and the meaning of personal pain in the context of political struggle. Sachs writes that 'the right thing to do is to stay and fight to the end'[19] but also that 'weakness of character' makes him want personal happiness, and he reproaches himself that 'negative considerations, such as the avoidance of shame and defeat, provide more powerful support for resistance in my case than positive ideology'.[20]

In condensing the materials of the diary into a play, Edgar has opted not to stress these self-searching reflections, but he has not underplayed the effects of the solitary confinement on Sachs. Freeman, one of Sachs's interrogators, reads to him from a little pamphlet on the effects of solitary confinement, which include trouble seeing and hearing, and the fear of going mad. He threatens extreme sleep deprivation as a further tactic that is 'degrading' (p. 58). Further on in the second act, Sachs asks to see a doctor because of physical symptoms that include dizziness, body spasms, out-of-body experiences, and a fantasy about cracking his skull open and watching as 'my brains burst out like pomegranate pips'(p. 67) – the horrific image from the *Diary*.

The other 'evidence' of Sachs's suffering from isolation is dramatized in his attempts to socialize with his captors. He tries through conversation to sustain human contact as long as possible. The one time he turns away decisively is when his captors have tricked him into believing he is to be released, only to rearrest him moments later. This cruelty is one of the most deliberate acts aimed at breaking Sachs, and Edgar follows the *Diary* quite faithfully, except for the way he represents the aftermath. In the *Diary*, Sachs says he did not want to go back to his cell and got the idea that perhaps he could 'derive some advantage from the situation'.[21] He asks the Colonel to discuss aspects of his conditions and is invited to the Colonel's office, where he requests some concrete items that would improve his circumstances (a chamber-pot, crossword puzzles, a bed in place of his mat, etc.). He gains some concessions before returning to his cell. Edgar changes these details to get maximum impact of the reversal of fortune from Sachs thinking he is free and asking to phone his mother, to the next moment when he is told he is again under arrest and collapses into a chair. He listens as his mother calls through and is told he is still there and is then denied any other information. In Edgar's version, Sachs stands and says, 'My cell, please. Now' (p. 47). The effect of this decision to seek isolation reinforces the seriousness of what has happened and the despair Sachs feels in this instance. It also contrasts strongly with Sachs's usual desire for conversation and contact, even with his tormentors. On this occasion, Edgar's fiction is that he prefers solitude.

Perhaps the most ingenious adaptation Edgar makes involves the metatheatrical aspect of the diary. Sachs writes that he considered writing a novel, but then decided it would be better if it were a play because of the audience: 'I want something better, more immediate, with live people standing up and voices sounding.'[22] He imagines the staging, himself as the actor, and the opening line: 'So this is what it's like.'[23] He decides he must find a way to make the audience understand his isolation and comes up with the idea of a blank screen which he will force the audience to look at for three minutes. Edgar refines Sachs's idea to make it theatrically viable. He places this scene right after the scene of the rearrest, the last scene in Act 1. He uses the diary materials to construct a monologue for Sachs about imagining and working on the play, including the original idea of a book and deciding, 'I wanted something more immediate, more active, more alive. So it had to be a play' (p. 48). Sachs describes the set, his cell, the draughts, the comb-cleaning, and the isolation. Then he comes to the problem:

> But as I think of it, I am aware, increasingly, the real problem is to show just what it's like, in isolation, the disintegration, and the horror of it all, to people who are not alone, because they are together, watching, as an audience, my play.
>
> (p. 48)

He decides that 'the best thing is, not in the play, but in the audience, for them to see' (p. 48). Edgar shortens the audience experience of this isolation to two minutes rather than three, and gives them not a blank screen but the image of Albie Sachs lying on his back in solitude. As in the diary, Sachs tells the audience they must not talk or read their programmes, but just 'sit and stare' (p. 49). The close correspondence between this *coup de théâtre* and what Sachs imagined and described in the diary works with both the truth claims of a 'verbatim' theatre piece and at the same time with the metatheatrical reflexivity of a quite different aesthetic.

Finally, we turn to the political questions of the play – what chances are there to be a good man living under a bad regime? Can one achieve a kind of heroism out of human frailty? What is required by the situation? What is worth remembering? What is the worth of individual struggle within a movement? The play makes a number of contributions to these considerations.

The characterization of Sachs (both his own self-characterization and Edgar's) posits an individual with strong political convictions who is being tested in a number of ways. The old challenge of US slang is particularly apt: 'Put your money where your mouth is', meaning, do more than talk in pursuit of your beliefs. Of course, lawyers are quintessentially talkers and their skill is based on conceptual verbal agility. Through his efforts to defend political activists, Sachs has contributed his skills to his cause. Also through his argumentation for legal reform, he participates in trying to keep the South African system from even greater repression. Still, it is not clear if this participation in the struggle against apartheid is sufficient. Acutely aware of his white privilege, Sachs wonders if his revolutionary sentiment is authentic and strong enough. Considering his white privilege, as it manifests in the jail ('I'm patted all over with petty privilege'), he meditates on its effects: 'And I abhor its cunning. What it's done to me, by splitting me from my comrades, isolating me. Removing me from that collective strength, that stops me being just a white man with an upset conscience, places me in history, and gives my conscience scale' (p. 51). Placed at the beginning of Act 2, this monologue stages Sachs speaking to a coloured constable who stands silently with a broom during the speech. Sachs discusses the necessity for armed struggle in the light of the escalation of government repression since the Sharpeville massacre and the banning of the ANC. But he also looks back nostalgically to an earlier time in the 1950s, which he calls 'days of innocence', when non-violence seemed a way forward, while now 'the sacrifices that we'd only sung of, suddenly came real' (p. 50). Suspicious that the motive of non-violence was really a lack of courage, he worries that he cannot find the hatred and rage to sustain his revolutionary commitment: 'But where do I locate that. Me, Albie Sachs, the boy who always broke up fights at school. The natural mediator. Where can I find my hatred and my rage?' (p. 50).

These remarks place his personal struggle not to give in to his interrogators within a larger social situation and problematize the role of a singular individual – within a political movement, on the one hand, and as a resister to the state apparatus on the other. They offer a larger conceptual frame for the next part of the act, when Sachs decides to talk to his interrogators. After a particularly hard session of questioning in which Freeman has mocked Sachs's role in the movement and his ambition to be a hero, Sachs agrees to speak to them. He rationalizes that the information they want is not relevant anymore because all the pending trials at the time of his arrest must already be over. He says it does not matter anymore, 'it won't hurt anyone'. He also admits that it gets harder day after day to find 'the stamina, sufficient stamina' (p. 73).

However, in the next scene, something happens to change his mind. The Sergeant, with whom he is on semi-friendly terms, laughs at a joke Sachs tells him about lawyers, and Sachs asks the Constable what it is like working under the Sergeant. The Constable replies that it is better to be one of his prisoners than one of his constables because he was formerly a prisoner himself. When asked about his crime, the Constable replies: 'Think he filled this kaffir up with water, and then jumped on him till he died' (p. 75). Sachs is devastated by this brutality, which, mentioned casually, cuts with graphic precision through any temporary bonhomie between Sachs and his captors. In the following interrogation, Sachs again refuses to answer any questions, and when the Sergeant takes him back to his cell, Sachs says, 'Just thank you. Thank you very much' (p. 76). This ironic 'thank you' is clearly for giving Sachs, through horrific example, the renewed strength to resist. Edgar takes this detail about the Sergeant direct from the *Diary*, but transposes it into the scene in which Sachs almost gives in to interrogation, thus building a theatricalized condensation of the temptations of defeatism and its resistance. The scene where Sachs decides he will talk to his captors, and then changes his mind, occurs in the *Diary*, but the reason for Sachs's change of mind is more diffuse – a conversation about the legality of torture seems to be the determining factor. Sachs concludes: 'How could I ever have thought of answering their questions? Just seeing them in the flesh provides me with sufficient emotional charge to withstand the pressure to give in' (p. 263). Edgar's creative mediation works through rearrangement in this case to achieve dramatic effect.

The contribution of this scene to the larger political problematic is to make it extremely clear how difficult it is to hold out against the temptation to give in, and it portrays the evilness of the apartheid system and the officials acting for the state as the counterpoint to an individual act of cowardice or persistence. Sachs heard the story about the brutal act by chance; if he had not heard it, he might have succumbed. In this case his (good and gentle) tendency to see his captors as individuals had obscured the face of the regime long enough for him to consider a bargain with the devil (I'll tell you what you want to know since I'm pretty sure it won't hurt anyone directly).

Albie Sachs is freed in the next scene and takes his celebrated run to the sea, Edgar following the *Diary* very closely. However, while this jubilant scene marks the end of the *Diary*, Edgar writes two more short scenes for his play – and they complete the political thematic with a characteristic Edgarian negotiation and retrieval. Edgar historicizes the events of the *Diary* by jumping ahead two years to the occasion of Sachs's rearrest for a second period of imprisonment.[24] The first scene makes it clear that the situation has worsened in the country, more violence and torture of prisoners is occurring, and Sachs too will have a more difficult time. The final scene begins with Sachs's taped statement under duress after 180 days of detention – he has been broken. The scene changes to Sach's office, and Danny Young, a prisoner Sachs recognized when he was first imprisoned, has come to see him. Sachs admits he lost the battle to withstand his tormentors. Danny says that everybody breaks, but Sachs feels that he has lost the elan he had when he first went into prison. Recalling the earlier passage on innocence, he says: 'When I went in, I was kind of innocent. And inside, I lost that ... And what it leaves you with's a kind of fatalism. Crippled spirit. What the hell' (p. 84). He clearly feels he's failed. But Danny tells him: 'I brought you greeting. There are many people, hope that when South Africa is free, we'll see you once again in Cape Town. Many people, won't forget, the things you did for them' (p. 85). Danny repeats 'They won't forget' three times, insisting that the one who resisted will be remembered over the one who broke, that it mattered that he resisted, that it should be honoured. Edgar underlines both Sachs's failure and his persistence in the end of the play. He is a flawed, finite human being, but he is also heroic – for his efforts, for his partial accomplishments, for his struggle against the devils. This is the Albie Sachs that is worthy of remembrance, not denying his finitude but because of it.

In its historical moment, *The Jail Diary of Albie Sachs* constituted a political performative insofar as it manifested an act of resistance to the apartheid regime through its reproduction of the acts of a living resister. The exemplar, Sachs, modelled resistance through behaviour which can itself be emulated by others – such is the inspiration and efficacy of the piece. The repetition of the performance is also a promise of future 'performances'. Other surrogates will stand in for the protagonist; other acts of resistance will follow.

The impact of the play on its audiences was certainly connected to their contexts. In the UK, white audience members with a sense of responsibility for the Commonweath were asked to consider their willingness to become involved in the struggle against apartheid through Sachs's personal example and doubts about his own strength and commitments. In the United States the anti-apartheid movement was more closely associated with the pan-Africanism of the time, and came to public attention largely through African-American organizing efforts, extrapolating from the civil rights struggle to the South African situation. Those theatre patrons who saw *The Jail Diary of Albie Sachs* were experiencing the struggle from a different perspective – a liberal white Jewish perspective that asked difficult questions about how to participate in a struggle against another group's oppressions.

A particularly theatrical affirmation of the impact of the play in a specific situation took place years later, in 1988. The real Albie Sachs had been continuing his work with the ANC, living and working in Mozambique. A car bomb, intended to kill him, caused him to lose an arm, one eye, and much of his hearing, and resulted in his return to Britain for medical treatment. There, on Sunday, 6 October 1988, he attended a special benefit performance at the Young Vic of *The Jail Diary of Albie Sachs.* On this occasion, five actors who had previously been in the play in various productions were on stage as he himself sat in the audience along with his mother and Dorothy Adams, a black woman who was in prison with him during his first confinement and who was the anonymous whistler he described in *The Diary*. After the play finished, David Edgar called the real Albie Sachs up on to the stage to speak to tremendous applause. In his memoir about the year following the bombing, Sachs recounts his thoughts immediately before he spoke: 'Everybody is waiting, this is the moment where the evening ceases to be about a certain part of my life and actually becomes another part of my life.'[25] Catching the moment of his own performance of self, Sachs reaffirms the relationship between the reality of his life and its theatrical demonstration. He delivers, together with the play as a structure and a vehicle, the documentary promise to provide access, although mediated, to the desired reality. The evening, taken as a whole, was a repetition, a 'first time', an aesthetic event, and a political event – truly, in Jill Dolan's phrase, a utopian performative.[26]

The play was widely produced and became part of a larger activism in the anti-apartheid movement in Europe and the US. Tony Taccone lived in San Francisco at this time, and was one of the six young actors and directors who founded the Eureka Theatre. The group of left-wing artists were especially influenced by the plays of Caryl Churchill, Trevor Griffiths, and David Edgar.[27] The company produced *The Jail Diary of Albie Sachs* in 1981. Taccone and Oscar Eustis (now Artistic Director of the Public Theatre in New York) directed Richard Seyd (a former member of Red Ladder – a socialist theatre company in Leeds – before he emigrated to the US) as Sachs. The week before they opened, Seyd received a death threat on his home answering machine, and a threat was left on the theatre's answering machine as well. They deleted the messages; Taccone says they did not take the threats seriously: 'We were kids. We didn't take it seriously. We were worried we couldn't get people to come to see the show, let alone blow us up! We were in a ninety-nine seat theatre in the basement of a church.'[28] The night of the first preview, after the show, someone apparently stayed in the building. A four-alarm fire ensued, caused by an explosive device planted by a professional arsonist, according to the fire officer. The next day, when the company gathered to assess the damage (they lost everything but the costumes), two actors in the cast who were in fact South Africans said it was surely the work of South African vigilantes. Sachs was scheduled to make a national speaking tour of the US within the year. To the astonished and bewildered company, they said, 'You don't get it. You don't understand. This is how things are now in South Africa.'[29]

The San Francisco theatre community rallied around the Eureka and helped them rebuild the production, and the Magic Theatre gave them space. One week later the show reopened. The large amount of publicity they received from the fire, and the admiration the plucky company garnered from the public, ensured a sell-out run.

## *Mary Barnes*

> I was absolutely a 60s baby, coming of age in '68, '69. I remember sitting in Manchester, which is a dreary, rainy northern city, with beads on and smoking joints and listening to The Doors. What's more, I was pretending I was in San Francisco. You know the principle of the 1960s, don't you? The British aren't particularly interested in the Beatles or the Stones, but are obsessed with The Doors and Grace Slick. When Allen Ginsburg said that Liverpool is now the centre of consciousness for the human universe, I always wanted to ask, 'Have you ever been there?'
>
> David Edgar[30]

> The mad things said and done by the schizophrenic will remain essentially a closed book if one does not understand their existential context.
>
> R. D. Laing[31]

> We didn't build the future, but we are no longer other, to ourselves.
>
> Brenda (community leader, Act 3)[32]

*The Jail Diary of Albie Sachs* could be viewed as a kind of verbatim theatre because David Edgar saw the playwright's task there as 'sculpting' the new work of art – the play – from the material available in the source work of art – Sachs's memoir. 'Sculpting' meant chipping away the excess material until only a pure core remained. With *Mary Barnes*, on the other hand, he took a consciously different approach. Although the source book here was also a personal memoir of a time of great trial for an extraordinary individual,[33] was also set in the socio-political context of the sixties, and also offered plenty of rich material for 'verbatim' playwriting, Edgar chose to regard it instead as 'a kind of trampoline, or linear row of pegs, on which various things would hang which would rush off down different avenues'.[34]

In his introductory note to the published version of the play, Edgar first describes the source book, *Mary Barnes: Two Accounts of a Journey Through Madness*, as a 'true story ... about a group of people who believed fiercely in a particular view of the nature of madness, and who attempted to live that belief in a peculiarly intense and passionate way'.[35] However, he subsequently points out that in order to bring out the truth of their efforts on the stage, he had to 'fictionalize the characters in the book ... [invent] many statements and actions by people involved ... telescope and even alter many of the events'. The result is that, although 'people often do and say things that were really said and done', words, characters, and actions have been switched around enough that Edgar finds it necessary to rename all the characters except Mary Barnes herself (p. 91).

Despite the eponymous title of the source for this play, and of the play itself, David Edgar sees it first of all as the story of a 'group of people'. Mary Barnes is, in fact, a member of this group, and although her story is paramount in the multiple stories that make up the play *Mary Barnes*, Edgar shifts the focus to the group in his adaptation for the stage. In the first instance this group is a therapeutic community, but one constituted by its opposition to then conventional therapies for dealing with schizophrenia (usually involving drugs and frequently electro-shock treatments), along with a conviction that many of the values and practices of the conventional world are themselves the sources of insanity. Although most of this community's creators would have described it as apolitical, its aim to create an island of living well in the midst of a larger significantly deranged society makes it by necessity political. It is obviously 'attending to and amending a set of arrangements', in Oakeshott's formulation. From the outset, this new *socius* is confronted with numerous problems of managing the borders between its domain and the larger society, as well as all the difficulties inherent in attempting to organize itself internally in ways conducive to its *raison d'être*. In this way, the therapeutic group of *Mary Barnes* comes to provide a locus for the investigation of the sixties phenomenon of alternative communities, as well as the dynamics of human community generally. As the character Brenda eventually comes to remark about a community like hers: 'I just, sometimes, wonder if it's possible at all' (p. 137).

*Mary Barnes* returns to the problematic sketched out earlier in considering *The Jail Diary of Albie Sachs:* a fundamental question for all political analysis has always been how to coordinate the life of the individual with that of the society, one central formulation of which is, 'Can one live a good life in a bad regime?' *Mary Barnes* directly investigates one modern solution to this conundrum: libertarian constitutionalism. Libertarian thought, at its core, seeks to minimize the connection between the nature of the regime and the life of the individual by the prescription: 'that government governs best which governs least'. Two distinct but closely related propositions underlie this position: first of all, no one knows absolutely what the best life for any given individual should be, so the best solution is to let each individual choose for him/herself as much as possible; and, secondly, no one other than an individual her/himself has anywhere near the same interest in the outcome of any choices made as the individual her/himself does, so only that individual should make the choices concerning him/herself.

By contrast with classical and medieval thinkers, then, the 'modern' western choice (beginning, at least, in the sixteenth century) is to make freedom, rather than justice, honour, or salvation the central value of the regime. In the microcosmic world of the community *Mary Barnes* presents, this is exactly the kind of regime that is desired: one with so much freedom that it can accommodate the 'eccentric' and 'chaotic' behaviours often associated with 'schizophrenia'. Tremendous efforts are made to eliminate all elements of hierarchy, authority, rules, organization, or any other distinguishing principles that might give some members power or influence over others (thereby making some more free than others). Not only does this community seek to expand freedom to the very fullest within its boundaries, it implicitly calls for the same change in the larger society, because it locates the source of 'schizophrenia' in the many ways in which the larger society (and its microcosmia, such as the family) is overtly or covertly repressive. In this instance, the *Mary Barnes* community also represents many other 'alternative' communities developed during the sixties: most of them were founded by people who felt themselves oppressed by conventional society and sought to make small-scale utopias where freedom was maximized for all.

Kingsley Hall, where Mary lived and was treated, was a therapeutic community established by R. D. Laing in London's East End. Between 1964 and 1970 a group of Laingian psychiatrists set up an exemplary community and treatment space where non-traditional forms of therapy could be developed and deployed. As with many 1960s collectives, this one aspired to egalitarian principles and to allow as much freedom as possible to patients to find and take their own paths toward recovery. R. D. Laing was the leading proponent of this alternative approach to madness. Through important publications as well as his clinical practice, he popularized the critique of psychiatry, as commonly practised (using shock and drugs), as an inhuman response to others' pain that did not help them and in fact often harmed them further than their original state of mind.

In a series of best-selling books (*The Divided Self*,1960; *The Self and Others*, 1961; *The Politics of Experience*, 1967; *The Politics of the Family*, 1971), Laing set out the thesis that schizophrenia is the result of a divided self formed of contradictory messages in early life, usually from one's parents, which leave the person in a contradictory double bind. Behaviour and especially language that might seem babble actually could be understood as a metaphorical code that signals this internal psychic impasse. Combining existentialism and Marxism, Laing understood psychosis as induced by a combination of social and familial interaction that shaped subjectivity: 'By the time the new human being is fifteen or so, we are left with a being like ourselves, a half-crazed creature more or less well adjusted to a mad world. This is normality in our present age.'[36] Laing was extremely influential in the sixties, achieving a kind of guru status in the anti-psychiatry movement and in popular culture. He lost most of his influence, however, in the 1980s because significant scientific research had since shown that schizophrenia can be treated, at least in part, through new pharmacology and psycho-surgical techniques. His personal life and eccentricities, much in the public eye, also aided in his discreditation, as well as the general disapprobation which came to mark the rejection of 1960s ideals and counterculture more generally. Daniel Burston, who has written two books about Laing and edited a special issue of *Janus Head* on Laing's legacy, has described his importance in terms of the history of psychiatry at the time and the diagnostic contribution Laing made:

> *The Divided Self* was published in 1960. At the time, and for another decade afterwards, psychiatry had little evidence to

> support – much less prove – the view that schizophrenia is basically a neurophysical disorder . . . That being so, Laing's eloquent appeal to treat the schizophrenic as an anguished, despairing person, rather than a bundle of irksome neuropathology, struck a deep and responsive chord in and out of the mental health field, particularly in view of the coercive atmosphere, and the pervasive apathy, anonymity, and indifference of most mental health hospitals, and the horrifying side-effects of drugs, lobotomy, and electro-shock.[37]

Edgar very carefully (and probably wisely) kept the play well away from the figure of Laing. Hugo in the play is representative of Laing, who lived at Kingsley Hall in its early days. In the words of one reviewer, Hugo is 'a laconic guru who takes a paradoxically authoritative back seat to the efforts of Berke [Eddie] – portrayed as an ebullient American academic'.[38] Although Laing is the theoretical mind behind the experiment, the play and the book it was based on are first and foremost an account of the relationship between Mary and her therapist Joe Berke, and between Mary and the community. Laing saw a production of *Mary Barnes* in New York in 1983, and it was the first time Edgar met Laing. He did not try to interview him when researching the play because, as Edgar put it, 'I talked to a good few people who had been at Kingsley Hall, but I decided not to meet Laing himself, fearful that – like kippers in the fridge – his presence would end up flavouring everything.'[39] It would not do to have the focus deflected from the central subject of the play – the attempt to form a radical ideal community.

All of Edgar's plays from the mid to late seventies are predicated on the assumption that the bright days of the sixties have disappeared, and, indeed, have been followed by a backlash against the perceived excesses of that decade, a growing political conservatism which might even lead to the emergence of a significant fascist movement (*Destiny*), the appearance of a more oppressive state apparatus (*Albie Sachs*), or resurgent class-based oppression (*Nicholas Nickleby*). Edgar thus moves to contextualize the time and place of *Mary Barnes* immediately, using references to the Beatles, clothing, male hair length, and similar features to point toward autumn 1965 in the East End. (The play does not name the actual place,

Kingsley Hall, which in its earlier days served as a community centre, a rallying point for pacifists, suffragettes, social/educational service campaigners – a very 'political' place – and even Mahatma Gandhi's residence in the thirties, while he was negotiating with the British government.) The actual experimental community there began in 1965, was most intense during its first two years, then slowly faded until it lost its lease in 1970 and closed up shop, though some of its members continued its practices elsewhere.[40]

We have seen that in his earlier work Edgar attempted to keep personal elements away from his characters so they would better embody the abstract principles or positions they were designed to typify. In *Mary Barnes* he sought to reverse that practice, and now to write a play in which 'the personal *was* the political'.[41] He also worked to create a play with a significant number of female characters. Writing plays about explicitly 'political' subjects – given the gender orientation of the times – had previously meant writing about almost entirely male characters, a point not missed by fledgling feminist theatre artists, who complained that the theatre was as bad as the Left in its focus on masculine subjects. Edgar also sought to use the vantage point offered by the intervening decade to examine in some detail the successes and shortcomings of the 1960s for audiences in the late 1970s. The appeal of all these factors – plus the fact that the play was a great opportunity for skilled actors and directors – meant that within five years it had performances in Birmingham, London, New Haven, Sydney, Geissen, San Francisco, Los Angeles, and New York.

Saying 'the personal is the political' and dramatizing it are two different things, however. David Edgar achieves their dramatic embodiment through a play that contrapuntally juxtaposes a large number of contrasting elements, beginning with a set that is directed to be split between the highly personal space of Mary's bedroom above and the large and open public space of the community below. These spaces allowed the staging of comparisons between the intimately personal 'love story' of Mary's relationship with Eddie, her therapist, and the multiple cooperating/conflicting relationships of the evolving therapeutic community itself (see Fig. 9). Patti Love and Simon Callow, who played Mary and Joe, plunged into a fully emotional approach to

Fig. 9 Self-portrait of Mary Barnes, from *Mary Barnes: Two Accounts of a Journey Through Madness* by Mary Barnes and Joseph Berke.

their roles, meeting the real Mary and Joe, and working intimately with each other. Callow's comments on their work give another dimension to the 'personal is political' performatives involved in the production:

> The subject of schizophrenia and its handling is harrowing, and Patti was already daring to go further into the experience of it than I've seen an actor go. In a sense, mine was an easy performance to give: it was just a question of reacting to Patti. It was important however to be scrupulous about the professional means of these people; they were doctors and not amateurs. The relationship between Patti and me continued, *mutatis mutandis*, off stage as well as on. *Mary Barnes* is the only production I've been involved in which really followed the Strasberg path in its quest for total emotional reality, and Patti's performance is the only 'Method' performance I've acted with. It was exactly what was needed. Any kind of technical reproduction would have been offensive.[42]

In addition to the set spaces and the acting, Edgar's script allowed for a number of other strong contrasts: Mary's qualified 'cure' was juxtaposed with the electro-shock-induced 'cure' of Angie, another former member of the community who is forced by her family to leave the house and undergo conventional psychotherapy. The childlike language and non-verbal physical communication between Mary and Eddie contrasted with the sophisticated linguistic communication of the psychiatrists. The community's aims to connect with the people of the surrounding quarter came up against the hostility that grows between the groups. The psychiatrists' view that persons with mental difficulties, like Mary, cannot clearly distinguish between metaphor and reality contrasted with their own inability to see (or acknowledge) that their pretence of a community without rules and hierarchy – and the resulting power imbalance – is repeatedly shown to be false.

This list could go on, but the point should be clear: a vital effect of the cumulative impact of all these juxtapositions is to create a play with a number of different axes of unresolved tension, leaving the audience no simple route to resolve all the complexities. Yes, Mary is 'cured', but she is not fully recovered. Yes, her 'cure' avoids the evils of drug and electroshock therapy, but that seems to be achieved at an unacceptable cost of manipulative behaviour by all concerned. Yes, the psycho-therapeutic experiment 'worked', but not completely, and at a cost (of resources and to other 'patients') that would be unacceptable and unsustainable. Yes, communities without rules and hierarchy are achievable, but perhaps only for short spaces of time, or by certain kinds of personalities.

The play opens in the public space, with one of the main characters self-consciously changing out of his bourgeois 'uniform' into more casual clothing, clearly symbolizing the transition from the larger society into that of the community. (Later, he will signal his departure from the group in protest by resuming his suit and tie.) For most of the first act, the play alternates between scenes set in the public space dealing with the community at large, and those set in Mary's private space, dealing entirely (or primarily) with her. As time goes on, though, Mary re-enters the public space, and most of the scenes of Act 2 are set there. But she is gradually taking over the space, and by the end of the second act she plays the last scene entirely in the public space, albeit almost entirely by herself.

The opening scenes show the various members of the group arriving in 1965 to inaugurate the community. It is obvious that most of them already know one another, and they have leased this house specifically for their experimental purpose. Keith, the first one we meet, is not a member of the group but a member of a rock band that has been using (and continues to use) the basement of the house for practice; he is the group's connection with the neighbourhood. Keith will reappear in the middle of the narrative arc, to help the group understand why their interaction with their neighbours is producing not community but hostility, and in the play's final scene, as he tries to help Angie connect with her past, the past of the experimental community (which has been forcibly erased from her memory). Keith also helps establish the ordinary person's perception that Mary Barnes – who, at this point, is not behaving too extraordinarily – is 'loony' (p. 100).

In the second scene, Mary announces that she has come to have a breakdown (and two scenes later, in Hugo's summary of her back story, we learn that she has been waiting a full year – until the experimental community could be started – to have this breakdown). She will undergo what is loosely called regression analysis, since she believes that her problems began with being born 'wrong' and one of her aims is to rebirth herself, now in a better environment. Eddie, a psychiatrist from the States who has been introduced in Scene 3 (the stand-in character for the 'real' Joseph Berke, who co-authored the book *Mary Barnes*), volunteers to work with Mary on this project. Over a long period, marked by Mary's most extreme kinds of behaviour, he succeeds in finding ways to help her experience the regrowth she has wanted all along. The whole community generally participates in – and is affected by – this process, but Eddie has to endure the enormous difficulty of dealing with Mary's ferocity, possessiveness, narcissism, and manipulation, all of which eventually drives him to behaviours he does not expect of himself (such as punching Mary in the face).

In the course of this long process, Eddie tries giving Mary crayons at one point, hoping that this will appeal to her expressive side in a way that will move her away from making designs and sculptures with her own excrement. This initiative succeeds, and leads her to switch to painting with her hands. Eventually (by Act 3) she begins to gain recognition for her painting from the London art scene, but in the process she has taken over the domestic space of the community with her paintings, leading to more internal conflict within the group over how much room she should be given.

Meanwhile, as she has 'gotten better', she has become an assistant to other 'patients' as they travel their own journeys, especially a young woman named Angie who arrives at the beginning of Act 3. By now it is 1968, so three years have passed since the group began, and Mary is able to act as a helper to people such as Angie, but only to the degree that they repeat fairly exactly what she has gone through. She tries to get Angie to replicate her experience, as she will later insist on a similar formula for her brother. In neither case, and for different reasons, is her prescription appropriate – but she is unable to see this. She identifies it as a failure of the community that it cannot help her brother (also conventionally diagnosed as schizophrenic) – and, indeed, that inability does point up the fact that extreme freedom helps some but hinders others.

All of the major male characters in *Mary Barnes* are psychiatrists, although two supporting roles go to patients Laurence and Simon (Mary's brother). All of the major female characters are 'patients', except Brenda. This imbalance makes the task of creating effective and valid female characters difficult, and the play does not quite succeed in this respect. The exception is Brenda. She is with the community from start to finish, is involved in more of the events of its life than any other character except Mary herself, is the most consistently left-wing community member (in the conventional sense of left-wing), and although she does not have any long speeches, she has some of the best lines in the play. She is exemplary of the kind of second-wave feminist who came to consciousness in the sixties – participating in the communities and movements of the sixties as an adjunct to the male leaders and experts, but beginning to see that if the principles of equality and freedom and the destruction of traditional power imbalances they espouse mean anything at all, they require liberation of women from the traditional places they have in society (including countercultural society).

So Brenda is introduced at the beginning as a non-psychiatrist among psychiatrists (she does not recognize Wilhelm Reich's signature device, for example), yet she is also clearly one of the founders of the community, and she will serve it throughout as the overseer of the household. (The men do assume a share of the mundane activities, but often only with her prodding and organizing.) She is forever responding to situations by making coffee, she is frequently cast in the traditional woman's role of mediator, yet she is the one who observes at the beginning that they have moved to the place they have chosen ('Our liberated zone', she calls it) because here,

> ... where the people work. People work with their hands.
> Where mental pain and suffering is not a pastime for the middle classes.
> Where people's heads are fucked up by the way they're forced to live their lives.
> Round here.
>
> (p. 96)

This kind of glorification/romanticization of the urban proletariat is typical of Brenda's outlook on their endeavours, and she repeats this act several more times. In the end, she is the one who pronounces summary judgment on the whole experiment. One of the psychiatrists, perhaps the most insightful one, has asked her what will happen now, and she replies:

> I don't know.
> I know . . . I think I know. . .
> (*Pause*)
> For me, it was best of all. . . Just to see ourselves, each other, all our, lumpy nakedness. To hear our voices, all their, I don't know, their, rasping melody.
> Capture our lives in their, messy majesty.
> You see?
> ZIMMERMAN: Of course I see.
> BRENDA: We didn't build the future. But we are no longer, other, to ourselves.
> (*Pause. With a smile.*)
> We've closed the door behind us. And, who knows, what lies beyond, the point, beyond the pale.
>
> (p. 164)

Brenda is, in a way, the first in a considerable line of Edgar's female characters (including Floss in *The Prisoner's Dilemma* and Alex in *Playing with Fire*) who finish out plays by taking the measure of the moment, and rededicating themselves to the actions they have been pursuing. They are more than survivors: they have assessed realistically the gains and losses from the experiences dramatized in their situation, and – even when the going remains difficult and there is no external source of value to prove to them their activity is absolutely right and/or will be rewarded with success – they pursue what they see as the good (empowerment, equality, justice) because, in reality, there is no other choice worth doing. Edgar celebrates minor victories of self-knowledge, courage, and fair-mindedness through these characters, even though he also ironizes them and does not hide their weaknesses. Despite Brenda's protestations about not knowing the future, the audience – living in the seventies – knows some of it, and it is not hard to imagine Brenda as a leader of a women's collective in the early seventies, as second-wave feminism really gets under way.

Brenda labelled the community 'our unsacred family', and Hugo (the R. D. Laing figure) had suggested at the very outset that they should eat together every day in the public space. Consequently Edgar stages two scenes that have deliberate resemblances to Last Supper meals, on the one hand, and political meetings like those in *Destiny*, *Maydays*, *The Shape of the Table*, and *The Prisoner's Dilemma* on the other. These events reveal ways in which a number of individual factors – age, ambition, personality, skills, empathy – combine with external events, ideological principles, prejudices, ritual, and social dynamics to produce the patterns of cooperation and conflict characteristic of family gatherings, public meetings, and community events. Hugo has said: 'We must avoid hierarchies, chains of authority, unspoken rules. Or we should at least speak our unspoken rules' (pp. 97–8). This was certainly a major ambition of many countercultural groups during the sixties, but outsiders were always sceptical about such equality being sustainable.

At the first of the two such dinners dramatized, the psychiatrists begin by bonding through focusing on the common enemy: conventional psychiatry. Brenda tries to alter the direction slightly by providing a traditionally Marxist position, suggesting that mental illness is a product of the reduction of humans to commodities. The psychiatrists do not take this up, but one of them is prompted to tell of 'drapetomania', a piece of pseudo-science from the *antebellum* southern United States which claimed that drapetomania was a mental illness which only applied to 'Negro' slaves, encouraging their fantasies about running away. Edgar may be being a little sly with this allusion: the historical creator of the notion of drapetomania claimed that it was caused by an excessive sense of equality between masters and slaves (though that point is not made in the play). Beth, one of the 'patients', partly gets this reference and responds to it.[43] Her answer, though, leads to open conflict, first between Brenda and the 'shrinks', and then among the 'shrinks' themselves: Brenda continues to maintain her left-wing views about authority and state violence, but Douglas and Eddie begin to fall out about the role of perception in authority and violence, while Hugo attributes these evils to hypocrisy and self-deception. Mary responds to the increasingly conflictual atmosphere by picking a fight with Beth, and this is headed for serious struggle when the action is interrupted by the breaking of windows by people from the outside neighbourhood – expressing their unhappiness, so it is thought, with the community for bringing into their midst 'nutters, perverts, and layabouts' (p. 119). In response to this vandalism, Douglas calls the police, and by calling in heretofore invalid outside authority, begins the erosion of their 'liberated zone'.

The second dinner scene, although it presumably takes place some time later than the first one, begins with Hugo trying to regain the earlier 'us against them' unity that the psychiatrists had at the beginning of the first meal, but Douglas is not having any of it. Douglas is hostile from the first, and subsequently Hugo matches him. Things deteriorate from there, Douglas charging the others with dishonesty for not acknowledging that there are informal rules structuring life in the community. Some of these have to do – from Douglas's point of view – with the excessive licence granted Mary Barnes, who, he notes, has expanded from her room to fill the house with her paintings (which now cover many of the walls). He claims that she is, bit by bit, taking over the life of the community. This leads to open physical fighting between Mary and one of the other patients, Laurence, and to Douglas's departure from the house. It also leads to Mary using biblical language and symbols (bread and wine) to take on a redemptive role in keeping with the Last Supper theme. This, too, because of her religiosity, seems to be part of her recovery process.

In assisting in that recovery, Eddie has taken a kind of leadership role, exhibiting initiative, persistence, imagination, flexibility, and a kind of bravery. However, he does not thereby become a role model for the rest of the group. In a therapeutic community, it would seem, leadership is specific to certain situations and persons. Hugo also clearly acts as a leader on occasion, but it is more in the style of a guru than a general community leader. Because of these features, which appear to be specific to the specialized nature of this kind of community, the narrative does not really allow for the exploration of one of the major questions for sixties' countercultural groups: how do such egalitarian communities provide leadership when they need it? Psychotherapists are accustomed to operating in environments where they are in the dominant positions because of their expertise, but limited in their capacities for initiating action because of the very nature of the therapeutic process, which relies on the patients to act while they react. Because of limitations like this, Edgar's ambition for one dimension of *Mary Barnes*, that it should provide an opportunity to examine a range of sixties-style groups, is not fully realized. On the other hand, what is amply demonstrated is that in 'leaderless groups' everyone has to lead, and if some opt out of the role and responsibility for the whole, it falls apart. Arguably that is what happens by the end of *Mary Barnes.* As with Albie Sachs, the question of human limitation and finitude lingers as a coda.

At the Eureka Theatre in San Francisco both the real Mary Barnes and David Edgar came to town and attended the opening night performance, in March 1981. Tony Taccone remembers the company's excitement – and a bit of anxiety – about having them come. Mary Barnes stayed with Taccone's family during her visit, and he recalls a particular anecdote. The first night she was there, after everyone had gone to bed, he heard noises downstairs and went to investigate. He found Mary playing with his 5-year-old son – they were sawing a log for the fire with a small plastic saw. 'It was so profoundly innocent and genuine. She knew it was playing. She was playing with my son.'[44]

## *Albert Speer*

> Because, yes, I cannot admit what I have not admitted and remain alive.
> But if I did, I could die the man I might have been.
>
> Albert Speer, Act 2[45]

David Edgar's play, *Albert Speer*, bears a different sort of relationship to its namesake in comparison to the two earlier plays. First, *Albert Speer* is twice removed from its sources, being the adaptation of a biography. Second, the aura of the actual human being behind the name – the living person who affected his historical moment – towers over the play like Banquo's ghost. Although like Speer, Albie Sachs occupies a significant place in public consciousness, the monstrosity of the Holocaust and the world-determining consequences of Speer's actions make their respective public iconicity incommensurable. (In the case of *Mary Barnes*, Joe Berke is not the widely known figure Mary Barnes was in her day; and now, after her death, the public that knows her is certainly smaller than in the 1970s, when her art was first coming to attention, while Joe Berke is even less of a public figure outside the therapeutic community or among historians and other scholars of psychotherapeutic techniques.)

Without doubt, the public debates about the truth or falsity of Speer's self-representation overshadow the different kinds of receptions the other memoirs received in their time. However in our time, Albie Sachs, still very much alive, is widely honoured for his role as architect of the constitution and one of the first justices in the new South African Constitutional Court, appointed by Nelson Mandela and serving until he retired in 2009. In 2005, in *Home Affairs* vs *Fourie*, he wrote the opinion legalizing same sex marriage in South Africa. He has therefore increasingly become a celebrated international public figure, with his own aura and gravitas. In Speer's attempt to refashion his identity after his release from prison, and in his publication of the memoirs and international speaking tours, we cannot help but remark his obsessional attempt to seek the kind of public validation that has come to Sachs without self-promotion and fully from his good works.

In the case of Albert Speer, his contested public image still resonates beyond his death, in 1981, among several generations still living, for whom the direct memories of the Second World War and the Holocaust continue to be momentous, and for new generations of students who explore in school the history of the Nazi era and the personages responsible for it. Indeed, following Derrida's notion of hauntology, the spectre of Albert Speer adds a negative valence to the play, which is all the more powerful for its ephemerality.

The play is an adaptation of Gitta Sereny's biography, *Albert Speer: his Battle with Truth*, and takes its place among a number of influential accounts of Speer, including his own memoirs, *Inside the Third Reich* and *The Spandau Diaries*. The entire subject of 'Albert

Speer' is itself a contested documentary terrain with various archival records at the heart of interpretations of his life, his actions, and his motives. To write a play about Speer is to enter public discourse about how he should be judged. This judgment is impossible without recourse to the archives, and indeed, the biographies of his life become themselves part of the archive to be consulted.[46] While Edgar adapted Sereny's book for the stage, he also theatricalized his own version of the evidence, the documents, the personage that gave the play its title. And at certain points the tension between the biography and the play text reflects more about the shaping hand of the authors than might be guessed at face value (see Fig. 10).

In this chapter, we can attempt to highlight and discuss only a few of the most important aspects of Edgar's monumental play. Acclaimed by a number of the critics, and requiring fifty actors and multimedia scenography, Edgar utilized the full resources of the Lyttleton Theatre to create a kaleidoscopic panorama of Speer, his life and times. The mixture of fantasy and reality embedded in the

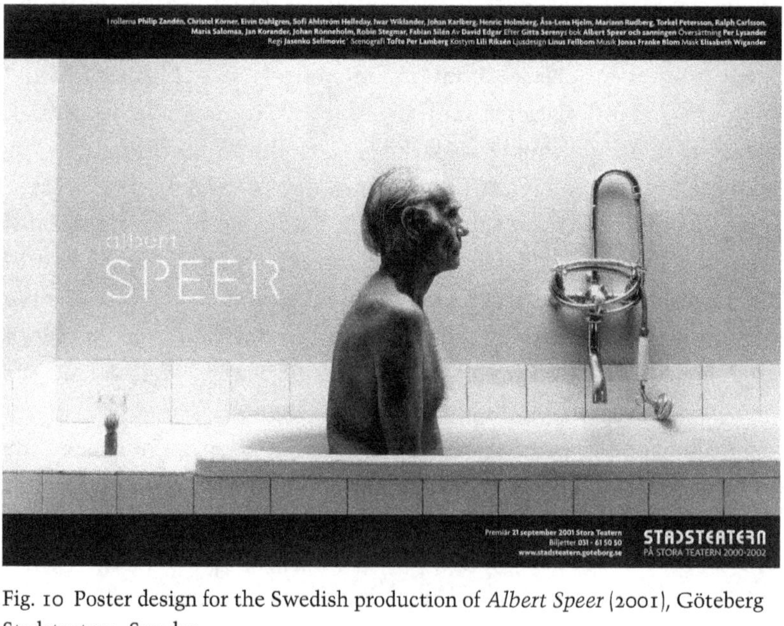


Fig. 10 Poster design for the Swedish production of *Albert Speer* (2001), Göteberg Stadsteatern, Sweden.

text extended to the staging (dreams and nightmares, flashbacks, footage of the war and camps bleeding into the material set – all these effects created a powerful spectacle).[47] We first identify the epistemological hybrid of fact and fiction as a key attribute of this work, differentiating it from the two earlier plays by the larger amount of fictional invention it displays; second, we move on to the Faustian framing of the play and its call to judgment as a key feature of both dramaturgy and thematic focus; and third, we close with a discussion of Speer's decision(s) to reach for celebrity as a world-historical figure and the consequences of embracing this performance-based life. The crucial moral question of individual responsibility for the evils of the regime will of course come into our discussion, but perhaps less centrally than in the Sereny biography or in Speer's own quest. We think the confounding paradox of public performative man (chimerical, unstable, unverifiable) is as crucial in Edgar's version of Speer as the older philosophical question about the good man in a corrupt system.

In an article about the play, written five days after his mostly positive review of the production, Michael Billington criticized Edgar for mixing documentary and fiction in a hybrid approach to the topic, preferring the Tricycle's strict verbatim version of Nuremberg (1996) or Harold Pinter's faction play, *Ashes to Ashes*, supposedly inspired by Pinter's reading of Sereny.[48] He faults *Albert Speer* for mixing documentary and fiction: 'As an examination of Nazism, it falls somewhere between the chilling sobriety of fact and the unfettered use of the dramatist's imagination.'[49] We think Billington missed the point of the exercise – the attempt to consider Speer rather than Nazism *per se* as the object of inquiry, and to go beyond the limitations of the trial testimony to place an entire life in context. The play (and the biography as well) focuses on the individual in relation to his role as a public figure, first as a member of the Reich leadership and then as a commentator on his own participation in the regime. It also dramatizes his family relationships and his last love. The judgment it elicits from audiences is a summary judgment on the quality of a life. Neither the legal focus of Nuremberg nor the analogical and tangential metaphors of *Ashes to Ashes* grapple with this project. Edgar's play wants to be (and is) a part of the public discourse around the biographies and commentaries that focus on Speer – his name, as the title makes clear, is the focus of the project rather than, say, a 'Life and Times of the Third Reich' or Brecht's *Fear and Misery of the Third Reich* or *The Resistible Rise of Arturo Ui*.

In his first memoir, *Inside the Third Reich* (1969), Speer maintains an objective, not terribly personal, voice as he goes over in close detail his memories of the Hitler years. Then, in his account of his prison experience at Spandau, *The Secret Diaries* (1975), a different, more personal voice of introspection and observation becomes available. One has to read his accounts with discerning attention to his characterizations of his own actions, his descriptions of others (especially Hitler), and his own judgments on the regime. Sereny got close to Speer and many of the key figures in his life, and writes with an insider's knowledge to conclude with some sympathy that Speer 'was unique among Hitler's men in the intensity of this inner battle of conscience'.[50] Reading the memoirs, it is clear that Speer carefully separated himself from the other leadership figures of the regime in order to legitimize his view of himself as different from them, more discerning, more able to offer to the world an account of the meaning of what transpired (and therefore less guilty of the evils they perpetrated). For example, his emphasis on the combination of an autocratic authority (dictator) and the newly developing tools of technology allow him to act as if from above, in an omniscient warning voice speaking to the future. In *Inside the Third Reich*, he quotes himself in his summing-up at Nuremberg:

> Therefore, the more technological the world becomes, the more essential will be the demand for individual freedom and the self-awareness of the individual human being as a counterpoise to technology. Consequently this trial must contribute to laying down the ground rules for life in human society. What does my own fate signify, after all that has happened and in comparison with so important a goal?[51]

That this self-characterization, coupled with his admission of responsibility for the actions of the regime as one of its leaders (something no other defendant at Nuremburg was willing to do), succeeded in setting him apart as an historical actor with conscious and self-reflective abilities and insights is indubitable in the light of the millions of copies of his books sold and the significant public attention given to his opinions and personage after his incarceration.

Speer exemplifies David Marshall's formulation of a 'public subject'. In *Celebrity and Power: Fame in Contemporary Culture*, Marshall refers 'to a representation of individuality and personality that operates in the public sphere', in short, as a celebrity.[52] Viewing celebrity as a form of public subjectivity explains how the power of celebrity comes to entail ethical questions. Celebrity is not just a matter of the skill displayed by the celebrity in his or her achievements; rather, representations of individuality and personality are embodied in performers whose appearance both promises and limits access to an intimacy of the 'real'. While celebrity can bring with it powers that are associated with leadership, charisma, even prophecy, it also brings the vulnerability to exposure that makes the distinction between private and public life meaningless. Because celebrity performances only expose one or sometimes several aspects of a person, the celebrity lives with an ever-present danger of being caught out by the display of some traits or behaviours not explicitly part of the *intended* display. This leads to major and continuing efforts to control the representations of the public persona, something clearly evident in Speer's actions from early in his career. Thus everything concerning Speer turns on the epistemological questions of 'facts' in relation to unverifiable 'private' material, graspable only through public performances. The mixture of fact and fiction Billington faults in the dramaturgy is only an aesthetic expression of the problem of the public subject that is the subject of the drama – it is almost a metatheatrical commentary through stylistic means.

Edgar was able to write (and Trevor Nunn to direct) a grand epic play on Brechtian principles – surely historicized by the passage of time and creative attention to juxtaposition and relief as techniques of deliberate *Verfremdungseffekt*. This is the type of play at which Edgar excels, and he is at the top of his craft in this project. The scenes exhibit an economy of selective image and direct action that achieve a tight dramaturgy, especially laudable in the light of Sereny's 700-plus page biography and Speer's equally capacious memoirs (not to mention the extensive body of additional scholarship). Edgar considered Speer through careful study of the archives and, of course, the lens of Sereny's text. The resulting drama shows the playwright pursuing his defining creative insight concerning negotiation and retrieval. In Edgar's view, Albert Speer was engaged in trying to negotiate his life through a Faustian bargain, and then in the later portion of it, post Spandau, to attempt a retrieval of self-respect, dignity, and authority through a new self-fashioning performance that finally failed.

Without offering a systematic account of the balance of fact and fiction in Edgar's play, we do want to point out some important strategic dramatic effects he creates for the stage. The play begins and ends with Speer dreaming. In the opening dream, set in the 1970s, he experiences the nightmare of the Nuremberg trial with a different outcome: instead of twenty years in prison, which was his sentence, he dreams he is sentenced to death by hanging. 'Not – yet', he protests upon waking (p. 8). In the final scene, Speer's nightmare features Hitler mocking his claim not to have known the full fate of the Jews. Again he protests 'Not yet', but his time is up; it is the moment of judgment and final accounts. He continues:

> Because, yes, I cannot admit what I have not admitted and remain alive.
> But if I did, I could die the man I might have been.
> *To 'us'.*
> Of course, it wasn't that 'I could have known'. That I was 'blind'.
> Because, yes, one cannot look into a void. If I 'turned away', I knew.
> I knew. I helped to build a boneyard.
> Yes. I knew.
> And now, at last, I need never speak nor think nor dream of any of these things again.
>
> (pp. 146–7)

The specifics of these dreams are invented, although Speer did experience dreams of Hitler coming back to haunt him.[53] Also, more importantly, Edgar invents the final admission of Speer that he knew. This is not in Sereny, and it is not in any account of Speer's last days. The closest evidence in Sereny's biography is a statement Speer made in 1977 in support of a legal action in South Africa attempting to block publication of the pamphlet 'Did Six Million Die? The Hoax of the Twentieth Century'. Speer wrote that he still considered 'my main guilt to be my tacit acceptance [*Billigung*] of the persecution and the murder of millions of Jews'.[54] However, when Sereny translated his statement into English for publication, he asked for a footnote that parsed the word *Billigung* to mean 'looking away, not by knowledge of an order or its execution. The first ... is as grave as the second'.[55] This distinction continued to matter to Speer as the thin ground of his less than total guilt until the end of his life. By having the fictional Speer admit unequivocally that he knew at the moment of his death, Edgar makes his own judgment that Speer had to have known and also dramatizes the link between this admission and the moment of death, which strengthens the Judgment Day motif that structures the play.

The references to Faust that shape the play are part of this motif, and demonstrate the creative design of Edgar's version of Speer. The first page of the printed text, before the list of characters, contains two citations, one from Marlowe's *Dr Faustus* and one from Speer's *Inside the Third Reich*.[56] That Speer saw the analogy between himself and Faust, Hitler and Mephistopheles, is a factual claim based on the memoir. Edgar makes these equivalencies part of the scaffolding of the play – using the postponement of reckoning ('not yet') as a structural device in tandem with flashbacks to further the echo of the classical play within the contemporary one. In addition, he stages the key temptation, the moment when the bargain is sealed, in 1940, when Hitler takes Speer with him to Paris and 'lays the world at his feet'[57] by ordering him to build a new Berlin greater than Paris.[58] Coming out of the flashback, Speer's spiritual interlocutor, the Spandau chaplain Casalis, says, 'So you had your Mephistopheles.' Speer answers, 'And he had his Faust.' Later in the second act, in a fictional conversation between Casalis and the rabbi Raphael Geis, Casalis spells out the spiritual/material situation for Speer: 'Rabbi, I have a fear. That the only way he could admit what he admitted was by denying what he has denied. I taught him to confront as much of what he knew as he could deal with and remain alive. That to save his life he had to sacrifice his soul' (p. 131). In a sense, this is a second Faustian bargain – the price for continuing to live and to try 'to become a different man' (p. 16) is to deny full knowledge of the Holocaust, even in the face of a great deal of evidence against him. The effect of the strong Faustian motif on the play is to frame the judgment about Speer in moral rather than legal terms, taking into account the whole of the lived life of the man in question, and also to set up his paradigmatic 'Everyman' import.

Speer can be interpreted not only as himself but also as speaking for the ordinary German citizens who wanted to plead that they did not know about the murder of the Jews as national policy. Indeed, Speer's two memoirs were greeted with passion both by his former friends and colleagues, who felt he had betrayed them by admitting too much, and by others who felt he had offered a defence for unconscionable behaviour by German citizens. Whether he confessed or quibbled about what he did not know, he upset people from diametrically opposed factions. He also, of course, won sympathy and respect from people who thought that the prolonged examination of the conscience and desire to atone redeemed him from his blind sight.

We have used religious language here deliberately (redemption, atonement), with full knowledge of its Christian resonances. If Faust sets up the paradigmatic action of the final judgment and the weighing of all the deeds of a life, the performance of penitence becomes one of the most powerful and yet contested 'acts' in Speer's repertoire. This emphasis on ritual and performance underscores both his surrogative role for common German citizens and his exemplary role as leader and public figure. In this context, we can see how Edgar figures Speer as a failed actor. The choice of Marlowe's *Doctor Faustus* rather than Goethe's *Faust* is critical too for the judgment. Faustus is damned to hell for selling his soul in Marlowe, while in Goethe's poem of Enlightenment reason and human progress, Faust repents his evil bargain and is saved by God. Depending on which version one applies to Speer, he can be redeemed by his final admission. But since Edgar is a secularist who cites Marlowe and not Goethe, and since the last scene is the playwright's fiction, there is good reason to conclude that Edgar's Speer is not redeemed at death. This is one of the points of tension between the play and the biography, for Sereny's judgment is much milder, closer to Goethe than to Marlowe. In her closing lines she writes:

> I came to understand and value Speer's battle with himself and saw in it the re-emergence of the intrinsic morality he manifested as a boy and youth. It seemed to me it was some kind of victory that this man – just this man – weighed down by intolerable and unmanageable guilt, with the help of a Protestant chaplain, a Catholic monk and a Jewish rabbi, tried to become a different man.[59]

Edgar made another dramaturgical decision relevant to his view of Speer as a performing public subject. Speer chose a high-profile public persona when he emerged from Spandau, much to the distress of his family, who had hoped to find some relief from public scrutiny and a retreat into private life. In conceiving the scenes of the play, Edgar made a large number of them stage Speer's performance of self for the perception of others, often in public situations, but even within 'everyday life'. The first clear indication of the import of this theme comes early in the first act, when Speer asks Casalis to help him change: 'You spoke about a journey to becoming someone else. I wondered if you felt that anyone could leave their past behind, and become a different man. Or if there are crimes – and criminals – so terrible there is no price too high for them to pay' (p. 16).

Casalis says he thinks Speer is capable of change, but that 'to be born again... he must confront the truth of what he was before' (p. 17). Following on from this early scene, we watch Speer's efforts to construct a self that would transcend his past.

The first act of the play is retrospective, as Speer retells his life through the Hitler years to Casalis (and us). Casalis's presence makes Speer's account rhetorical – an act of persuasion as he tries to explain himself and his early thrall to Hitler. Edgar dramatizes the scene, recounted in Sereny and by Speer himself, of his first lunch at 'the merry Chancellor's Café' in Hitler's jacket, when Speer was looked at and sized up by members of Hitler's entourage. Speer interprets this scene for Casalis in terms of his excitement to have been 'plucked from nothing, to be chosen as the brightest and the best of my profession' (p. 29). Later in the act, in a scene at Hitler's quarters at the Berghof, Edgar imagines a game among Hitler's group where they are all trying on his large peaked cap and impersonating his manner. No one fits the cap until Speer puts it on: it fits. The rise to the 'second man in Germany' is staged through a series of performances for others, even involving costume pieces. Edgar also shows him wielding power through his address to party members at the Ministry of Armaments, when he orders: 'full mobilization of up to twenty million workers from the conquered territories' (p. 56). He is seen addressing the powerful Gauleiters, ordering them to stop consumer production or face prison. While many scenes in the first act dramatize conversations between Speer and Hitler, and some between Speer and his family (father, brother, wife), the thread of the narrative moves ahead through Speer's public performative acts and their reinterpretation.

The second act is largely made up of public scenes, with the exception of the family dinner party organized to welcome Speer back after his release from Spandau, and even that has the formality and the estrangement of a public occasion – because he and his family members barely know each other after twenty years of his absence, and because he has planned and orchestrated it for 'public' effect, choosing foods such as foie gras (which no one likes) and buying his wife a watch (bungling the inscription by misremembering her birth date). This scene, one of the most excruciating in the play, shows Speer trying to orchestrate his family to 'play' according to his 'scenario', and failing. When he reveals that he intends to write his memoirs, this upsets his wife Margaret so much that she leaves the room. His daughter Hilde explains why: 'After twenty years of watching us grow up, and building our own lives... For it to be... the only thing we're known for. To have it all raked up again' (p. 107). Speer however, presses on: 'I am determined. I will write the book. I think I owe it to the world' (p. 107).

The next three scenes take place at publishers' parties or public lectures, and involve speeches and formal performances to different groups of people. The memoir has been written and has become exceptionally popular worldwide, and yet each scene is marked by dissonance. Rudi Wolters, Speer's lifelong friend who bribed the guards to allow him to smuggle letters out of the prison to his family, appears at the first book launch and asks to speak with him privately. He dislikes the memoir and does not hide it, mocking his friend's 'performance': 'It would never do for the great post-Nazi rent-a-penitent to profit from his crimes. Having resolved to walk into his dotage in a hairshirt, renouncing all the vanities and luxuries of life for locusts and wild honey' (p. 112). But Wolters has come about another matter, which involves explaining that he has edited *The Chronik*, an office journal that he kept for Speer between 1941 and 1944. There were originally five copies of this document, but three of them were destroyed or disappeared, one turned up at the Imperial War Museum in London, and the original one was buried in Wolters's garden until Speer was released from Spandau, whereupon Wolters gave him a copy. Speer sent it to the federal archive in Koblenz. However the (discredited) military historian David Irving compared the Imperial War Museum copy to the Koblenz copy and found they did not match, and wrote to Speer about it.[60] In the play, Edgar reverses this, and has Wolters tell Speer about these events. Wolters goes on to say that he has taken out certain incriminating bits – minutes of meetings in 1941 to plan the eviction and evacuation of 80,000 Jews from Berlin, and also notes in Speer's handwriting commenting on the action on the 'Jew-flats'(p. 116). Speer is taken aback by this, insists he may have known about the removals but not where they were going to be sent, and in the end instructs Wolters to destroy the original manuscript, which shows the deletions and changes.

This story, quite complex and not very dramatic, becomes theatrical through Edgar's skilful plotting. The arrival of Wolters interrupts the great fête that is going on to celebrate the success of Speer's memoir. Then, although Wolters manages to get Speer alone and to tell him about the problem of the *Chronik*, the pressure of people wanting Speer's autograph (nice irony) means that people are constantly knocking at the door and interrupting their discussion. This structure of interruption and threat is then compounded by Wolters's searing attack on his old friend for hypocrisy in the memoir: 'You flagellate yourself in hindsight actually to justify your actions at the time' (p. 116). The result is a scene focused on the public performance of Speer before his admiring readers, on the one hand, and his need to put out a 'brush fire' regarding the *Chronik* (through destroying evidence) on the other, all the while being mocked for pretending to be someone Wolters clearly thinks he is not.

The construction of this scene is all Edgar. Not only does he change the account in Sereny of the circumstances of the *Chronik* incident, he also transposes and condenses the events into the two scenes at the book signing. In Sereny's account, the revelation of information takes place in letters between Wolters and Speer over a period of twelve days, and with no face-to-face meeting at all. The comment about locusts and honey came similarly in a letter.[61]

Edgar presses on in the next scene with more public performance images of Speer. He is giving a lecture at a university a few years after the publication of his first memoir. In this scene Speer speaks, is heckled, intervenes to keep the heckler(s) from being removed and insists on answering their questions. After several bouts of question and answer, a heckler produces documents that are read out to show Speer was at a conference in Posen during which Himmler explicitly spelt out the Final Solution. At one point, he addressed Speer directly. This proves, says the heckler, that Speer has been lying and did know about the extermination of the Jews because he was in the room. Speer is very shaken, but denies being there, saying he was at the meeting in the morning but had to leave. The last lines of the scene read: 'I was not. I cannot recollect. I wasn't there' (p. 128). The scene points up the role that Speer plays in public – until the damning indictment destroys his credibility. This recalls David Marshall's comments about public subjects being vulnerable to exposure, to the display of some traits or behaviours not explicitly part of the intended display. Surely this is what happens in this scene.

Edgar's dramaturgy is not based on the sequence of events in the Sereny book or in another major biography on Speer by Joachim Fest.[62] Instead of hearing this at a public speech, Speer probably read the article by US historian Erich Goldhagen in *Midstream Magazine*. He was terribly upset by it and spent the next several years investigating every means possible to prove it was not true that he was at the meeting. He obtained two affidavits, saying that he had gone on from the meeting in the afternoon to Hitler's headquarters in Rastenburg, from a colleague who claimed he had driven there with Speer, and from the conference organizer saying he was sure Speer left Posen after lunch and that Himmler was short-sighted and could not have seen Speer in the semi-darkened hall. Speer worked out a detailed defence of his position with lots of detail about the length of time the car trip would have taken, and the probable time he spoke with Hitler, which would not put him in Posen at the time of Himmler's speech. The closest any of this comes to a disruption at a public lecture is Sereny's account that Speer was worried that some journalists might bring this up at a book launch in Munich.

The reality is more interesting and actually weakens the case: Goldhagen embellished his documents beyond their true contents. He added to Himmler's speech: 'Speer is not one of the pro-Jewish obstructionists of the Final Solution. He and I together will tear the last Jew alive on Polish ground out of the hands of the army generals, and send them to their death and thereby close the chapter of Polish Jewry.'[63] In one respect, at least, Edgar did follow Sereny: the scene is designed to show Speer deeply shaken by this charge, and the charge presented in such as way that it is likely credible. Sereny herself comments on this whole event: 'The fact is that the more Speer tries to explain away awkward facts, the clearer it is that he is trying desperately to avoid facing the truth. There is simply no way that Speer can have failed to know about Himmler's speech, whether or not he actually sat through it.'[64]

The last major scene before the closing scenes of the play stages Speer's meeting with death camp survivors (who do not actually appear on stage). The event has been brokered by two of his spiritual advisors, Casalis from the Spandau days and Rabbi Rudolf Geis, with whom Speer had a significant relationship after Spandau. We glean what transpired from their conversation. Casalis reveals that the reason Speer wants to meet survivors has to do with the Goldhagen affair. Speer's own account of his reason (in the play) is slightly different:

> Rabbi. It has been nearly thirty years. Nobody could go on asserting his own guilt at full volume all that time and remain

> sincere. I wake with it. I spend my days with it. I dream of it. *But what I say about it has inevitably grown routine.* And now that I have proved – to my own satisfaction, yes – my innocence of yet another charge. . .the danger is that in considerable relief at that I say – well if that's all right, then there's no guilt at all. So if you will forgive me, sir, I need this meeting. Because I need to know . . . What it was like, to be on the receiving end of me.
>
> (p. 134; italics added)

This is a very strange admission. It is hard not to think Speer is using the meeting to freshen up his resolve to play his part of penitent to the full. He seems to be indulging in a streak of masochism because the pay-off will fortify his performance. On the other hand, he is also staging this meeting, just as he staged the other events of his public life. Surely, he may be thinking, if people see me meeting with death camp survivors they will finally believe me. Edgar leaves the scene's ambiguity, but it certainly resonates with the previous scenes of Speer managing his public image.

In the remaining scenes of the play, it becomes clear that Speer is having a more and more difficult time maintaining his role. As he says to the audience, 'Because if I knew, and if I *knew* I knew, then everything becomes a lie' (p. 135). In the final scene, confronted in his dream (during his stroke) by Hitler, he admits finally he knew: 'I knew. I helped to build a boneyard' (p. 147). Speer dies because the performance is over, and it has failed. He dies because he has lost his wager with the devil. He dies because he cannot sustain the self-deception, if indeed that is what it was.

In 2005 a new conclusive set of documents were discovered that proved Speer did know – at least at the time – the full horror of the camps:

> The documents uncovered by the Berlin historian Susanne Willems include a Third Reich report from May 1943 that refers to a 'Prof Speer special programme' to expand the Auschwitz camp so that it could serve as a death camp. The report, on which Speer made copious handwritten notes in the margins and over the text, refers to the fact that Auschwitz's role as a work camp

had 'recently been expanded to include the solution to the Jewish question'.[65]

The three plays discussed in this chapter confront more personal forms of failure than any other plays in Edgar's *oeuvre* – and more personal forms of heroism, too, in Albie Sachs and Mary Barnes and Eddie/Joe Berke. Certainly, if Edgar set out to hone his techniques of psychological realism in the earlier plays, he had done Lukács proud. *Albert Speer* shows a playwright at the height of his powers, able to combine acute individual representation with an epic dramaturgy that historicizes the incidents of the narrative and employs a wide range of gestic and other theatrical effects. Roger Allam as Hitler and Alex Jennings as Speer turned in extremely distinguished performances, and most of the critics agreed it was an important achievement (see Fig. 11). Irving Wardle sums *Speer* up as 'an evening of solid craftsmanship, made remarkable by two superb performances and a readiness to transgress the supposed certainties of history'.[66]

Fig. 11 *Albert Speer* (2000), National Theatre. (*l to r*) Roger Allam as Hitler and Alex Jennings as Speer.

More interesting to our understanding of Edgar, however, might be Charles Spencer's letter to *The Times* in response to the review of Benedict Nightingale, the *Times*'s reviewer, who commented that the actors brought 'gravity and anguish' to the role of Speer, and 'charm' to that of Hitler 'before his deterioration into the monster we know'. Spencer wrote: 'These comments reveal the danger, and to some the offensiveness, of fictionalising historical characters responsible for ghastly crimes. The process inevitably humanises such monsters and invokes understanding, if not forgiveness. This is evident even in the plays of Shakespeare.'[67]

We assume there are a number of Charles Spencers in London, and that it is not the same Charles Spencer who is the theatre critic for *The Telegraph*, and who wrote in his own review of *Speer* that 'the audience is completely under the spell of theatre at its most intelligent and enthralling'.[68] However, this other Charles Spencer raises in a fairly mild-mannered way the issue of the dangers of representations of evil. Other commentators, such as historian Andrew Roberts, claimed Edgar was presenting Hitler as 'fascism with a human face'.[69] This discourse raises one of the core issues about censorship that Edgar himself has often addressed in defence of others' work. In his essay for *Race & Class* previously quoted above in Chapter 2, Edgar answers his critics with an impassioned appeal to the value of the dramatic imagination:

> By enabling us to imagine what it is like to see the world through other eyes (including the eyes of the violent and the murderous), artistic representation develops capacities without which we cannot live together in societies at all. Defence of free speech is not primarily a matter of the rights of the speaker but the rights of the listener. In that sense, we all have the right not only to offend but to be offended. Without it, we are all impoverished and disarmed.[70]

This seems like an especially effective commentary in light of the specific moral problems raised by Speer. Edgar fully engaged with the nature of performance through the medium of the theatre to elicit a soul-searching examination of humans as creatures whose self-fashioning performances are never completely congruent with the self they purport to display.

# 6 Socialism's aftermath

## *The Shape of the Table, Pentecost,* and *The Prisoner's Dilemma*

The collapse of 'really existing socialism' in 1989 caught many political commentators by surprise because it happened so quickly and decisively. Within a year, however, David Edgar had joined fellow playwrights Caryl Churchill, Howard Brenton, and Tariq Ali in exploring the consequences and changing circumstances of those events.[1] Beginning with *The Shape of the Table* (1990), his closest look at practical negotiation and the transfer of power in a formal political setting, Edgar wrote three plays over the next decade which form a trilogy following the unfolding drama of post-Communist politics.[2] The other two plays, *Pentecost* and *The Prisoner's Dilemma*, were written five and ten years on, respectively, when the politics of immigration and refugees generated deeply divisive fault lines for all of Europe. The former Eastern bloc countries faced extremely difficult problems establishing workable democracies because they were troubled by ultra-nationalism, ethnic conflict, racism, financial instability, and a lack of effective leadership – not to mention external pressures and 'assistance' that were often internally perceived as meddling and arrogance on the part of the West. These three plays are Edgar's most detailed treatment of the problem of democracy itself, and it is no coincidence that in their moment they addressed issues that the West, no less than the former East, was finding increasingly intractable.

There are at least two ways to view Edgar's preoccupation with this material: first, as a writer and activist on the Left, the end of the cold war and the collapse of the USSR and its eastern and central European (ECE) satellites meant a serious confrontation with the question of what was 'left of the Left' in terms of ideology if not programme, historical lessons if not future objectives. Almost overnight 'socialism' became identified in the West as a failed project, and conservative scholars and commentators were quick to begin the rhetoric, now only too familiar, of a 'new world order' in which capitalism was the triumphant global system and socialism was relegated to the dustbin of history. Probably Francis Fukuyama's *The End of History and the Last Man* (1992) is the key touchstone text for the popular conviction that western liberal democracy/capitalism would be universalized as the final form of human government/economy.[3] Thus obviously for a committed writer on the Left, like Edgar, it was important to examine the changes that were underway in order to understand what was happening and also to begin a debate about what price the new democracies would pay for their fledgling arrangements, and what liabilities their communist histories and their years of satellite politics would have for attempts to reconfigure their polities.

Edgar, like most of his Left playwright colleagues, was under no illusions about the oppressions of the Soviet system, but the viability of an alternative form of democratic socialism, that might evolve in the West while *perestroika* changed hard-line policies in the East, was still at least a possibility before the events of 1989 utterly changed everything. For Edgar, however, as early as *Destiny* the spectre of disillusionment with political systems had never been very far away; from *Maydays* on, this disillusionment focused directly on left-wing politics and ideology. While Edgar had been reworking and rethinking what might be a viable political framework to which he could give allegiance, the watershed collapse of Communism forced a new assessment in the light of political realities. Edgar candidly told *Living Marxism*: 'By the end of the eighties I didn't quite know which direction I was going.'[4]

The second key to understanding Edgar's commitment to writing plays about central and eastern Europe during this period is the recognition that the changes in the East reflected back on issues and events taking place in the West. The Thatcher government fell and John Major became prime minister just about the time *The Shape of the Table* premiered. The questions examined in the play – written before Thatcher was forced out – about how rapid change happens and how political elites negotiate regime change suddenly had an uncanny application closer to home. The war in Bosnia (1992–5) and the western involvement in the conflict in Kosovo at the end of the decade threw the spotlight back on western democracies and their alternating inaction and intervention in the region.

Scholars and political commentators in the various countries of the former Soviet bloc began to question the parallel 'orientalism' that seemed to characterize their representations in the West, and the desire to 'rejoin Europe' was matched by resentments concerning the way their own cultures were patronized or subsumed by the 'occidental' others. What was being called 'revolution' in the western press was often perceived as 'restoration' by countries who traced their genealogy to pre-Soviet political formations, nations, even empires. Meanwhile, and of no small matter, 'Old Europe' developed fears of being overrun by immigrants from the East and refugees from a variety of worldwide conflicts, leading to the concept of 'Fortress Europe' and the question of the future size and shape of the 'New Europe'. If these questions lie at the heart of *Pentecost, The Prisoner's Dilemma* also turns back on the West to ask whether 'liberal interventionism' ever really serves the interests of those in whose country the intervention takes place.

Thus in delving into the historic changes in central and eastern Europe as a locus of inquiry and analysis as well as dramatization, Edgar also simultaneously reflects back on the assumptions of his own culture and politics as a western European and more narrowly as British. If the plays are Edgar's most detailed treatment of the problem of democracy itself, as we claim, they are also his most classical formulation of political issues: What constitutes participation? What is the basis of sovereignty? Is democracy inherently antagonistic internally? What is the appropriate balance between freedom and equality? Can pluralism alter patterns of misunderstanding and prejudice, making them less susceptible to demagogic exploitation? Countries undergoing regime change are particularly open to such analyses. That these questions ricochet between East and West, and apply in different measure to all states and nations, makes the trilogy both extremely specific in its historical referents and broad-based in its philosophical entailments.

This combination of specificity and generality characterizes Edgar's dramatic style during this period. Edgar hones his realist techniques, following Lukács's preferred formulation for typical characters engaged at the nexus of the individual and the social, to show how thoughts and feelings grow out of the life of society, and how experience and emotions are parts of the total complex of reality. The two later plays also see the emergence in Edgar's dramas of complex female protagonists, not perhaps for the first time in his work – one thinks of the women in *Maydays*, which ends at Greenham Common, or the female characters in *Mary Barnes* – but certainly historically linked with second-wave feminism. Edgar represents new possibilities in western politics for women while formulating a gender critique of western 'cowboy' diplomacy. The classical formulation of political problems benefits from another dramaturgical technique established in these plays. Edgar argues that he writes 'faction', a form that, as he described it in 2004, 'takes real events and fictionalizes them in order to allow the writer to present what she or he regards as the essence of the process being dramatised, without being encumbered by the need to present facts literally'.[5] Edgar refuses to name the country in *The Shape of the Table* as 'Czechoslovakia', even though the comparisons are patently obvious; and although he uses Bulgarian as the native language for the country in *Pentecost*, he denies it is Bulgaria (and indeed, the generic does outweigh the specific in this play, which could be set in any number of ECE countries). Similarly in *The Prisoner's Dilemma* the country in question has features that might evoke Bosnia or Nagorno-Karabakh, but Edgar insists on a no-place capable of associations to a number of places.

We shall have a lot to say about this particular technique and its relationship to documentary theatre, on the one hand, and tragedy, on the other, and shall also want to probe the consequences of this aesthetic choice for a theatrical politics. (Ironically, the term 'faction' has also played an important role in an ECE context: In the late 1970s a large literary/political debate took place in the former Yugoslavia concerning Danilo Kiš, an intenationally known writer who used the term 'faction' to describe his own work. The circumstances and objectives were different than Edgar's, but Kiš's primary distinctions between fact and fiction and the attempt to describe a practice which creatively combined the two was similar.)[6]

In the discussion that follows, we will start out with some observations about the plays in the context of historical developments in ECE and some recent scholarship from experts on comparative politics, ethno-cultural relations, and minority rights. The purpose here will be to call attention continually to the relationship between the fiction, its factual context, and its possible interpretations, including highlighting where differences of perception might appear between the representer and the represented.

Then we move to the question of the means of representation – the developing Edgarian dramaturgy – with special attention to the deployment of 'faction' and its assets and liabilities for each of Edgar's political dramas.

## Defining some terms

One of the most interesting discoveries we made while researching the trilogy was that definitions of terms we took for granted in other contexts – such as 'eastern Europe', 'ethnic conflict', 'liberal pluralism', and 'Leftist' – were context-specific and needed initial unpacking and continued vigilance in order to ensure we were clear and precise in our usages. The term 'eastern Europe' itself has a centuries-long history of being used to make some peoples 'other',[7] but it took on a special valence in the cold war era. As has been pointed out by 'Easterners', it is part of the binary logic of East and West that shifts depending on where the East is perceived to be by the speaker. Thus Milica Bakič-Hayden argues that in the Balkans, people 'subverted their own identities by orientalizing one another'. She claims that orientalism is a '*subjectivational practice* by which all ethnic groups define the "other" as the "East" of them; in so doing, they not only orientalize the "other", but also occidentalize themselves as the West of the "others"'.[8] We started noticing that referring often to 'the East' and 'the West' in our text repeats the binary formation, but does not disaggregate 'the East'. Yet it is difficult to write about the general principles considered here, or the generic characterization of them in Edgar's plays, without falling into this practice. We will refer to specific places and to newer names for the territory under consideration such as 'ECE' whenever possible.

Ethnic conflict is not so much an ambiguous term in itself (although ethnicity is of course a fraught term), but the way the phrase has been deployed rhetorically in international media and commentary has often linked the term to tribalism and to an idea of irrational violent hatred. The scholars we read taught us to decouple these linkages from a one-sided and pessimistic notion of ethnic difference, and to re-examine how such terms are used. For example, Patrice C. McMahon writes:

> While it is understandable that violent ethnic conflict attracts a great deal of attention from academics and policymakers, ethnic pluralism – common throughout the world – does not necessarily lead to violence. Like violent ethnic conflict, ethnic cooperation also requires an explanation. Even research that allegedly focuses on managing ethnic conflict does not spend much time on the avoidance of conflict or how de-escalation takes place.[9]

Looking at Edgar's plays, he seems to shift around in his attitudes towards this issue. Arguably, *Pentecost* is his most despairing play, yet it also figures a utopian performative of community building at its centre. In *The Prisoner's Dilemma*, conflict framed within ethnic diversity trumps fledgling attempts to build a bicultural state, but the play offers an understanding of what alternatives exist to separatist solutions and suggests that sometimes these can work, or are at least worth striving to achieve.

'Liberal' has become a thoroughly chimerical word in the new century. Associated with freedom or liberty, when connected to equal rights, social welfare, and regulation of finance or environment, it is considered progressive or 'leftish'. However, it can just as easily be associated with economic liberalism, free trade, low levels of regulation, and smaller government. In this latter cluster, it is a conservative political position; in the last decade, neo-liberalism has been linked to globalization and becomes synonymous with US policy as well as multinational corporations, the World Bank, and the IMF. This etymology of 'liberal' is further complicated by political scholars who refer to liberal democracy or liberal pluralism as a practical system of governance that entails minority group rights. In describing the kind of governments desirable for ECE countries, political scholars will speak of liberal democracies to indicate majority rule plus minority rights. While we will follow their example, we are uncomfortable with the ambiguities of the terms and the range of possible political positions they may signify. ECE scholars have noted the double standard on the part of the West when the Council of Europe or the European Union sets rules for ECE countries before they can join the EU while carefully sidestepping the application of those standards to their own countries. A case in point involves Recommendation 1201 of the Council of Europe Parliamentary Assembly (adopted in 1993), which stated in Clause 11: 'In the regions where they are a majority, the persons belonging to a national minority shall have the right to have at their disposal appropriate local or autonomous authorities or to have a special status, matching this specific historical and territorial situation and in accordance with the domestic legislation of the State.'[10] According to Will Kymlicka, a political philosopher known for his research on democracy in multicultural societies, this recommendation, while not legally binding, went some way to upholding a universal principle concerning minority rights and mentioned territorial autonomy (TA) as one possible mechanism for achieving justice. Since then, alleges Kymlicka, there has been 'marked movement away from the endorsement of TA'. The reason given is that it would be applicable as a universal principle – West as well as East – and a number of western countries that accepted the principle nevertheless did not want 'their laws and policies regarding national minorities subject to international monitoring'.[11] Thus the appeal to liberal democracy or liberal pluralism may be received cynically by many, as characterized by Boris Tsilevich (journalist, scholar and Member of the Latvian Parliament since 1998) in the challenge, 'Why don't you [westerners] take these aliens and treat them as you admonish us [easterners] to do?'[12]

Finally, the question of what the signifier 'Left' means in today's global world, or more narrowly, in Europe or the ECE as we consider it here, is not easy to answer. Within certain countries of eastern and central Europe, to identify a former communist who has retained his/her political power may be to call someone 'left' who is hypernationalist and against minority rights. Following the politics in ECE by referring to Left and Right may just be a prescription for confusion. Meanwhile, it seems to us less and less accurate to describe Edgar's evolved political stance as simply 'Leftist' when it is difficult to say exactly what that term now means. Political terms of this sort are always relational, and in the present climate, that includes a broad group, because the majority governments in the UK and much of western Europe are neo-liberal rather than liberal, and much less libertarian than David Edgar. This difficulty will continue to plague us, and will be addressed again in our conclusion.

### *The Shape of the Table*

In 1985 Mikhail Gorbachev became General Secretary of the Communist Party of the Soviet Union, energizing a younger generation of Soviet leaders (and citizens) who felt cheated by their political-economic system because it had not delivered the material wellbeing they had been promised. It was not merely that the USSR's economy paled by comparison with those of western Europe and North America; absurdly, one of the two greatest powers on earth – from their point of view – was being left behind by South Korea and Taiwan. Gorbachev rapidly initiated a number of changes trying to reform the Soviet economy and polity – loosely summarized under the concepts of *perestroika* and *glasnost* – and many of these were successful in the short run. However, over time the tasks of reform may have been too great, the reformers may have moved too fast, or the Soviets' form of communism may have simply been too brittle to be capable of the massive and rapid change necessary.

Whatever the reasons, Gorbachev's reform efforts within the USSR not only fell short for that regime, they (and their failures) had decisive consequences for the Soviet-style regimes of central Europe. Unlike the Soviet Union, most of the ECE polities were still led by their founding generation, who were highly resistant to any kind of change, and had maintained themselves in power almost entirely by the forces of the secret police and other agencies of repression. As demonstrated in Hungary in 1956 and Czechoslovakia in 1968, the ultimate trump card of these regimes was the ability to bring in the USSR's Red Army to deal with any domestic opposition. But Gorbachev declared in 1988 that this form of interventionism was no longer available, and that the ECE regimes were now 'on their own'. This announcement, and actions that followed, brought to the fore a large array of dissident movements and ideas that had already been building in ECE countries, such as the Solidarity movement in Poland throughout the 1980s. Taken together, these events set in motion a string of 'revolutions' in central Europe in 1989–90 that brought these regimes to an end in startlingly rapid and relatively non-violent ways (Romania excepted).

As we have noted above, several playwrights on the Left responded quickly to these momentous historical developments with new theatrical writing, and it was not surprising that David Edgar did as well. It was certainly time to complement his critique of left-wing ideology in *Maydays* with a corresponding investigation into 'actually existing socialism' through a new play. But in creating such a play, it is also clear that he saw other possibilities present in the circumstances:

> There are two great political stories. One is about how you give up power – the story of *Richard II* and *King Lear*. The other is about how, when you've got power, you avoid turning into the people you've taken it from – *Henry IV*, I suppose. Both of these were present [in the 1989 events] and people were concentrating on the second one – which comes into the second half [of *The Shape of the Table*] – but apparently ignoring the first [how power is given up]. That's where I started from. The second thing I was interested in was the wonderfully strong images we saw on television of the great events in the streets; bells in Prague, flags with holes cut in the middle in Romania, the sparklers on the Berlin Wall, and so on. I wanted really to look behind all that at what was going on in the meeting rooms. One is very struck by the contrast between these grand, simple, majestic images and the detailed reality of the negotiations.[13]

*The Shape of the Table*, then, is certainly about what went wrong with 'actually existing socialism', but it is also about power and the transfer of power, the effect of power on those who lose it and those who newly possess it. It is also about political negotiation, and the interconnections between great, dramatic events in the streets and the representation of those events in the process of regime change. It is about one of the curious dimensions of majority rule, that in an unusual historical space where armed force and other coercive practices are temporarily unavailable (almost a Lockean 'state of nature'), sheer numbers are decisive (and the only source of legitimacy). And it is about the central question that was being little asked at the time: not 'How do we escape our past?' but 'What kind of future will this bring?' and 'How do we even think about that future comprehensively now?'

To explore these questions, Edgar created a play extraordinarily unlike those he had written in the past. Known for having single-handedly halved unemployment among actors with his huge casts, Edgar here has written a play with less than a dozen actors. Famous for plays whose timeframes are measured in decades rather than years or months, here he limits himself to barely more than a few weeks. There is just a single set, and in it only the table really changes. *The Shape of the Table* is a miniature, focusing down on the macrocosmic questions at its centre through precision and subtlety.

The question, then, for Edgar was which central European revolution should he use to examine these questions in such detail. Here he makes an interesting compromise with his concept of 'faction'. As we have noted, he explains 'faction' as taking 'an event, a syndrome or a process and fictionalis[ing] it, changing not only names but characters and incidents, in order to present a model of real and usually identifiable occurrences to an audience who are invited to test what they see against their experience of the happenings to which it relates'.[14] Following this, Edgar should have abstracted from ECE in that year a fictional model of the extraordinary changes taking place there; instead, he has abstracted a model which has obvious and extensive similarities to Czechoslovakia's people and events. Not only is Pavel Prus a 'dead ringer' for Vaclav Havel, and Viktor Spassov an incarnation of Alexander Dubček, but the political movement Public Platform is clearly the echo of the actual Civic Forum – even the dates specified for the action of *The Shape of the Table* are almost exactly the dates of the 'Velvet Revolution' in Czechoslovakia. (And, if we carry this further, Josef Lutz has a great deal in common with the younger Gustáv Husák, the last Communist Party leader in Czechoslovakia.)[15]

Edgar has said that one of the strengths of 'faction' as a way of exploring historical situations is that the audience is encouraged to avoid testing the play for exact verisimilitude with their understanding of actual realities, but instead can focus on the questions and issues raised by the abstract fictional model behind the play. Then, for *The Shape of the Table*, why not seek out the elements of central European regimes and their histories which were common to them all, and focus the play on these? Why call attention to actual history by reminding audiences specifically of events in Czechoslovakia, instead of constructing a model that draws upon all six Soviet bloc ECE countries (Bulgaria, Romania, Czechoslovakia, Hungary, Poland, and East Germany)?[16]

The answer is that Czechoslovakia contained certain elements that Edgar wanted to highlight in his consideration of what kind of regime change is possible. Alone of all six central European regimes, Czechoslovakia had a genuine and sustained experience of reform from *within* the communist movement: Dubček's effort was led by real Marxists (including, for a while, even Gustáv Husák), seeking a 'third way' between Soviet-style communism and western capitalism. Even though this movement is presented in the play as existing only in the historical past, it is presented to be taken seriously as a valid option, an effort to avoid a simple binary choice between the USSR and the capitalist West.

And there may also be another reason for reminding the audience that this fictional country is much like Czechoslovakia. Of all the countries of ECE, only Czechoslovakia had a viable pluralistic democratic government surviving throughout the interwar period, a functioning democracy that was brought back to life in the immediate post-World War II period, until the Communists seized power in 1948. Thus in the debate over how to understand the change in ECE in 1989–90 – was it 'revolution', 'reform', or 'restoration'? – Czechoslovakia has the strongest case to lay claim to the last characterization.

This may seem like a minor debate over terminology, but it was an important issue in the various processes through which Soviet rule was ended in ECE. To label these changes 'revolutionary' was in a European sense to indicate they were progressive, radical, perhaps even violent transformations, since the model for such revolutions in Europe is the great French Revolution, followed by that in Russia. To understand them as 'restoration' was to see them as a 'return' to valuable aspects of the past, with differing degrees of conservative emphases. (US Americans have always understood 'revolution' in this latter way, since an examination of all the specifics of iconic documents such as their *Declaration of Independence* indicates that it was a call for a 'return' to the *status quo ante* the Seven Years' War.[17] Most US Americans thus work with a model for 'revolution' which is essentially – though, perhaps, not so visibly – conservative or restorative.)

So, 'faction' is employed to fictionalize Czechoslovakia's history in order to make it plausible to enlarge the range of possibilities theoretically open to reformers, as well as, perhaps, to make the 'revolution–restoration' argument a live one. At the same time, there are some ways in which the country of *The Shape of the Table* is *not* Czechoslovakia – for example, there is no ethnic split in the play's country, in spite of the fact that Czech–Slovak rivalry is an integral part of Czechoslovakia's politics, was a central factor in the Prague Spring, drove features of the 1989 changes, and led to the splitting up of the country three years later. Clearly, Edgar wanted to focus the explorations of this play in a different direction (he would take up ethnic rivalry in ECE in his next two plays, most directly in *The Prisoner's Dilemma*). In addition, the country in *The Shape of the Table* could bring to mind firing on demonstrators in Germany, details of the Polish negotiations, and smart, potentially more liberal communists in leadership roles in Poland and Hungary who resembled Kaplan and Vladislav in the play.

Thus, *The Shape of the Table* is not about a completely fictional ECE regime. It is about one very like Czechoslovakia – but still different enough that the audience should not see the play as if it were a *roman-à-clef* to be 'solved'. As Edgar has said of this style of drama:

> What I am saying is that dramatic fiction can uniquely illuminate certain aspects of public life: and the dramatic power

> of drama-documentary [his earlier term for 'faction'] lies in its capacity to show us not that certain events occurred (the headlines can do that), or even, perhaps, why they occurred (for such information we can go to the weekly magazines or history books), but *how* they occurred: how recognisable human beings rule, fight, judge, meet, negotiate, suppress and overthrow.[18]

In light of Edgar's concerns and aims, but also in light of the actual play he wrote, how should *The Shape of the Table* be viewed, then? Three possibilities come to mind.

One approach begins with the fact that the play's narrative arc is almost 'palindromic'. It opens with Pavel Prus a prisoner and victim of the repressive policies of the regime led by Josef Lutz, and ends with Prus's inauguration as the first president of the new regime, in which Lutz is now a prisoner. The process through which this complete reversal of status has taken place is the negotiation of a deal (or series of deals) behind closed doors – a cynical view might be that one elite has simply replaced another elite; it is all just a matter of power.

A second way of reading this same series of events would note that at the outset it is Prus, the prisoner, who acts on principle, while Lutz, the First Secretary, seems ruthlessly pragmatic in his behaviour. As the play proceeds, though, Prus seems more and more pragmatic, while Lutz begins to show a principled side, even a kind of lost idealism. This view would begin to posit an inverse relation between principle and power: those who are out of power, or who do not have any chance at it (and the responsibilities of governing), are able to refer their words and actions to ideal values and keep their principles bright and shiny; the closer they come, though, to exercising actual power, the more they apparently must compromise these ideals and dirty their hands with the practical realities of actual governing.

A third view would see idealism of any stripe as the source of the problem. Late in the play Prus says:

> Do you know what the real slogan is of this revolution? If you can call it that, with not a window broken?
>
> LUTZ: Yet. No, tell me.

> PRUS: 'Back to normal.' ... Please, no more adventures. No more heroism. Certainly no more unimaginably splendid futures. Just, let's get back to the normal, ordinary way of doing things. The way that works. The way they do them in the West.
>
> (pp. 80–1)[19]

'Back to normal' means accepting the fact that humans are fundamentally flawed, that the effort to reach for the stars routinely leads to disaster, that it is better to be content with a regime that at least provides for basic material needs and some freedoms for many – but not all – people, even though it means putting up with crime, unfairness, and the pursuit of naked self-interest.

All three of these views undergird conventional ideological positions, and Edgar clearly wants to explore their significance. But they do not cover all important standpoints, and it should be obvious that we think Edgar's own position is different from all three, albeit more fully developed in some of the other plays than this one.

As the play opens, the scene is dominated by a single massive table covered with a tablecloth (see Fig. 12). In the minimalist dramatic economy of *The Shape of the Table*, this is the only feature of the set that will change in the entire course of the play. The first of such changes occurs exactly halfway through the play, when the Communist prime minister, Michal Kaplan, acknowledges that the opposition has forced an opening up of consultations about the country's political future, by dramatically whisking off the tablecloth to reveal that what had seemed to be a single large table is in fact a number of smaller ones (which can presumably be organized in a large number of possible arrangements). As he does so, he quotes Prus's earlier words to the effect that: 'I think we're entering, or we have entered, now, your magic land where everything is possible, and things aren't always what they seem' (p. 48). As the next scene opens, the tables have been rearranged to form three sides of a square, indicating that differing, even contentious, views will now be expressed from the different sides – but nothing is resolved. By the following, or penultimate, scene, the third side of this U shape has been removed, indicating that the communists are no longer present at the table. Finally, for the last scene, only one small table remains, a place for Lutz to place his coat, and then to sit at, as the lights fade on communism in ECE. The table has been shaped by events, and has contributed to the shape of events.[20]

Painter explains the use of the table as a symbol by picking up Kaplan's revelation that the initial large table is not a single table:

> Edgar's device is on one level comparable with the use of the cherry orchard in Chekhov's last play, where the orchard's changing status and the first attempt at destruction of the trees signify the end of one era and the emergence of new hope for the future. In Chekhov's play we find ambivalence: there is both sadness and hope in the symbol of destruction, just as the changing shape of the table in Edgar's play signifies a mixture of despair at the failure and potential for the future. The elegiac quality is unmistakable in both plays.[21]

Kaplan's quotation of Prus's remarks about a magic land alters their meaning, but refers us back to an image Edgar has brought to the

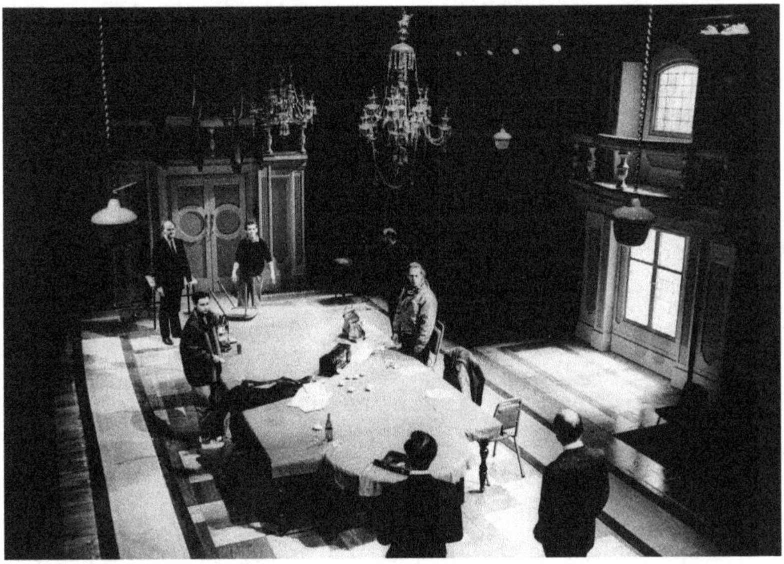

Fig. 12 *The Shape of the Table* (1990), National Theatre. The central object for regime change – the table.

forefront for understanding these large historical events: Prus at one time had written a study of fairy-tales (for which he was imprisoned). He brings this up very early in the play, and points out that fairy-tales have common elements: they all take place in a special time, outside of regular history; they often involve the passing of a good king and a struggle for succession; they often involve secret books, rooms, potions which confer special powers but simultaneously create special problems, and they usually have happy endings. Along the way to those endings, however, things are often not what they seem to be. Edgar explains the analogy thus:

> There is a rhythm to fairy tales, and Marxism has equivalence to that. Feudalism gives way to capitalism; then capitalism creates in its own belly the means of its own destruction, the industrial proletariat; and then the industrial proletariat takes over. The dialectic of thesis – antithesis – synthesis is there in most fairy stories. Also there is the morality-tale element; plus the element of wanting to live happily ever after – there are many ways in which the Marxist story and the fairy story are equivalent. But now that the grand story is off the agenda – a story that we have all ingested, even without realizing it – it will be interesting to see how we live.[22]

There is an elegiac quality running throughout *The Shape of the Table*, and this is one of its centres: for Edgar, the implosion of Soviet-style regimes at the end of the 1980s was not simply ridding the world of a number of dismal, incompetent, and frequently vicious systems; it was simultaneously the loss of one grand vision of human history. Even if that vision had been wrong, it encouraged people to think of society in a comprehensive way, to view humans in an egalitarian fashion, to understand that having a grand narrative means knowing what the end of the story should be – and it is the ending which gives the middle – the present – meaning. The only end now in sight as the play concludes is 'rejoining Europe' – but what is Europe now?

One of Edgar's problems in dramatizing how this all happened is the speed with which the changes took place – few had foreseen the pace of ECE changes. He turns this to theatrical advantage, explaining:

> Each scene ends with some sort of resolution and a sense of what happens next; then the next scene comes and the goalposts have moved and the stakes are upped. The character you think has just won is suddenly out on his ear. And each shift is a surprise to somebody. Each is a moment when you think you've gotten to a point of rest and you haven't.[23]

One effect of this rapid change of circumstances, power relationships, and success/failure is that, although the time covered by the play is very short, the rapid developments greatly enhance the opportunity to see multiple dimensions of a character. This is not so much character development – the time is too brief for that – but time-lapse photography images of the various persons centrally involved in the dramatic action, allowing us to see them in a wide variety of circumstances in a short space of time. As in Edgar's *Destiny* and *Maydays*, no main figure is painted as an incorrigible villain; good or evil results are presented as the outcomes of complex human processes of (not always conscious and rational) decision-making, which involve differing motives, ambitions, career positions, time horizons, misinformation, values, and prejudices. A notable example of this is Josef Lutz, well summarized by Painter, who claims that

> The character grows from a position of lying bureaucratic ugliness to that of moral voice. In the first scene this working class First Secretary shows his capacity to contemplate violence against the demonstrators and his unjustified faith in the inclination of the Soviet Union to come to his aid. In the second scene he lies about the reaction of the 26th February auto plant meeting and is demoted to Chair of the General Federation of Trade Unions; however, by Act Two, Scene One his moral conviction about 'reneging on our promise to end the crime of capital accumulation and the exploitation of one man by another' begins to sound less like automatic Communist jargon and more like sincere protest in the face of frightening future possibilities. Lutz's rediscovered moral integrity is heard clearly in the final scene when he debates with his successor.[24]

Since, in real life, the play's audiences have known leaders such as Lutz and Kaplan only as the hardline, grim, and ruthless personalities we first encounter in the opening scene, Edgar works hard to make Lutz's more idealistic side believable: he has survived Buchenwald, the front lines against the Nazis, imprisonment for a period by his own party for alleged 'Titoite' deviation. He shows a keen intelligence and strong capacity for the ironic examination of discrepancies between words and deeds. And, most significantly, in the end he is willing to accept responsibility for the failure of the revolution in his country, saying he (and his colleagues) have betrayed the working class – it is not the system that went wrong, it is 'pilot error' by individuals like him. He has been corrupted by the insidious effects of power, just as he warns Prus that Prus will be. Only if audiences are willing to find this calling up of the idealistic vision of the younger Lutz – when he and his comrades envisioned 'futures of an unimaginable scale and splendour, in which the immense and boundless untapped energies and talents of the masses would be liberated, every peasant would be Aristotle, every worker Michelangelo' (p. 79) – only if they can find this valid can they accept Edgar's proposition that, along with the gains so obvious in ECE revolutions, something vital is being lost as well.

This combination of gain and loss is apparent in the play's treatment of the question of the freedom gained through the collapse of communism. This is discussed, even debated, most directly by Spassov and Prus in Act 2, Scene 2. Prus has observed that the Communist state has given people 'what they need, not what they want' (p. 73), and claims that what they want is 'freedom'. When Spassov asks whether that is freedom 'to' or freedom 'from', Prus suggests that the old regime at least provided security, protection against starvation, ill health, discrimination, and criminal violence at the price of denying individuals the opportunity to excel, to choose their own leaders, to do anything they please, to take advantage of others, to be lazy and irresponsible.

This complex and sometimes paradoxical consideration of freedom is dramatized in a number of ways throughout the play. For example, in the final scene Lutz notices that the administrative assistant Monica Freie has been retained by the new regime and he approves of that (fearing, as he does, that discrimination against women will increase, along with discrimination against those who worked for the former regime). However, it turns out that continued employment is not actually desired by Freie, who had thought she might be pregnant, and would be free of having to work – but, ironically, only by virtue of assuming the limiting role of parenthood. At the end of the prior scene Kaplan has reported that the new freedom has resulted in racist attacks on foreigners and Roma. Liberty turns out to mean that anti-Semitism is once again surfacing. Lutz observes, and Prus agrees, that there is a kind of freedom from being in prison where pretence of any sort is no longer necessary. And everyone continues to be free under both regimes to go on smoking, a kind of 'voluntary' self-enslavement.

The action of *The Shape of the Table* progresses from the opening scene, where the Party is clearly in charge, as it always has been, and the only question is how best to manage the occasional celebrity dissident, such as Prus, as well as the public demonstrations, which have been growing, to the final scene where the former 'vanguard of the proletariat' is busy reconstituting itself as just another political party, while its former leader is in prison, and the very same dissident is now being inaugurated as the new president while the crowds ring the bells. In the process, not only do Lutz and Prus exchange places, so do the old and new regimes, but also the play dramatizes this trade-off through a mirror-image account of the negotiating process.

In the first scene we only know about the public opposition to communist rule through the views of the rulers, and the way they use such information in jockeying for power among themselves. Not only are the public demonstrations offstage, almost all of the dissidents are as well. However, by the second scene – only one week later – things have begun to change, but we still know of the changes only as reflected through the Party leadership. Different members of that leadership, though, are by now taking different positions on what to do about the public clamour. The most hardline leader of the group visible to us – the Party Secretary Josef Lutz – has been effectively pushed aside for a more pragmatic manager in the person of the prime minister, Michal Kaplan. Kaplan clearly feels that he can arrange a transition to a system in which the Party's predominance is maintained.

A day later, with the third scene, we begin to see the dissidents in action: younger, on average, than the Party and government officials they are challenging, divided by background, experience, and temperament but all coming from solid middle-class backgrounds – all of them 'workers' in one sense or another, but none of them from a truly working-class origin. Their 'demands' are still fairly limited, timid even, and they are careful to be playing loud music while they discuss things so they cannot be heard on bugging devices. As cautious as their positions are, though, they are unexpectedly threatening to the Party representatives, but the majority of the latter see a way out of this challenge by revising the wording of the dissidents' demands in ways that do not alter the fundamental status quo, in terms of who is in power, how history is understood, what real changes might be made in the economy.[25] Furthermore, in the early part of this long scene, we, the audience, are still being presented primarily with a picture of the Party regime in action – sometimes self-contradictory action – as the group still dominating the scene.

However, as time goes on we see more and more of the dissidents' activity, as well as more and more of their internal disputes. At one crucial point, the Prime Minister is led to concede a number of points demanded by the dissidents, and the locus of power begins its massive shift.

> MATKOVIC [a dissident leader]: And the fact that the development of a full independent sovereign national life is now 'the restoration of a fully independent so and so forth . . .' that would indicate that we were once sovereign and then lost that sovereignty?
> (*A slight pause*).
> KAPLAN: Yes, that certainly might be implied.
> MATKOVIC: Perhaps in the period we were in receipt of fraternal international assistance?
> (*Pause*)
> KAPLAN: Well, you could put that interpretation on it, clearly.
> MATKOVIC: And last, I note, 'the principles of socialist democracy' are now 'the principles of socialism and democracy'.

KAPLAN: Are they?
(*He takes the document and looks at it.*)
Well, so they are.
MATKOVIC: With the implication that the two are not in all ways necessarily identical.
...
VLADISLAV [Apparatchik and government minister]: Well, that would appear to follow, yes.
MATKOVIC: So, it would be at least theoretically possible to have socialism without democracy
VLADISLAV: Unlikely, but conceivable ...
MATKOVIC: Or indeed the other way round.

(pp. 47–8)

At this point, however, it is only a beginning; some formulaic concessions by the Party that the Prime Minister clearly feels are not decisive. By the end of the scene Kaplan has ceased to be the primary spokesperson for the government, acceding to the dissidents' demands (that role has passed to Vladislav), and the stage is set for the dramatic appearance of the former reformer, Viktor Spassov. Many of the positions advanced by the dissidents and now grudgingly conceded by the government had been reforms Spassov – from within the Party – had sought to implement twenty years before.

The crux of the negotiating struggle comes in the long scene that opens the second act. It is clear that Kaplan and the rest of the old regime leaders still think at the outset that the situation can be handled by admitting a few tame outsiders to minor governmental positions, making some significant but not regime-altering adjustments to the education system as well as to the economic regime, and going through the motions of a judicial inquiry into the government's handling of some dissident activities. They are quickly disabused of these illusions when the Public Platform group responds with a much tougher and more extensive set of demands than they had been promoting only the previous week. Lutz, in particular, is outraged by these demands, regarding them as betraying the Party's commitment to the working class, challenging the dissidents' credibility as representatives of the people (whom, he claims, they in many ways disdain). Milev, on behalf of the Party, attacks the dissidents for going well beyond what they had already agreed to only seven days ago. Public Platform concur that they have gone beyond their prior agreements, but argue that they have been pushed by events, especially the continuing demonstrations in the street, and they claim that they need to represent this public voice. They also threaten that the public protests will only get worse if their demands are not met.

This forces the Party group to withdraw for a caucus, leaving the audience to see only the interaction of the dissident committee. In that interaction we can begin to see the usual sort of differences that happen in political negotiations: specific individuals weigh the value of various objectives differently; particular individuals have differing assessments of, and capacities for, risk, and calculate the likelihood of success differentially. In the immediately preceding scene, Matkovic had warned that it is harder to recognize when you are winning than when you are losing in negotiations, and that is clearly the case here. However, they begin to sense that they *are* winning – and Prus counsels that they do not want to win too quickly, because they need Kaplan to remain in power long enough and effectively enough to turn things over to them.

In the process, the youngest member of the dissident group, the student Zietek, begins to treat Spassov – who has been making useful, incisive contributions to their negotiating deliberations – as an unwanted relic from the past, and this leads to the intervention of the one woman in the group, Victoria Brodskaya. In the most powerful and passionate speech in the entire play, Brodskaya summarizes the evils of the existing system, and condemns their weak and pragmatic approach.

> I'd ask them why they are prepared to lose factories but not the party branches. Why they'll give up education but they won't let go the police. I'd ask them why the fact of power seems to be so much, much more important than the things you do with it. And I'd ask them how they feel about a 'so-called socialist society' which promises a new Jerusalem but offers tangerines. In which

> the rule is, if you want to eat, then keep your mouth shut. Which pledges the collective liberation of all humankind but actually makes people greedy, selfish, cynical and sly. In which no-one actually feels responsible to anyone or anything beyond themselves. And who the hell they think we are. And what they take us for.
>
> (p. 62)

She then returns to being the secretary, and is not heard from – substantively – again.

The Party group re-enters at this point, and more or less gives up: Kaplan announces he will see the transition through, but then resign, likening himself to the US ambassador to (South) Vietnam taking the flag with him as he left by helicopter while Saigon was 'falling'. The President (of the old regime) similarly has announced his impending retirement, and it now becomes clear that the dissidents have secured not only their demands, but a whole new regime. Power has now changed hands. We are led to see Kaplan in the image of the cartoon character who runs off a cliff and keeps going successfully as long as he does not look down: Kaplan argues implicitly and explicitly that they have now looked down and have seen they have no support, and so they are leaving/falling.

In his review for *The Observer*, Michael Coveney characterizes the structure of the play this way: 'The first act is witty, elegant, funny; Edgar's most stylish writing to date. The second act – after the surprise resignation of the avuncular prime minister and a unifying rendition of the national anthem – is dominated by two long, beautifully wrought debates .'[26] Other reviews suggest that part of the audience missed this element – once Public Platform had won out, things seemed to them 'resolved'.

In the most important respects, the negotiations – and, in one sense, the play – are over at the end of the first scene of Act 2: in another sense, there are several crucial matters – perhaps the most crucial matters – still to be considered: with the old regime at an end, what does the future hold for the forces now unleashed in ECE? The former regimes had met some needs, ignored others, and simply suppressed many forms of disorder. What will now happen to the social fabric of these nations?

Furthermore, what are we to make of Spassov, and what to make of Lutz? What should be the future of neo-Marxist reformism, and what of Marxism itself? Even more, do we lose more than just these ideological viewpoints when they disappear from the historical scene? Might we not also be losing a way of looking at history and human possibilities that began in the humanism of the Renaissance, progressed through such processes as the Enlightenment, the French Revolution and nineteenth-century political development, but has encountered serious difficulty in the face of numerous challenges in the twentieth century? Marxism may have shown itself an inadequate answer to the comprehensive questions about human life in society, but at least it has raised the questions: will this kind of inquiry now wither along with Soviet-style Marxism? As David Edgar put it in his 2008 attack on Left defectors among intellectuals and artists: 'Until very recently, almost everybody disillusioned with the far left felt there was still a viable near left they could call home. Now, that appears to be changing.'[27]

In Act 2, Scene 2, Spassov and Prus consider why the people in the streets can enthusiastically welcome the former's return to the public stage while at the same time consigning him to the dustbin of history. The two wholeheartedly agree that Spassov's reformist efforts twenty years earlier contributed directly to the much more extensive reforms of the present, and that he and his colleagues had a perfectly valid base in Marxism for the changes they undertook. But Prus gently tries to show him that – although Spassov never sold out to the West – he has lost legitimacy in the eyes of the present reform movement because he has not protested publicly in the meantime, has not gone to prison for his efforts, belongs to a period of the nation's history that is now seen as over and done with. Partly this is due to the rigidity of his Marxism, which has led him to look for valid protest only in specifically politico-economic actions, and thereby he has missed the fact that cultural events have become the new avenues of protest. But, partly it is also, as he himself ruefully observes, that he remains a Janus-like symbol – on the one hand, the leader of a singularly intelligent, courageous, and progressive reform movement; on the other, a symbol of national humiliation when that movement was crushed by Brezhnev's Soviet forces. He still makes a case for a third way, a neo-Marxist approach to social organization that tries to avoid the negative features of both classic Marxism and classic capitalism. In the end, though, he must surrender to the inevitable: Prus, rather than he, will lead the new reform.[28]

During their discussion in Act 2, Prus and Spassov have talked about a number of features of a politico-economic system neither capitalist nor communist – both in theory and practice (referencing Sweden for the latter). The play suggests that the dynamics of the cold war have now marginalized such concerns in creating a false dichotomy between capitalism and communism – false in the sense that there are more choices in the world than just these two, and therefore, that the failure of one should not necessarily lead to the institutionalization of the other. But, just as Spassov has been simultaneously honoured and dismissed through the rough processes of history, so too this important concern with 'thinking outside the box' is likely to be lost in the rush to change/return to 'normal'.

Similarly in Scene 3, the last scene of the play, the dialogue between Prus and Lutz is partly concerned with the corrupting and misleading effects of power, but also with the loss of the enterprise of seeking a comprehensive form of socio-economic organization that allows all the members of a society an appropriate place in its decision-making and an appropriate share of the benefits produced. This is the second of the two debates Coveney highlighted and which most reviewers missed. It is not an argument that Soviet-style communism was a good thing and will be missed. Rather it is an argument that communism was one form of effort to construct a better world that could be more equitable and more egalitarian. Lutz argues that the effort failed in his country because he and his colleagues were not up to the leadership tasks required; but it is clear that the system failed as well. Now, as Prus points out, people want to stop trying to achieve such a great society. Edgar presents this as understandable, but unfortunate. Marxism had been one answer to the question of how best to organize society. The fact that it has now been shown to be a false answer does not mean the question – and other possible answers – should now be abandoned, although it looks like that is exactly what will happen. The symbol of this loss is the final situation of Lutz, who one reviewer identified as 'a Lear-like figure'.[29]

Words are the lifeblood of most plays, and in their centrality as a medium we may not notice how important they are in themselves. One of the extremely powerful dimensions of this play is how it brings focus to bear on language and how many ways it may be more than a mere signifier of an action or an event; how in many ways it may be the action itself. A Czech reviewer, Martin Hilský captured this well:

> I find two extraordinary qualities about [Edgar's] play. The first is the way in which he dramatizes the language of political negotiations. The play focuses upon the shape of the negotiation table and the shapes of words in which these negotiations are conducted …
>
> He cleverly demonstrates the political drama of hair-splitting. When at one stage the opposition makes the government representative change 'the principles of socialist democracy' to 'the principles of socialism and democracy', the implication is that they may not always be identical, that there indeed may be democracy without socialism, and it takes no imagination at all to conceive of socialism without democracy.
>
> However, Edgar's political lesson is more general: his revolution is presented as a change of language and public discourse, and that the changed rhetoric may not always be an after-effect of political change but its prime agent and source.[30]

In the Shavian tradition, Edgar has always been particularly concerned with words, names, language. This is one element in his approach to playwriting that all by itself has made him an exceptionally powerful dramatic explorer of politics, because – in the end – the currency of politics is language.

## *Pentecost*

> The traditional isolation of language communities is more and more giving way to the polyglot world of Edgar's drama.
>
> Marvin Carlson[31]

Of the three plays we are treating as a trilogy, *Pentecost* has been the most widely produced in Europe and North America. Unlike *The Shape of the Table*, *Pentecost* does not require detailed attention to the minutiae of political negotiation; nor does it, like *The Prisoner's Dilemma*, expect audiences to follow an imaginary civil war somewhere in ECE, piecing together details of geography and language in order to figure out the plot. It is not that *Pentecost* is less complex (it is not), but it features a series of broad plot strokes that make it easier to follow, and it also reflects back on the West in ways that may make it more palatable for certain audiences, enabling them to identify with its concerns. This play has also been critically discussed more widely by scholars than Edgar's other two plays in this set, which suggests that a sense of its popular appeal may need to be measured against its scholarly critique. We take a close look at the play below in order to address the nature of its politics and its dramaturgy and the way these support or undermine each other – which may reveal something about its popularity.

Like Brecht's *The Caucasian Chalk Circle*, *Pentecost* develops a first storyline only to interrupt it with a second. In both plays, the two plots come together in the end. Arguably, the first part of *Pentecost* is framed as a romantic comedy.[32] A museum curator and an art historian investigate the possibility that a mural discovered in a south-east European church predates the development of perspective normally attributed to Giotto in the fourteenth century. Their growing attraction to each other as well as to the validation project is interrupted when a group of asylum seekers breaks into the former church where the fresco is being uncovered and takes over the plot, shifting the tone as well as the substance to the issue of who has a right to a place in the 'New Europe'. In the destruction that occurs at the end, not only the refugees' quest, but the question of the painting (destroyed in the blast) and the fledgling romance all come to nothing. In this elegiac if not tragic ending, *Pentecost* differs sharply from the reconciliation of *Caucasian Chalk Circle*, with its utopian ending to the Brechtian parable. On the other hand, *Pentecost* is a parable of sorts, and some of its formal elements function as utopian performatives.

As we noted above in Chapter 2, romance is a seldom-remarked attribute of a number of Edgar plays in which a pair of characters share a verbal flirtation – witty, quick, and erotically charged, reminiscent of Hollywood movies from the 1940s, or certain scenes from Shaw. Here, Gabriella Pecs, from the National Museum of the imaginary country, and Oliver Davenport, a British academic, open the play with a comic scene in which Gabriella tries to get Oliver interested in the painting she has discovered on the wall of a church, which had been under layers of paint from previous centuries (see Fig. 13). Oliver plays hard to get, and so a familiar gendered ritual unfolds in which Gabriella gradually wins him over to her cause, in part because it interests him, and in part because Gabriella's passion and wit attract him. He is himself unable to explain why he has decided to help her verify the originality of the fresco, and when she presses him, Oliver ends the scene with the line, 'Because . . . because . . . This is Illyria, lady' (p. 13).[33] This citation from Shakespeare's *Twelfth Night* links the play to Shakespeare's canonical romantic comedy, and also, as Stanton Garner Jr has noted, 'underscores the mythic overtones that southeastern Europe has occupied in the western cultural imagination'.[34]

Fig. 13 *Pentecost* (1997). (*r to l*) J. Michael Flynn and Mary Shultz as Oliver and Gabriella at the Tony Award-winning Berkeley Repertory Theatre.

The dialogue between Oliver and Gabriella is carefully constructed to reveal the back story of local history while creating a special relationship between them that consists of sparring, sexual innuendos, and clever exchanges, such as this one that turns on an allusion to an ancient language in the area, Old Nagolitic:

> OLIVER: But I take it you're persuaded that the painting was elsewhere.
> GABRIELLA: You forgive please: 'take it'?
> OLIVER: I—presume.
> GABRIELLA: Old Nagolitic too has its peculiarities.
> OLIVER: You stagger me.
> GABRIELLA: Words for 'to' and 'from' are actually interchangeable.
> OLIVER: This would explain the taxis.
> GABRIELLA: But only if cab driver speak Old Nagolitic.
> OLIVER: Which has been a capital offense since— . . .
> GABRIELLA: Blah-di-blah.
>
> (p. 7)

Part of the pleasure lies in the differences between their usages of English. Following the gender logic, Oliver commands English, the 'masculine' and imperial language which Gabriella has learned well but with distinctive lapses or idiosyncrasies. The allusion to the archaic language of the region is the butt of the joke here, but of course it also establishes the cultural differences and reinforces the hierarchies that are going to be interrogated in the play. Meanwhile these two people are beginning to finish each other's sentences. Their relationship warms as the verbal exchanges increase. There is even an interlude in which a businessman from Sweden and a young prostitute come into the church, looking for a place to have sex, leaving Oliver and Gabriella to witness their graphic bargaining. They are speaking in German, which Gabriella translates for Oliver. When it gets to the point of imminent action, Oliver reveals their presence and cuts the transaction short. Why is this scene here? On the one hand, to raise the sexual tension between Oliver and Gabriella and parallel it with a rougher transaction between West and East; on the other hand, to reverse the language competency for a time so that Gabriella is the one who is conversant with multiple languages while Oliver clearly only has English. This, and the fact that Gabriella exhibits good instincts and hard work in her investigation of the painting, make her a suitable match for Oliver (who, it will be noted, does not have to establish his credentials – she has assumed them).

Of course, this is not really the important focus of the play. Rather, the parable-like construct of the dramaturgy gestures to a coupling of East and West that would signify the expansion of Europe to include new members from the East, and the possibilities for fruitful collaborations between 'Old Europe' and the newcomers. (However, for those who see what happened after 1989 as a 'restoration', the old–new paradigm would not work. In addition, the dark features of the interlude with the Swede and the sex worker figure the power differential and ongoing exploitation of the East by the West.)

The country is a Bulgarian lookalike, or as Edgar coyly puts it in the stage directions, 'The language of "our country" is in fact Bulgarian, although Bulgaria is not "our country"' (p. xx). Following his logic of 'faction' in which the fictional country may be a composite of a number of applicable locations, we should think south-east Europe rather than a particular country. Gabriella describes the church's religious history more specifically: 'When we are Hungary, it Catholic, when we are holy Slavic people, Orthodox. When we have our friendly Turkish visitor who drop by for a few hundred years, for while is mosque. When Napoleon pass through, is house for horses' (p. 5). Elements of this description might apply to a number of ECE countries, but Edgar has mixed in enough distinguishing features to make it impossible to identify any one actual country. Clearly, Edgar is attempting to synthesize the post-communist region in this play, not to engage particular national histories.

Edgar explains this creative decision under the banner of 'faction', which has already been discussed as an aesthetic strategy, but in relation to this part of our analysis, it seems important to both criticize and defend this dramaturgical choice. We can do this by pointing out its parallel in the argumentation of contemporary political scholars writing about nation-building and the types of democracy coming into being across eastern Europe during the 1990s. A number of these scholars, whether from the East or the West, affirm the unique specificity of each particular nation and its history and context, while simultaneously offering a macro-level interpretation of the problems faced by all: low-capacity state institutions, chronic financial instability, weak civil societies, ethnicity as the primary source of identity in the public sphere.[35] Thus Edgar knowingly avoids the topical reduction of the ideas of his play – the theories about how things work – to one location. This justifiable tactic does, however, make him susceptible to the major objection of many East Europeans to the non-specific overgeneralizations they fear from the West. Seeing the play as a parable or fable in Brecht's sense helps ameliorate the difficulty to some extent, but of course, not entirely, for the play theorizes an East–West relationship, not a state to state relationship, or even a specific intranational situation. Thus the East–West binary, with its consequent power dimensions, inheres within the play's formal structures.

In terms of the generic properties Edgar gives 'our country', we find that they are depicted with an eye to a critique of western presumptions. Gabriella expresses what is at stake in her projection of western judgment: 'You think we don't know what you say? East Europe. Where even crooks don't know what icons worth. Where you pick up masterpiece for string of beads. Where everything is ugly and pathetic. Where they botch up socialism and make even bigger botch of market system too' (p. 10). Czaba, the Minister for Conservation of the National Monuments, arrives to see the painting and decide whether or not Gabriella and Oliver can continue their work, mentioning in passing that he apologizes for not attending an official dinner with Oliver some weeks before, because 'sadly, our currency is choosing that night to make bungee-jump, and I am otherwise engaged' (p. 17). The difficulty he will have in deciding who has the primary right to the painting rests, he explains, in a new Law of Restitution stating that all property expropriated by the state since 1940 should be returned to its rightful owner – but of course as two clerics, one Orthodox and one Catholic, demonstrate by their arguments, there are multiple claims not only for churches but also for 'factories and country houses' (p. 18).

As Edgar weaves in the characteristics common to many countries in south-eastern Europe, he invents a model for thinking about the commonalities among them as well as continuing to poke fun at western presumptions. Oliver provides a running gag when he imports a lot of fancy technological equipment (computers, faxes, etc.) into the church to aid in the restoration work. This equipment is apparently paid for by German and Italian corporations who are underwriting the project on Oliver's request, but Oliver does not seem able to work the equipment himself, although he is possessive about it and shoos others away. The irony is that the common soldiers who appear to be 'guarding' the space know how to use the computer, as does Czaba, who explains it to Oliver; and when Oliver still cannot cope, Czaba gets his secretary to help him print out his document. Thus Edgar gets a laugh at Oliver's expense, debunking the European presumption that eastern Europeans are 'backward'. The play is full of this sort of comic effect.

More complex and not at all comic is the exchange between magistrate and priest. Anna Jedlikova comes to judge whether the painting will be allowed to be removed from the wall of the church and moved to the National Museum. She confronts Father Karolyi, the Catholic priest who left 'our country' in his youth to escape sovietization, and who now has come back to help build the new nation. Jedlikova knew his father and resents his having left. Their sharp exchange rehearses the complex relationship between those who went into exile but returned wanting to create something new, and those who remained and lived through the Soviet period, and who honour a history 'newcomers' do not share. Jedlikova finally spells out her concerns clearly:

> OK. I tell you what I think. You leave, you stop to be a witness ... And now, already, here, our past is being erased. And exiles with new names come back, and restore old names of streets and squares and towns. But in fact you cannot wipe it all away, like a cosmetic. Because for 40 years it is not normal here. And so we must remember.
>
> (p. 38)

Through these and many other small scenes and details that are not essential to the plot but are extremely essential to the fable Edgar is creating, he registers a number of features common to many ECE countries. By personalizing them through characterization and the fiction's specificity, he gestures both to the generalities and to the particularisms inherent in the macro situation.

The main matter of the first act is, however, the fresco itself. A scene likened to Giotto's *Lamentation* in the Arena Chapel in Padua, is thought by Gabriella to predate Giotto and thus implies a huge revision of the history of art. She has managed to uncover some of it (the face of the Virgin holding Christ's naked body) using hydrogen peroxide. In the course of the act, the outline of the entire painting is revealed using proper cleaning materials that arrive with the electronics. Following up on archival research, Oliver and Gabriella discover that there is a letter from one Signor Vegni in 1425 describing the fresco and comparing its technique to Giotto's, and that a canto in the country's national patriotic poem also describes it, dating from the early 1200s – well before Giotto started his painting, in 1305. The action rises in Act 1 as it looks like East and West, female and male – Gabriella and Oliver – might team up to make 'the biggest art find since the unearthing of Pompei' (p. 25).

However, just as plans to remove the fresco and move it to the National Museum seem to be proceeding, a spoiler appears. He is Leo Katz, an American art historian from Cornell University. The answer to Gabriella's question to Oliver whether Katz is a journalist reveals the potential spoilage: 'In the sense that Pol Pot was an urban redeveloper' (p. 31). Indeed Katz wastes no time in complaining about his treatment on the national airline, condemning the record of 'our country' during German occupation, when 80,000 Jews were sent to the camps and many others died *in situ*, and revealing that he is a key witness in a lawsuit to block removal of the painting from the church. Katz, as Oliver recognizes, is on one side of a scholarly struggle between those who believe modern restoration methods homogenize and commodify artworks, destroying the material evidence of their history, and on the other side, art specialists whose techniques of restoration and conservation 'clean up' the artworks for long-term viewing and display. Katz has been summoned by the other priest – the Orthodox Father Bojovic, who has orchestrated the lawsuit to block removal.

The dramaturgy now shifts to a triangle: the artwork at the apex, and Gabriella and Oliver against Katz and Bojovic. Actually, however, it is also a triangle in which chivalrous Oliver defends Gabriella against the unwanted attack of the 'villain' Katz. The problem with this characterization is that although Katz does in fact appear to be an unsympathetic and boorish interloper, he is also very smart and quite right about a number of things. First, he discredits the provenance used to back up the likelihood that the painting predated Giotto by pointing out that ultramarine, a powdered lapis lazuli used in colouring the Virgin's robe, was not used in Europe until the middle of the thirteenth century – which makes it unlikely it was painted any earlier. Second, he charges Oliver with conspiring with Deutscheletronic and Peruzzi to make the painting a 'celebrity artwork' that will travel the world. Third, his arguments about the need to retain history echo Magistrate Jedlikova's comments on witnessing, and thus make at least a plausible motive for his opposition beyond sheer meanness:

> But paintings do grow old. Their history is written on their faces, just like it is on ours. And like the history of people, or of peoples, either you acknowledge it, and try to understand it, or you say it never happened, nothing's changed, and you end up doing it again. Hey, do you know, there were names here on the wall, from when it was a torture chamber, which they scraped away?
>
> (pp. 45–6)

Jedlikova pronounces that the procedure to remove the painting must cease and the painting remain in the church. Gabriella is devastated by this news, but she is equally angry at both men, believing one is an ignorant scumbag (her word) concerning her nation while the other, Oliver, has betrayed her. The stakes for her have had to do with the standing of her country and its culture in relation to Europe. Speaking to Jedlikova in her prepared statement supporting the restoration and removal of the fresco, she had said:

> And yes, it probably was painted here by foreigner. But maybe too you understand what it is meaning to us if despite all Turkish occupation, despite Mongol yoke, still this painting made, and wanted, asked for, and appreciated here. Maybe then we may feel

> bit more universal, bit more grown up, maybe even bit more European.
>
> (p. 42)

Now, the full outline of the dramaturgy is visible thus far: the desire of eastern European countries to verify their cultural credentials in order to rejoin Europe (even if for some it is a restoration to which they are completely entitled) comes up against the tendency of the 'Old Europe' to measure everything in terms of its own cultural values and to look down on 'outsiders', while duelling with upstart North Americans for supremacy and superiority. This tension has underpinned the romantic comedy and also the mystery of the painting's true origin with a far deeper geo-political axis.

The contest for western belonging and supremacy has been fought to this point completely within the hierarchy of European Enlightenment modernity. However, at the end of Act 1, this abruptly changes when a group of refugees bursts into the church, taking Oliver, Gabriella, and Leo hostage. The group demand European passports and safe passage to a new European home. This event ruptures what now appears to have been a self-contained world of narcissistic self-reflection within the narrow horizon of a totalizing West. It demands an urgent reassessment of the human parties seeking legitimation and belonging in a global context, making the argument about the *Lamentation* seem almost quaint (see Fig. 14).

The second act reminds audiences that 'Europe' is a constantly shifting, extremely sensitive flashpoint. The people who have taken over the church seeking asylum are identified as coming from a number of trouble spots – certainly at the time of the play's premiere, in 1994, well before Kosovo – but many still in the present moment of this writing: Palestine, Kuwait, Azerbaijan, Ukraine, Sri Lanka, Afghanistan, Bosnia, Mozambique, and Kurdistan. Several of the asylum seekers are Roma, one of the ethnic groups most downtrodden and oppressed in the former Eastern bloc. Suddenly the struggle is not intra-Europe, but global.

The new dilemma is described most aptly by Boris Tsilevich, who points out what he calls the West's dilemma between 'moralizing and burden-sharing':

Fig. 14 Tony Taccone began his tenure as artistic director of the Berkeley Repertory Theatre in 1997 with this production of David Edgar's *Pentecost*.

> On the moralizing side, these countries declare full adherence to the obligations of international conventions and urge the newly democratic states of East Central Europe to undertake similar obligations as soon as possible. With a policy objective of burden-sharing, the Western countries also want the new democracies to accept as many refugees as they can. Meanwhile, the old democracies are in the process of strengthening 'fortress Europe' and implementing increasingly restrictive policies toward asylum seekers. In these circumstances, even honest attempts to share good practices can understandably be perceived by the newly democratic European states as a way to make the poorer ECE countries accept refugees whom the West itself is trying to get rid of.[36].

The second act stages its new multiplicity of cultures primarily through language. In the first act, English has largely been the language of intercultural discourse, with the native language (represented by

Bulgarian) serving to alienate the presumption of English as 'natural'. In the second act, English is not always the compromise language that can negotiate cultural difference; Russian and Arabic become alternative languages for communicating cross-culturally, and everyone speaks his/her own language at some point. In an interlude in which the refugees are waiting for an answer to their ultimatum, they tell stories to each other in their own languages; through pantomime and partial translations by those who know the languages, the group comes to understand each others' stories and recognize some commonality. Marvin Carlson, in his commentary on the 'macaronic stage', points out the parallel between the action of the characters and that of the spectators: 'Each character finds his or her own way into the play's discourse with whatever language skills are available and each spectator learns to do the same.'[37]

This constitutes the Pentecost scene – an epiphanic interlude when, for a short moment, it seems that peoples of many languages can understand each other and share certain archetypal narratives, similar enough to hint at the universal while different enough to mark the particularity of each person's culture and history. This moment stands in ironic relationship to references to another Bible story, the Tower of Babel. In the first act, the government minister Czaba makes a joking reference to the scaffolding and stairs being built up to the painting; he calls it 'Babel's Stairway', glossing Led Zeppelin. In the last scene of the play, after government forces have blown a hole through the painting in order to rush the refugees, killing a number of them and Oliver as well, Czaba describes the bugged conversations he overheard among the group as 'fucking Tower of Babel' (p. 103). Thus the parabolic structure sets up two possibilities based on Judeo-Christian traditions:[38] (1) the cacophony and misunderstanding at this crossroads of the world will end in destruction, like the Tower of Babel; or (2) the possibility for reconciliation and communication across languages and cultures will be cultivated through an act of grace, which can transform the community. Beginning when the government agrees to give passports and safe passage to only some of the refugee group, excluding others, we see the second possibility begin to fracture until it is literally blown apart.

Edgar has woven into the last turns of the plot a final revelation about the painting, which comes just before it is destroyed. Oliver explains that in fact, the painter was Arab, and he used Arabic geometry and optics to develop perspective, painting with the blue ultramarine colour that only Arabs had in the thirteenth century. He interpreted the *Lamentation* differently, too, for his figure of St John is not comforting the Virgin but admonishing her to get over her grief and remember her faith – that her son has gained victory and is with Allah. This interpretation seemed impossible, Oliver reasons, because of a mistaken view of the medieval period: 'We have this mindset, still, about the mediaeval period. That everybody knew their places, no-one moves. To each his own walled garden. Whereas actually mediaeval Europe was a chaos of diaspora. Every frontier teeming, every crossroads thronged' (p. 98). With the destruction of the fresco, the possibilities for overturning the dominant western view and exploring a new account of humanism are lost, an account which, as Sean Carney has observed, would point to heterogeneous and multicultural origins. But Carney, in his perceptive analysis of the play, faults Edgar for writing tragedy, and faults the form for its catharsis, its *pharmakos* (Oliver's death), and thus its capitulation to inevitability. Because the play ends with the words inscribed on the Statue of Liberty ('Huddled', 'Yearning', and 'Free'), Carney concludes:

> The play seems to offer just such a pacifying tragic vision that asks acceptance, rather than response, from an audience. From this perspective, *Pentecost* lapses into a lax liberal humanism that valorizes Western democracy as the cure for the world's ills: it seems that we live in the best of all possible worlds already, if only the rest of the world was prepared to realize it. *Pentecost* thus endorses precisely the neo-conservative agenda that Edgar so trenchantly critiques in his earlier essays and plays.[39]

There is much in Carney's analysis (more detailed than we have been able to characterize here) that seems worth considering. Particularly in light of the cautions with which we began, underlining the self-absorption of the West, and the overblown sense of western entitlement and hegemony criticized by many in the East, there is a way in which the play seems to retreat to a default position aligned with liberal ideology and Judeo-Christian mythology. Edgar does not offer a clear way out of the tragic impasse to which the drama comes by the end, it is true; and an elegiac pessimism pervades the last scene, which is surely an aftermath both dramaturgically and philosophically. Yet we would like to look closely at that final scene in terms of an offsetting admonition or warning, which, like the Arab painter's gesture through the St John figure, transforms the meaning of the final tableau.

Rather than seeing the final action as resulting from the confusion of the Tower of Babel or the failure of a sentimental harmonious polyphonic 'speaking in tongues', we contend that the violence resulted from concrete identifiable sources, and as in Brecht's famous strategy of the 'Not/But', the spectator is given a privileged seat apart from the fray to ask and see how violence could have been avoided, what else might have happened. In addition, in a typical Edgarian ending, the emphasis is on retrieval of the scraps that allow humans to begin again. Although *The Prisoner's Dilemma* features the clearest figuration of this retrieval, *Pentecost* also stubbornly insists on a tangible kind of 'keeping on'.

The government plan to storm the building followed European and American counter-terrorist game plans, according to Czaba. The Europeans advised negotiations while the US advised sending in 'the cavalry' if it went on more than two days. When the refugees threatened to shoot a hostage or destroy the painting in order to show they 'mean[t] business', the American plan won out. In addition, there was a crowd of a hundred skinheads outside threatening violence and pushing the authorities to act. That they were implicated in what took place is indicated by the empty pram with a swastika spray-painted on its side (a Roma baby had been among the group of refugees in the church). Czaba offers the following explanation to Gabriella and Leo: 'We are young, poor country. Our industry is junkyard and our currency confetti. So, no, we cannot be dumping ground for everybody's rejects' (p. 103). These words are very similar to the words that Gabriella herself had spoken to Leo in the first act in a moment of anger when Leo had criticized the skinheads for beating up Vietnamese, Roma, and Ukrainians. She had exploded:

> I don't see just because of war, we have to be trashcan for world misfits. Or Ellis Island for all huddled masses en route to wild west. OK, so bad things happen. Very bad. But that is since 50 years ago now actually. Why should we be world transit camp? Why should we get rid of Russian army and get Russian dregs and scum in place?
>
> (p. 40)

'Dumping ground for everybody's rejects' sounds very much like 'trash-can for world misfits'. Only now Gabriella, having found a connection to some of those misfits (the young woman Cleopatra and her baby, whose pram is disfigured with the swastika), accuses Czaba instead of agreeing with him. Left with Leo at the play's close, Gabriella takes up from the pram the small notebook where Cleopatra wrote words in English she was trying to learn. Leo recalls that Oliver has said 'we are the sum of all the people who've invaded us' (p. 104), and in a kind of litany, survivors Gabriella and Leo read out the words that carry the traces of those invaders; words such as 'roadblock', 'shrapnel', 'checkpoint', 'ambush', but also 'exchanges', 'school', 'buffet', 'diaper'. The last three words are the Statue of Liberty words: 'huddled', 'yearning', 'free' (p. 105). The retrieval of these words, and their acknowledgement, is a kind of witness-ing, or to echo Jedlikova's Act 1 admonition, 'We must remember. We must not eat our names' (p. 38). The Statue of Liberty words are not elegiac in this context, they are ironic and provocative – the country whose rhetoric adorns its harbour now advises violent actions against those same huddled masses. The border words of Europe testify to the violence of 'Europe' – East as well as West. In a sense Edgar has proclaimed 'a pox on both your houses', but in another sense, the retrieval and reiteration of the personal history of one of the refugees is an act of witnessing by two people, one from the East and one from the West, who have survived and now bear responsibility into the future, even if all they can do is insist on telling the story.

This is, it seems to us, the way the play circles back on the tragedy with something more to offer than catharsis. The density of the text and the complex weightings of many factors in infinitely mobile and ambiguous moments of performance make questionable any totalizing claims for meaning. We read *Pentecost* in this fashion because we are predisposed to look for these patterns alongside other similar patterns in Edgar's *oeuvre*. *The Prisoner's Dilemma* ends with a parallel gesture of retrieval – perhaps clearer and stronger than the last scene of *Pentecost*, but ultimately of the same kind (see below, pp. 261 ff.). As failure of social efforts, democratic initiatives, or political negotiations are an ongoing theme of Edgar's works, the need to find a way to represent failure and yet to move beyond it, to keep on keeping on, is essential for his dramaturgy. These gestures may not always work or may work less successfully in some of the plays, but they do exist in every play he has written since *Destiny* (except perhaps in *Speer*).

### *The Prisoner's Dilemma*

> The Americans thought a few meetings would solve it, as if it were a personal quarrel. In reality, we were divided by a mountain of corpses.
>
> Aliya Izetbegovic, President of Bosnia, 1995[40]

> Are you near a breakthrough? I am very eager not to miss it.
>
> Jan, Act I, p. 53.[41]

> It seems unlikely that the play has changed greatly since its July 2001 premiere. The world, however, has.
>
> Lynn Gardner, review of London production, 2002[42]

If *The Shape of the Table* skipped over the question of the intra-national ethnicity that complicated the situation in Czechoslovakian politics, then the third play in this trilogy takes up ethnic conflict as a major focus. More precisely, the play addresses the way ethnic conflict plays out in a fictional set of circumstances designed to show both the intransigence of the parties to the conflict and also the historical and cultural reasons why the problems seem, and often are, intractable. At the same time, Edgar severely critiques an approach to conflict resolution that conceptualizes human relations through a prism of games and calculated role playing, and demonstrates a style of western diplomacy that can hurt rather than help reach realistic solutions to complex problems. Ethnic conflict, as noted in our introduction to this chapter, is itself a highly charged term rhetorically. For our discussion, we will broadly use the definition that it is 'substate disputes between groups of people who believe that they are members of different identity groups; it is *discord* among groups whose ethnicity has political consequences – including violence'.[43] 'Ethnicity' has an attributed biological relationship (even if only imagined). This definition focuses on ideology over biology, and it emphasizes the political form that the discord takes, noting that it can involve violence but also a variety of other possible manifestations. This approach is obviously wider than what is needed for the fictional situation depicted in *The Prisoner's Dilemma*, but it is important to the broader political thinking that lies behind the play. As usual, Edgar intends the political issues to be embodied in such a way that they can be applicable through extrapolation to other countries and situations where the particularities may be different but the broad interactional outlines are similar to that of the fictional post-USSR republic of Kavkhazia and its Muslim Drozhdani minority.

Ethnicity organizes individuals into collectives, providing a group identity that becomes one means of organizing a world – and understanding and affiliating with a past and a future. Political scientist George Schöpflin describes post-communist multi-ethnic countries thus:

> Dealing with ethnic others is burdened by infinitely greater problems of lack of trust, of solidarity and absence of shared codes of informal communication. Different ethnic groups differ not least because they have different doxic baggage. They make the world differently and believe that theirs is the best and only morally legitimate way of doing so.[44]

Edgar takes up the challenge of showing how these ethnic collectivities organize their worlds in order to complicate and reject the commonplace disparagement of 'ethnic hatreds' – it is not that they are primal, irrational, and/or barbaric; it is rather that they are logical, coherent, based on certain interpretations of history, and made bellicose by the lack of security and political strength in the region.

A number of ECE countries after the fall of the Soviet Union found themselves with one or more minority populations within their borders, borders that were often established for geopolitical reasons that had nothing to do with the identities of peoples living within them. The fictional country Kavkhazia is depicted as a former Soviet republic that contains a Christian majority and a Muslim minority with a long history of conflict and mutual distrust. In order for the play to do justice to both sides of the conflict, Edgar had to make both groups transparent enough for audiences to understand the legitimacy of their positions, and had to balance and humanize their leaders so that neither party could be seen to be primarily at fault in the actions that follow. At the same time, they had to be intransigent enough to show how diplomacy can fail, even with significant efforts on both sides to reach a just peace.

As Lynn Gardner noted in her review cited at the beginning of this section, the careful equilibrium in *The Prisoner's Dilemma* was tipped through the coincidence of real events, the premiere coming literally two months before 9/11[45], while its London production began four months after 9/11.[46] The play also stands in relation to a number of critical world conflicts of the 1990s, including the Middle East, Rwanda, and Northern Ireland.[47] Nagorno-Karabakh (1988–94) and the protracted conflict in Chechnya, in its second phase in 2001, bear close resemblance to the conflict in Edgar's fiction. The war in Kosovo (1998–9) was probably the most obvious conflict in audiences' memories where the indecisiveness of the West was followed by the subsequent NATO bombing campaign. The role of the West, both European and American, is a crucial component of *The Prisoner's Dilemma*. These associations bring back the question of the value of 'faction' as a political aesthetic.

Faction functions well for Edgar when it allows audiences to contemplate a number of associated real-life scenarios and gain new insight on the basis of comparison and contrast with the fiction presented. It works less well when it seems to overgeneralize a macro analysis from an outsider's position, or when the historical instance underlying the faction is clearly obvious. This latter case applies, in our judgment, to *The Shape of the Table*, where the shape of Czechoslovakia looms undeniably over the play.

In reference to the ghosting of *The Shape of the Table* by the real history of Czechoslovakia, there is a conundrum concerning the epistemology of documentary. Is the play making truth claims about the historical situation or not? Should one weigh the characterization of Prus, Spassov, and Lutz against the real Havel, Dubček, and Husák, on whom they are (or might be) modelled? If one does, then a richer field of thinking about their political agency unfolds, provoking re-evaluation, for example, of Dubček's role in the Prague Spring. If it is just a fiction, then Edgar ducks the evidentiary burden but also weakens the urgency of intellectual engagement with the historical reality.

In the case of *Pentecost*, the critique of Sean Carney and Stan Garner that Edgar appears to embrace a humanist universalism and tragic pessimism gains new (negative) valence in light of eastern European perceptions of western arrogance and complacency cited earlier. The notion that eastern European countries are unable to govern themselves is subtly reinforced in this view. On the other hand, in the case of *Pentecost* the critique of western arrogance is indeed clearly woven into the text, and because it is not any one country, the challenges facing the 'New Europe' (ECE and western Europe) in light of a host of problems including immigration, asylum seekers, self-governance, and human rights are all able to be examined.

We find the solutions to these problems less than completely satisfying in the first two plays, for the reasons given above. However, in the case of *The Prisoner's Dilemma*, the larger philosophical questions seem to emerge beyond the confines of historical specificity and without the taint of western complacency. In the trade-offs between peace and justice, the question of whether settling for the possible is a defeat or a limited (but realistic) win – the central philosophical dilemma – has salience for a range of countries and situations, and does not depend upon a precise historical referent. In addition, Edgar harshly criticizes the role of western intervention without retreating to an isolationist stance. The contingency of events suggests that alternative scenarios and behaviours might have produced a different outcome in the fictional world posited by the playwright, and might represent alternative solutions for other real world scenarios.

We think that faction is not better than docudrama, nor is it worse, but rather that each genre has its assets and liabilities, and each play must be weighed in the crucible of its triangular relationship to its moment, history, and performance event. Edgar's writing about faction has become more developed and more oppositional as the last decade has brought discussion of fact-based forms to the fore. We defend his development of faction in his own work, noting what we see as increased success in his use of the form through the trilogy and into the decade of the 2000s, when *Playing with Fire* shows a full mastery of faction (see Chapter 4 above).

In the case of *The Prisoner's Dilemma*, Edgar's published version is especially indicative of how he would like the play to work as a faction. Before each act he has compiled a list of pithy quotations from a number of sources; this is a common practice with his work, and these citations are often important reference points for the associational framework woven into the plays (and of course we have lightly mocked that at the beginning of our discourse on the play). For *The Prisoner's Dilemma*, Edgar quotes from several game theorists and conflict resolution scholars as well as Shakespeare, novelist Amos Oz, and a number of political leaders ranging from Gerry Adams to Shimon Peres to Bill Clinton. At the end of the play text he has published 'War and Peace after the Cold War: a Selective Chronology'. Beginning with 1989 and the fall of the Berlin Wall, he includes key political events concerning Northern Ireland, South Africa, the Arab-Israeli conflict, the Gulf War, the break-up of Yugoslavia, and the wars in Bosnia, Kosovo, and Chechnya. As his descriptions of these events entail both ethnic conflicts and claims for independence, many of which involved multiple diplomatic negotiations often brokered by the US, the UN, or the UK, it is easy to see the connections to the fictional plot of *The Prisoner's Dilemma*.

For the original London production, Edgar and the RSC partnered with the Oxford University Research Group on Conflict Resolution to sponsor a two-day conference entitled 'Theatre of War, Theatre of Peace: Dealing with Conflict in the 21st Century'. The conference took place during the first week of the London production and both its panels and audience involved scholars, aid workers, and journalists from many of the places cited in the Selective Chronology. This event served to make explicit the factional status of the play as a kind of fable or even allegory that had multiple possible applications to actual situations. You could find evidence of how this worked in other places, too, such as the *Financial Times*, where Ian Shuttleworth commented that when the fragile agreement hammered out through Act I collapses, 'accusations and counter-accusations fly about the real and potential harm of events on the ground, about state sponsorship of "independent" groups, about the historical legacy of old events, which are all too familiar to me as a Northern Irishman'.[48]

For the play, Edgar uses the ingenious device of staging a weekend seminar of instruction in conflict resolution and interactional role-playing for participants who will become deeply engaged in international diplomacy, humanitarian aid efforts, and nation-building in the main action of the drama. (Elsewhere we have written at length about conflict resolution theory and inter-actional gaming as a diplomatic strategy in relation to *The Prisoner's Dilemma*.)[49]

The seminar participants apply the games by simulating a diplomatic situation in which they play assigned roles. The stage manager of these theatrics is an American professor, Tom Rothman, who seems, during the course of the play, to turn into a suspiciously Richard Holbrooke-like orchestrator of a scenario which replicates the Prisoner's Dilemma game presented at the seminar.

The major rhetorical figure governing the play is analogy – both as a mode of comparison and also a reasoning device. It can be defined as an 'inference that if two or more things agree with one another in some respects they will probably agree in others'.[50] This characterizes the *modus operandi* of game theory – proponents believe that if the conditions can be set up such that they match the rules of the game, the outcome will emerge according to those rules and the two situations will prove analogous. Through the dramaturgy of the first scene, Edgar plants this notion and its critique deeply into the substructure of the text, allowing it to return and 'score' in a number of ways further on.

Analogies govern the structure as well as the content of the first scene set-up: the classroom where the seminar takes place functions as a stage in that an audience watches the simulation (Tom Rothman 'emerges from the audience' to join the seminar members and Nikolai Shubkin 'speaks from the audience' [pp. 7, 14]). Thus the analogy between classroom, theatre, and simulation techniques is explicit. The simulation is also a ceremony – what Edgar in *How Plays Work* identifies as a format based on formal public gatherings in which 'the situation (the location, its milieu, the associated activity) provides the means by which the action of the scene is revealed'.[51] The simulation itself replicates a formal diplomatic negotiation between two sides in a country torn with internal dissension in the form of an indigenous rebel group – analogous not only to the fiction unfolding in the rest of the play, but also of course to a number of real-life situations supporting this 'faction'.

Game theory as taught by Rothman proceeds through several additional analogies to games such as Chicken and the Prisoner's Dilemma. The game models are taken from film (*Rebel Without a Cause)* and television (police procedurals involving interrogation of suspected burglars), thus continuing the theatrical mode of 'learning'.

While Chicken as a bluffing/daring technique is analogous to parties in a negotiation refusing to back down until it is too late to avoid war, the Prisoner's Dilemma employs a divide-and-conquer structure that can only be defeated by mutual trust – analogous to disputing parties in a negotiation risking compromise without knowing if the other side will also compromise. Compromise will avoid war, or at least ameliorate the situation, but if one side 'rats', it becomes a zero-sum game.

The actual Prisoner's Dilemma as presented to the seminar posits that two prisoners, interrogated separately, might each individually 'rat' on their partners and get a lesser sentence, but if both prisoners keep silent, they both get off. In order to work, this gain is dependent on both intelligence and trust in the other; both of these are near impossible – but not definitively. However, the most outspoken of the students and the main protagonist in the next part of the play, Gina Olsson, does not appreciate the possibilities: 'I would say the consequence of treating these things as a game is to ignore the fact that in this world some people have much power whereas some do not. And if the powerful extend an empty hand then the last thing that the powerless should do is shake it' (p. 14). Annoyed by too many inappropriate analogies, she explodes: 'An authoritarian dictatorship and a people's liberation movement are not in fact two criminals who have done a robbery together' (p. 22). Thus she objects both to the oversimplification of game theory and to a faulty analysis of what constitutes common interests. While the gaming produces facile analogies, the appeal to a win-win solution implied in the Prisoner's Dilemma scenario only works if it is genuinely in both parties' interests to avoid further conflict; something Gina is at pains to point out does not necessarily follow from the power relations structuring the simulated situation.

Apart from the actual arguments about the particular analogies, the most important affect in this first scene lies in the dissonance and impatience of Gina Olsson's responses (played brilliantly by Penny Downie), set over against the views of the other characters (see Fig. 15). For Tom Rothman, the American professor self-satisfied with his seminar and the contribution of game theory to real-world situations, Gina's points are smart but can be accommodated by the theory. For Nikolai Shubkin, former Soviet academic and (Soviet) Afghanistan War veteran, and by Act 2 a senior military officer of a new republic (Kavkhazia), the analogy might work, but history has overtaken it: 'But now maybe for brief moment we come out of cell into bright ray of light at least. I say we pray we do not miss our chance' (p. 15).

Although analogies themselves are under attack for their superficial truths, the dramaturgy based on analogy also has its affirmations. In one of Edgar's most amusing and skilful deployments, a joke is told to set up an analogy, then the joke is itself modified and retold a number of times to different effect – providing an excellent instance of playwrights' technique from *How Plays Work*: repetitions with a pay-off. The joke is a recital of the 'three great lies': 'The cheque is in the mail, my wife doesn't understand me, I'm from the UN and I'm here to help you' (p. 13). Initially told by one of the seminar participants (Patterson), it is designed to puncture Rothman's suggestion that a successful outcome occurs when the UN intervenes as a trusted party to solve the Prisoner's Dilemma. Nikolai later tells a version from

Fig. 15 *The Prisoner's Dilemma* (2001), Royal Shakespeare Company, The Other Place and the Barbican (2002). Penny Downie as Gina.

Soviet times that ends 'come up from your cellars you have nothing to fear' (p. 16), thereby analogizing the UN and the Soviet regime, while later still, in a pornographic version, the third lie is said to be, 'I'm not going to come in your mouth' (p. 22). Based on abuse of power in relationships between unequal parties in all three iterations, these analogies work pretty well in addition to their internal tripartite structure as jokes or fables. The final action of these jokes, moreover, is to undercut seriously any naive belief in these 'lines'. Within the terms of the play, this device further discredits the gaming techniques and also those powerful entities such as states or NGOs who deploy them. They strengthen Gina's identification of the inadequacies of gaming in real-life situations.

The notion that the interactions among nations and peoples, especially weak and marginal peoples, are a kind of play can be traced to the British appellation of the 'Great Game' to south and central Asian politics in the nineteenth century.[52] In *The Prisoner's Dilemma*, viewing the interaction between the Kavkhazi and the Drozhdani as a game puts the emphasis on it as a sport or contest, with the premium on skilful play rather than a just outcome. If what is prized is technical ability, then a game can be serious and a diversion at the same time, but identifying something as a game more commonly tends to trivialize it. The first scene-as-prologue sets up this critique to apply to the action of the rest of the play.

Repetition with a pay-off or 'drop-line' is used to an even more important end in connection with a major thematic operating throughout the play – the question of how accurate communication can occur in complex transactions such as diplomatic negotiations. Within the simulation, the character Floss Wetherby (who is a former actress and now an aid worker) protests: 'You say "cessation", I hear "surrender".' Her counterpart says: 'You say "people's army", I hear "terrorist conspiracy"' (p. 7). This exchange is elaborated into a discussion of the necessity of discovering in any diplomatic negotiation the 'gap between both sides' positions and their interests' (p. 10). Later, Nikolai points out that in different cultures this phrase 'I hear' can mean different things even if both parties are speaking the same language: 'In English mouth, he mean "yes, I agree, but of course I cannot say". While in America it mean, there's no need to repeat, I am rejecting what you say already' (p. 24). Nikolai is an observer who hopes to learn to listen carefully in order not to miss his chance.

The drop-line falls to Gina in closing the scene: 'You heard' (p. 25). This time it is an assent to a subtly proposed assignation between herself and the American character Al Bek, after a remarkably indirect and ambiguous preliminary courtship. Al himself is not sure Gina is agreeing to meet him and asks, 'Uh . . . do you mean . . .?'(p. 25). 'You heard' both echoes the earlier attention to the 'You say/I hear' analyses and departs from it in shifting the content from politics to personal relations.

This personal aspect contributes another important element to the play that is well developed throughout the scene – the interaction shows how people act roles and at the same time act as subjects; act as public or official figures, but also have a personal trajectory that becomes entangled in the official one. Thus Al Bek has a stake in the seminar's content because he is originally from Kavkhazia, and Irish graduate student James Neil, because he is hoping to become a diplomat and wants to network to further his ambition. Tom Rothman wants to be an actual power broker and will later hire Al Bek to help him. Floss really is a committed aid worker who is also an actress. Gina appears to be available as well as married, but is annoyed when personal information about her is disclosed to others. Thus each of the characters has a public and a private face, sometimes seemingly contradictory in either intentions or values. As the rest of the play unfolds, those personal attributes will occasionally prove decisive for the political actions, thus illustrating a key shortcoming of gaming: it assumes rational goal-seeking behaviour based on accurate and unambiguous information about the situation. It cannot account for the irrational or idiosyncratic behaviours of agents who operate with different values and beliefs in opaque situations. In conceiving the play, Edgar was influenced by the late Nigel Howard's writing on negotiation and the role of emotions such that, in Edgar's words, 'emotion (and therefore "irrationality") is not only inevitable but vital in negotiations. Sooner or later, negotiators must confront the intractable contradictions of their and their opponents' positions'.[53]

Fast forward eight years from the 1989 seminar scene. Disparities in power and resources have mediated differences of language, culture, and religion between the Drozhdani Muslim minority and the Kavkhazi Christian majority to frame an environment in which some have taken advantage of the situation to pursue violence and repression on the part of the Kavkhazi government. One result is the organization of the Drozhdan People's Front (DPF), demanding independence for their region and autonomy for their people. Past incidents of violence and mistrust on both sides fuel the conflict, primarily based on material sources of power. On the brink of civil war, the parties agree to high-level talks brokered by the Finnish government. Gina Olsson, working for the Foreign Ministry, is now the chief negotiator between the parties who meet for an Oslo-like weekend at her home.[54] Nikolai Shubkin also appears as one of two key representatives of the Kavkhazi side.

Hammering out the agreement turns on choosing proper words acceptable to both sides, as such documents often do – in this case the clincher is the replacement of 'renounce' violence (because it 'mean[s] it was wrong. You renounce drug-taking or adultery') in favour of 'relinquish' (because it means 'Voluntary. Not conceding rights or principles. Not implying it was wrong before') (pp. 55, 64). Using some of the devices of repetition with a difference that he deployed in the first scene, Edgar returns to the importance of finding out what the other side really wants/needs: the 'You say/I hear' construction echoes throughout the negotiations. The substitution of the word 'relinquish' in place of 'renounce' brings agreement because the differences of nuance in the meaning of the terms is able to be 'heard' by all parties. By the time this final agreement is forged, the scene ends on a feeling of great elation. Describing the original Stratford production, Ian Shuttleworth commented: 'I don't think I've ever before seen an audience so engaged on a semantic level that they spontaneously applaud a particular choice of word as a dramatic breakthrough.'[55]

The play, as we underlined at the beginning of this section, is focused on ethnic conflict. The problems between the Khavkazi and Drozhdani groups are classic for intra-national ethnic conflicts – language, religion, cultural memory, contested versions of history, combined with living in and amongst each other. The intractable nature of the play's situation is symbolized by the events of 22 November 1990 at a bridge, alternatively called Bazarat (Drozhdani) or Basda Brod (Kavkhazi). For the Kavkhazi, a riot was put down by the state, incurring some casualties; for the Drozhdani, a 'massacre of innocents' took place in which 37 persons, many of them children, lost their lives. The parties are divided over language (what to call this place), religion (is it a Christian pogrom against Muslims or a Muslim revolt against Christians?), and history (the disputed account of what took place). Standing in for such places as the Haram As-Sharif/Temple Mount in Israel/Palestine or the bridge at Mostar in Bosnia, this bridge captures the difficulty of 'bridging' differences in many varied but structurally similar situations. Progress can be made only if the parties to the negotiations move beyond their entrenched positions to an understanding of the other's perspectives. In this case, understanding is gradual and provisional, contingent on the ability of the two parties to imagine the other's position as understandable if not legitimate.

Personal stories help, such as the death on the bridge of the chief Drozhdani negotiator's sister. Kelima Bejta is the play's second major woman figure, a young and fiercely committed leader of her people who is also reacting to the personal losses that have marked her experience: 'I have sister die in what you say riot I hear pogrom. She is fifteen and she is sitting down on bridge and she is truncheon by your police and she fall to raging river underneath and she is drown. Like 37 other person. Sorry other rioters. So sorry actually children' (p. 40). The bridge is the *lieu de memoire*, the site of contested history, the 'doxic baggage' which Schöpflin argues makes it seem that there is only one morally legitimate way of 'making the world'. Thus Roman Litvinyenko, the Khavkazi editor who accompanies Nikolai, responds to Kelima from the Khavkazi perspective that what she sees as a massacre of innocents is understood by him as a riot when 'a legal march in commemoration of our national heritage . . . turns into a pogrom of Drozhdnevnayan Christians if Ministry of Interior does not intervene' (p. 40).

Eventually human factors of trust and a forged common goal – avoiding further bloodshed – briefly succeed. Over a period of days, Gina Olsson fosters a climate in which such a compromise can be reached. In terms of rational action theory, the parties act in their own best interests, but also in terms of the overlap between their interests and those of their opponent.

Edgar deploys the bridge as symbol in a second way. The contestants in this play, as with so many in real-world conflicts today, cannot reach a solution by complete separation from one another. All of the parties in the conflicts referenced in *The Prisoner's Dilemma* – blacks and whites in South Africa, Protestants and Catholics in Northern Ireland, Israelis and Palestinians, Serbs, Croats and Muslims in Bosnia – will have to continue to interact with each other in the future. Edgar calls attention to this necessity in the very final negotiating scene. The delegations are attempting to radically separate the two societies along a river, but find that they inevitably must leave a particular bridge in place because it serves both sides, although 'blowing' it (as one proposes) would have created a cleaner border.

The elation of the moment of compromise during the breakthrough in Gina Olsson's living room is shattered at the end of Act 1 when, at the signing ceremony in Geneva, the agreement breaks down. While the negotiators (Gina, Kelima, Nikolai, and Roman) arrive for the official ceremony, back in Kavkhazia, dissident elements on both sides sabotage the agreement. Roman, one of the chief negotiators for the Kavkhars, explains the problem in terms of the failure of elites to find common ground big enough for everyone: 'Room enough for us, of course. Those who enjoy fine food, fine wine, fine conversation. But problem is the people that are leave behind. The Islamic Centre and the Society of St Demetrius. So-called "extremists" on both sides. And so Pandora's Doll is blown apart' (p. 74). The leaders and/or diplomats who work out agreements often move too far – further than they can bring the rest of their constituencies. Then the agreements cannot hold. Arguably, this is a partial explanation for the failure of the Oslo Accords, when neither Arafat nor Peres (after Rabin's assassination) could guarantee the follow-through of their various internal factions. This scene is also about the failure of vision – a vision of a peacefully existing multi-ethnic state – to persuade enough people that it is possible and preferable to struggling for more limited self-interest.

By the end of the Finnish scene, Edgar has built empathy for both sides, involving us with the negotiators as human beings who have forged a fragile sense of community. This attempt to reach for a just peace has seemed both visionary and possible within the limited confines of the Olsson living room. The realities of the political situation back in Kavkhazia break the utopian moment of compromise and raise the spectre of a blind idealism, a well-intentioned but ineffectual diplomacy. Edgar could be said to be writing about the historic failures of the Left throughout this play, and here he addresses the failure of intellectuals and elites. As in the Prisoner's Dilemma game, the players have to be smart enough and trustworthy enough to work out that they would be better off if they keep silent (or in this case, kept the agreement). But as Gina tells Nikolai, in closing the first act: 'They ratted' (p. 76).

In Act 2, we see that as a result of the failed agreement, civil war has indeed broken out, triggering the predictable resulting violence and death. Two years later, the kinds of possibilities explored in Act 1 have become impossible. The parties are further apart than ever, and have committed more hostile acts against each other, increasing the distance between their positions. Edgar dramatizes another aspect of a failed Left, this time the humanitarian Left. Floss Wetherby, the third female protagonist and one of the original seminar members in Santa Cruz, is working for an NGO relief agency, delivering medical supplies at the disputed border zone of rebel Drozhdania. As the former negotiators and now field commanders Kelima (DPL) and Nikolai (Kavkhaz) struggle for control of a shipment of medicine, Floss realizes the impossibility of remaining neutral, supplying humanitarian aid without having it co-opted for use as part of the war. In a brutal lesson, Nikolai demonstrates the limits of Floss's position by forcing her to choose which of two innocent persons he will shoot in retaliation for a double-cross by the DPL. When she refuses to choose, he kills them both in front of her. Just as the civil conflict has progressed too far to go back to the Finnish agreement, so the violence and extremity of the war makes saving both lives an impossibility – all Floss could have done was to save one person. Because she could not make the adjustment to a less perfect solution, she lost doubly. Nikolai has thereby illustrated the worst-case scenario of the game of Chicken, the lose-lose outcome. This critique of idealism is harsh, and it is not Edgar's last word, but it is decisive for this scene. In fact, analysts studying Prisoner's Dilemma as game theory conclude that the best choice is, in fact, to rat – because it saves the participants from even worse outcomes and because the requirements necessary for achieving the most desirable outcome are unattainable (or almost always so).

In the final negotiation scene that forms the bulk of Act 2, diplomacy gets another chance, and fails again, although for a different set of reasons than those of Act 1. The American Tom Rothman began the play as stage manager of a simulation intended for an 'audience'; he ends by attempting to manage a 'real-life' bargaining situation on a large ship. Always meddling, now the Americans are calling the shots, and the California professor plays the chief negotiator (he seems to be part of the government). Rothman, continuing to have faith in the 'game', sets up the Prisoner's Dilemma situation by putting the Kavkhazis in one stateroom on a ship and the Drozhdanis in another, submitting to each of them a draft agreement, and pressuring both sides to sign. Gina Olsson has been sent for, presumably to deliver Kelima Bejta and the Drozhdani side by persuading them to sign.

The players, however, refuse to stay within the confines of the game – they break the rules when the Kavkhazi president, Yuri Petrovian, simply walks into the Drozhdani stateroom and begins to negotiate with them directly, making his own proposal. This action derails the US attempt to coerce the two sides into accepting a Washington-imposed agreement that weakens the government but does not give Drozhdania independence. The terms of the game are upset when the players think outside the script. Ironically, this thinking gives rise to a proposal for partition, which amounts to giving up on the vision of a peacefully coexisting multi-ethnic state. It is, however, similar to the previous scene in which Floss was asked to choose the lesser evil – this partition may give both sides more than they think they will gain staying together, although it will entail considerable ethnic cleansing and a closed Muslim society in Drozhdania.

Gina, who is no longer really a player, thinks partition is selling out: 'This is quite abject. This is a betrayal. Worse, this is a surrender … Of the spirit of a peaceful democratic multi-ethnic state with equal rights for all' (p. 122). For a brief moment, Gina had persuaded everyone to agree to a multi-ethnic state in Act 1, but the moment for this vision is past; it is not possible, and the little patch of common ground has shifted to preserving mutual independence by splitting the country in two and setting up a strong border. In the fiction imagined here, the decision to make this compromise is made not by the Americans, nor by the western Europeans (arguably in reality western powers usually manage to 'call the shots' and force their will in such situations). Here it is the will of the parties themselves, although Edgar never lets us forget that this agreement is made by individuals 'trapped' on a US warship, with bombing Kavkhazia threatened by Washington if talks fail, and all participants constantly aware of the larger geopolitical consequences of any decisions they take.

Edgar has taken us down a dark path toward a steadily receding solution. While making it clear why and how a peaceful multi-ethnic solution could not be agreed, he has also insisted that it was not because one side was intransigent or both sides were irrational; it was because a series of nearly successful steps toward overcoming distrust did not conclude, because violence escalated the conflict, and because neither side was willing to take the necessary risks to overcome the obstacles.

The last scene in the play confirms that, two years after partition, Drozhdania has become a fundamentalist Muslim country that represses dissent and curtails free speech. Written before 2001, Edgar was definitely not siding with the Kavkhazis in the end. Kelima has been portrayed as an exemplary leader of Drozhdania, and sympathy weighs with her and her people significantly throughout the play. Nevertheless, the decision for partition empowers the more extreme elements of the DPL. Rather than ending the play with only the ominous representation of the new repression, however, Edgar turns to the third important female character, Floss Wetherby, and gives her the last word and the last action: retrieval. Two and a half years after her terrible experience of war's brutality, and now in her early fifties, Floss is still in the region, apparently continuing her aid work, but in a different way. She seems to be falling back upon her experience as an actor to arrange play events (such as she might have known from acting school or coaching exercises) that structure the intercultural exchange of meanings associated with ordinary objects, and the performance of tableaux based on these. There no longer seems to be any obvious power relationship between her and her fellow participants (she is not distributing resources, or even 'teaching', and the 'young people' she is meeting with are there voluntarily).

When challenged in the meeting by paramilitaries to stop and leave altogether, she finds a way to continue by reactivating a 'riddle' first discussed in the first scene of the play: 'Some of you are liars. Some of you tell the truth. But only you know which you are . . . If I asked you to put up your hands if you want me to obey these men, what would you do?'(p. 137). None of the others put up their hands. In this fashion, she seems to model democracy *and* resistance, even after her previous experiences. She has learned to work with what she can achieve, where she cannot achieve the full goal. Starting over is always a possibility. Floss is only an individual, and arguably what she is doing will have slight impact. Yet it seems significant that Edgar leaves us with this image of Floss finding a way to make a 'comeback'. Her theatrical gesture is moreover an act of resistance. Although Floss is reduced to a gesture, that gesture is performative for the Drozhdani, and by one of Edgar's apt analogies, for an anaemic western Left as well. The Drozhdani also act performatively in their silence, finding a way to attempt to negotiate their new situation without giving up their interests. The last line of the play, the ultimate 'drop-line', is of course Floss to the paramilitaries: 'You heard' (p. 138).

Of course, we do not know what happens next. Do the paramilitaries put up with being outfoxed by Floss, or do they simply shut the proceedings down, or engage in (more) violence? Do these local young participants in the exercise calculate that there may be future consequences, for themselves or their families, from remaining at the meeting? 'You heard' is, of course, ironic, since there was nothing to hear (or see) in the non-action Floss called for: does silence really mean consent?

This inability to decide the ultimate effect of Floss's action is important to a design which does not simply reinstate her earlier naive notions of philanthropy. As Lila Abu-Lughod, an anthropologist writing on feminism and Muslim women, has cautioned: 'As anthropologists, feminists, or concerned citizens, we should be wary of taking on the mantles of those 19th-century Christian missionary women who devoted their lives to saving their Muslim sisters.'[56] Similarly, Floss's 'model' behaviour could easily slip into this mode of patronizing do-gooding. The ambiguity of the situation and its consequences helps curb the impulse to read Floss in this manner.

However, this final scene also refers us back to the opening, likewise a performance, of a role-playing simulation on a university campus. Floss was a principal actor in that drama, too, and she has been through a lot in real-world terms in the meantime; events that would have driven most other people out of active efforts to connect with people from other cultures (compare Gina's retirement to private life). Her present activity seems to have taken into account what she has learned from her earlier tragic experiences. As Abu-Lughod also notes, 'Where we seek to be active in the affairs of distant places, can we do so in the spirit of support for those within those communities whose goals are to make women's (and men's) lives better?'[57] Arguably, this is what Floss is now engaged in.

It is significant that Edgar figures the positive possibilities for a revived Left in terms of female protagonists. If the Old Left had a tendency towards patriarchy (and so too the 'New Left' of the sixties and seventies), then the remnants of the Left in the new century may be embodied by the female sex, at least so Edgar manages to suggest in this play, which more than any of his earlier plays shows the political potential of female leadership.

Finally, turning again to Edgar's representation of ethnic conflict within an ECE context, the play captures the problematics of a multi-ethnic nation. If the three options are government by majority rule, a form of federalism in which there is some autonomy and protection of minority rights, and a complete partition into separate nations, Edgar has clearly favoured the federal solution while nevertheless explaining why that is not always what the people involved will choose. He has dramatized failure while still insisting on the possibilities for success. He has acknowledged that often only compromise is possible, but urged that the struggle continue.

Sitting in the pit at the Barbican together with the NGO and aid workers who had gathered for the performance, we were thrilled by the play's complexity and brilliance, and to be together with an appreciative and knowledgeable audience. Looking back over the reviews now, we can see the usual divisions between those who find Edgar too intellectual and those who find his insight and complexity exhilarating. We think you can tell by the way critics describe the play whether they engage with the rich dynamics or fall back on journalistic formulas of description and judgment. As one example, Paul Taylor begins by describing the play as a 'long, involved evening' in the first paragraph, making the charge that 'the piece itself feels more like an academic manual of conflict resolution techniques than a fully fleshed-out human drama'.[58] It is clear Edgar will not be appreciated from the first words. On the other hand, Michael Billington, who is often cool about Edgar's plays, was precise in his positive comments on this occasion: 'David Edgar has always written well about the process of politics', he begins, ending: 'Edgar's forte is for the minute particulars of politics, and it is on this level that his intricately plotted play succeeds.'[59] Although this is hardly enthusiastic, it is fair enough. John Peter wrote one of the most engaged and enthusiastic reviews of the play, which we think recognizes the blend of artistic talents responsible for the whole:

> It [the play] tells of a series of negotiations. Michael Attenborough's direction is masterly in its lucidity – which is important, because Edgar has a complex story to tell. The talks are a labyrinth of subterfuges, lies, resentments, suspicions, passions. Words are fought over with the combined ferocity of medieval theologians and boxing promoters. You have to disentangle slogans from facts. Penny Downie plays the Finnish lead negotiator, and her beautifully understated performance is a scorching account of humanitarian frustration.[60]

In our estimation, this trilogy exemplifies Edgar's most mature and important work. It is international in its scope and character, based on deep research and complex creativity, addressing political ideas and behaviours that are critical to our globalized landscape and understanding of recent history. The balance of realistic characterization and epic form that has become his stylistic hallmark is fully realized in these plays, particularly in his women characters of *Pentecost* and *The Prisoner's Dilemma*. Taken together, they are also model history plays – creative embodiments of historical processes of struggle and change that can help those who come after understand what has happened and why, in the years after the end of the socialist era.

# Afterword

> I'd like to be a secretary for the times through which I'm living.
>
> David Edgar

> There is nothing wrong with being just a secretary. They are people who can have great influence, upon the course of things.
>
> *The Shape of the Table*

If David Edgar saw his public persona as a (Balzacian) secretary for his times in 1996, he is in an even stronger position to perform that role now, as he moves into the fifth decade of his prolific career. There are secretaries and there are Secretaries: Mikhail Gorbachev was a Secretary. And there are Secretaries-General – roles with a good deal more room for leadership and ability to shape affairs than those who merely record. We have shown that Edgar is a Secretary at least as much as a secretary, and that, with some of his fellow playwrights who also 'attend to arrangements', he is engaged in defining the cultural character of the new millennium.

Our study has aspired to examine Edgar's artistic and intellectual contributions to this project from the standpoint of sympathetic appreciation but also critical inquiry. We were hoping especially to understand the long trajectory of left-wing politics during the postwar years and into this new period, when it is not clear if the terminology of the 'Left' will even survive. Furthermore, we hoped to understand this conundrum through the prism of theatrical performance, where imagined embodied actions and scenarios present an ongoing repetition of political behaviours – negotiations in our parlance – showing the theatricality of politics as well as the politics of theatre.

Edgar's work provides a panoply of these imagined situations of humans 'attending to the general arrangements of a collection of people' (Oakeshott). Through the seven problematics of political theory we listed in Chapter 1, Edgar has forged a creative trail that tackles each in dramatic form, sometimes in multiple iterations. We formulated the questions as if in a textbook; however, the plays feature stories, events, characters, and imagery that seek to stimulate a theatrical knowledge always more concrete, embodied, and situated than the abstractions of political science or sociology.

Concerning the desire to understand the complex history of the western Left, what Edgar's plays do best is provide a multiplicity of ways of being, of paths taken and not taken, showing both the changing conditions of the times and the concrete choices that humans who considered themselves 'on the Left' made in different situations and contexts. The commentary and activism that accompany this creative work perform Edgar's personal itinerary of his journey, allowing us to study him as part of the equation in following out our questions.

It is difficult to judge whether globalization and neo-liberalism have weakened the specificity and salience of the concept of the Left beyond repair. It will surely continue to be useful as a descriptor of a specific historical past, and some term will continue to be needed to describe the aspiration and commitment to greater social justice, egalitarianism, and forms of law and polity that are inclusive in their membership and redistributive in their economics. For the foreseeable future, we think it is likely that the remainder of the Left will take the form of critique of inequitable and unjust forms of social arrangements, and their abuses of power.

We have now looked in some detail at twelve of Edgar's most important plays and selections from his extra-theatrical writing and activism, acknowledging the large number of his other works we had no room to give detailed consideration. It should be clear from what we have written that we consider Edgar unparalleled as a contemporary dramatist who combines technical craft, a prodigious intellectual range, and a talent for imagining dramas that catch the key political issues of his times. We have also argued that he is an important public intellectual within his generational cohort. However, even as we now conclude our study, David Edgar moves into his fifth decade as a playwright with new commitments and projects. It is tempting to speculate on what lies ahead.

The most recent play considered here is *Testing the Echo* (2008), but by 2010 Edgar had written *Black Tulips* for the highly successful series of plays on Afghanistan at the Tricycle under the title *The Great Game*; he had adapted Julian Barnes's novel *Arthur & George* for Birmingham Rep and Nottingham Playhouse; and had also adapted Ibsen's *The Master Builder* – his first Ibsen – for Chichester.

In the first half of 2010 he wrote commentaries on a number of important issues. In February 2010 alone, he published three such pieces. One examined 'Britishness' through a retrospective look at radical historian Raphael Samuel's *Patriotism: the Making and Unmaking of British National Identity*, comparing and contrasting the 1980s to the 2000s in order to read Samuel's three volumes in terms of 'the identification of two forms of patriotism – patrician and plebian – [as] the dialectic on which all three volumes rest', and to point out that Samuel's second volume, 'Minorities and Outsiders', advocated a 'more pluralist politics, one which starts from a recognition of diversity', *avant le lettre* of multiculturalism.[1]

In another piece, Edgar excoriated the BBC for its weakened public sector ethos (and its exorbitant salaries for top executives and star presenters). Here, he linked the critique to the state of public services such as municipal authorities and rails, concluding: 'it's clear that the failures of a selfish, incompetent and greedy private sector are being taken out on a public sector which, at its best, demonstrates that it is possible to combine innovation and creativity with other, more old-fashioned virtues'.[2]

In a lighter mode, he celebrated what he identified as a new generation of political playwrights that have come on the scene, proving that political theatre is resilient and has a good future. It has made a comeback in the years after 9/11 and the Iraq War, 'not least because these events reminded people that politics matters because politics kills'. He heralded the expansion of new writing in the subsidized theatre, and pointed out that much of it 'consists of plays by young writers – many of them British Asian or Afro-Caribbean, many of them women – set in semi-fictional or fictional worlds'.[3] Here is Edgar the promoter of playwriting and playwrights, welcoming the arrival of new writers to the tribe of British playwrights with whom he identifies and which he has actively championed since his own youth.

In Edgar's public life, his practices reflect the concern to 'keep on keeping on' we have described as marking many of his plays. The notion of being always within a process of negotiation based on paying close attention to the arrangements of his society in order to amend them 'by exploring and pursuing what is intimated in them' is the epitome of Oakeshott's description of the political – and Edgar's practice. Further, the commitment to retrieval, to finding the shard, fragment, or remnant from even the most disappointing and discouraging outcome, that can be taken forward to begin again, marks Edgar's own political trajectory as well as that of many of his characters, such as Albie Sachs, the women at Greenham Common (*Maydays*), Floss (*The Prisoner's Dilemma*), and Alex (*Playing with Fire*). This determination also expresses Gramsci's 'pessimism of the intellect, optimism of the will', which seems fitting for a new time of uncertainty. It is a chastened optimism, an extensively rethought understanding of the 'Left', that Edgar brings to his continuing secretarial performance as Britain enters an era of deliberately chosen austerity, which may further unbalance the society economically and which could have unforeseen political consequences as well.

Edgar is, in our judgment, still 'a man of the Left' insofar as he takes his performance of self forward in new and creative challenges to the problems of the day. With the UK election of the coalition of Conservatives and Liberal Democrats in June 2010, Edgar returned to a position of opposition that may prove more familiar and inspiring than the insider's critique of New Labour has proved to be. Judging from the recent work described here, we can see many possibilities for a fertile political imagination ahead. As the political landscape became clear, Edgar has immediately gone on the attack. On the eve of the election, he reminded voters that the historic alliance between progressives, intellectuals and the poor was in danger of disappearing[4] (a familiar warning that he has also used against the defectors (see Chapter 2 above). In July 2010, as Labour moved toward its own leadership contest, Edgar was cautioning Labour not to betray its historic compact:

> Surely, none of the leadership candidates wants to renege on a progressive alliance which built the welfare state, challenged poverty and equalised pay at the same time that it legalised homosexuality and abortion, liberalised divorce and abolished the death penalty. Ironically enough, social liberals appear to have stuck with Labour in the election. The new leader needs to rebuild the crumbling covenant between social progress and social justice.[5]

With this exhortatory intervention, Edgar as activist and commentator has taken on the new conjuncture. We expect there will also be a new play before long. Few people are better positioned than David Edgar to provide some illumination, some context, some ironic observation, and some continuing leadership in the times ahead.

# Notes

*[Electronic sources are fully cited in the bibliography]*

## 1 Introduction: political commitment and performative practice

1. Robert Hanks, 'Speaking in tongues', *Independent*, 26 October 1994, p. 2.
2. John Peter, 'Politics in the Picture', review of *Pentecost*, *Sunday Times*, 30 October 1994, p. 23.
3. He has written forty full-length plays in as many years, along with a number of shorter plays and a good deal of television and radio work.
4. His plays have been translated into many languages and produced around the world, especially multiple productions in Scandinavia, Germany, and eastern and central Europe (ECE). He has enjoyed a long-term relationship with Tony Taccone, the artistic director of Berkeley Repertory Theatre in Berkeley, California; and while his work has also been performed on the US east coast (New York and New Haven especially), California and the west coast have proved to be a hospitable North American home over the years.
5. In this volume, we will capitalize 'Left' or 'Right' when referring to the ideology or an aggregated sense of partisans sharing that ideology – mostly when it is a noun; in other instances, especially as an adjective, we will use lower case for 'right' or 'left'.
6. In 1994 he wittily characterized his then current position as 'the moment where libertarianism and Trotskyism overlap on a Venn diagram'. Quoted in Hanks, 'Speaking in Tongues'.
7. Edgar himself highlights *Nickleby* as a progressive or left-leaning adaptation of Dickens, stressing the analogies to the Thatcher years: 'A year into Thatcher, our audiences wanted to be assured that there was more to life than money'. Quoted in Susan Painter, *Edgar: the Playwright* (London: Methuen, 1996), p. 74.
8. It was subsequently broadcast on BBC Channel 4 in 1982, and has been widely performed all over the world since that time, including a major revival (and textual revision) in the US and UK during 2005/6. Theatre

historian Jim Davis calls it 'one of the crowning achievements of the British theatre *c.* 1968–80'. Email to the authors, 10 August 2010.

9. In a well-known self-characterization, Edgar has approved of Michael Billington's description of him as 'a secretary for our times'. Susan Painter begins her book on Edgar with this quotation and Edgar's comment on it, that indeed, 'I'd like to be a secretary for the times through which I'm living'. *Edgar the Playwright*, p. 1.
10. Ian Shuttleworth mentions this in his otherwise ringing defence of Edgar. '*Testing the Echo*, Tricycle Theatre, London', *Financial Times*, 7 April 2008.
11. David Edgar, 'Enter the new wave of political playwrights', *Guardian*, 28 February 2010.
12. This term was coined by Aleks Sierz in 2000 to describe the theatre of the 1990s and its young playwrights (Sarah Kane, Mark Ravenhill, Jez Butterworth, Joe Penhall). See *In-Yer-Face Theatre: British Drama Today* (London: Faber and Faber, 2000).
13. Graham Saunders, 'Introduction', in Rebecca D'Monte and Graham Saunders (eds), *Cool Britannia?: British Political Drama in the 1990s* (Houndmills: Palgrave Macmillan, 2008), p. 6.
14. *Ibid.*, p. 7.
15. Dan Rebellato, 'From the State of the Nation to Globalization: Shifting Political Agendas in Contemporary British Playwriting', *A Concise Companion to Contemporary British and Irish Drama*, ed. Nadine Holdsworth and Mary Luckhurst (Oxford: Blackwell, 2008), pp. 245–6.
16. Our position is different from a number of recent theatre and performance scholars, who also wish to separate politics from theatre in order to argue either that lumbering theatre with politics warps theatre (Alan Read) or that only when they are separated can theatre be seen in terms of its own ontology (Ridout and Kelleher). What these accounts have in common is the playing down of any direct intervention in political debate and the concentration on the formal aesthetic properties of theatre, as having their own internal politics, separate from the larger socio-political structures of society. (We cite Read below in relation to his reaction to *Playing with Fire*.)
17. There are a number of serviceable definitions of politics in current circulation in theatre studies. Besides Joe Kelleher's cited below, there is, for example, Peter Billingham's observation that for thirty years 'political' has carried 'a sense of the oppositional and interventionist', captured in the title of his book, *At the Sharp End* (London: Methuen, 2007), p. 11.
18. Michael Oakeshott, *Rationalism in Politics and Other Essays* (London: Basic Books, 1962), p. 112.
19. A term used by Jonas Barish in his study of the anti-theatrical prejudice, and cited and redeployed in Nicholas Ridout's erudite study, *Stage*

*Fright, Animals, and Other Theatrical Problems* (Cambridge University Press, 2006).

20. *Ibid.*, pp. 3–4.
21. Quoted in Joe Kelleher, *Theatre and Politics* (Houndmills: Palgrave Macmillan, 2009), p. 3. Original source: Stefan Collini, 'On Variousness; and on Persuasion', *New Left Review*, 27 (2004), p. 67.
22. Kelleher, *Theatre and Politics*, pp. 3, 16.
23. Dan Rebellato, 'Can theatre change the world?', *Guardian*, 12 April 2010.
24. Rebellato, 'From the State of the Nation', p. 246.
25. *Ibid.*, p. 248.
26. *Ibid.*
27. *Ibid.*, p. 252.
28. David Edgar, 'Provocative Acts: British Playwriting in the Post-War Era and Beyond' in *State of Play*, ed. David Edgar (London: Faber and Faber, 1999), p. 7; for another formulation of Edgar's definition from 2005, see 'Come Together', *Guardian*, 10 January 2005. He lists 'some or all of the principles that defined the so-called State of England play: non-domestic, contemporary settings, large casts, presentational and episodic structures, and narratives that placed the present in the context of the immediate past'.
29. www.merriam-webster.com/dictionary/state [accessed 17 July 2010].
30. Michael Billington, *State of the Nation: British Theatre since 1945* (London: Faber and Faber, 2007), p. 15.
31. Rebellato, 'From the State', pp. 253, 254.
32. *Ibid.*, p. 255.
33. *Ibid.*, p. 257.
34. Janelle Reinelt, *After Brecht: British Epic Theatre* (Ann Arbor: University of Michigan Press, 1992).
35. Quoted in Painter, *Edgar the Playwright*, p. 108.
36. Billingham, *At the Sharp End*, p. 36.
37. David Edgar, 'Secret Lives', *Guardian*, 19 April 2003.
38. David Marmet, 'Why I am no longer a "Brain-dead" Liberal', *Village Voice*, 11 March 2008.
39. David Edgar, 'Ten Years of Political Theatre, 1968–1978' in *The Second Time as Farce: Reflections on the Drama of Mean Times* (London: Lawrence and Wishart, 1988), p. 29. This essay originally appeared in two issues of *Socialist Review* (1978) and was reprinted in *New Theatre Quarterly* (1979), and is one of the best historiographic sources on this period, frequently cited by scholars and critics alike as a 'classic' essay.

40. See chapter 1, 'Theatre of Agitation and Propaganda: early work' in Painter, *Edgar the Playwright*, pp. 13–27.
41. See, for example, Edgar's 'It's an agitprop structure, still, in a funny kind of way . . . each scene makes its own point', quoted in Painter, *Edgar the Playwright*, p. 33.
42. Rebellato, 'From the State', p. 248.
43. David Edgar, *Plays: One* (London: Methuen, 1987), p. viii.
44. Edgar, 'Ten Years of Political Theatre', p. 28.
45. Edgar, *Plays: One*, p. viii.
46. Georg Lukács, *Studies in European Realism* (New York: Grosset and Dunlap,1964), p. 6.
47. As, for instance, in the first definition offered in the Merriam Webster Dictionary.
48. We are not suggesting that Brenton and Hare have not written well about Shakespeare and contemporary playwriting; indeed, both of them have done so over the years. But these are not systematic approaches to craft, the way Edgar's book is, and we think *How Plays Work* showcases Edgar's primary concerns as well as inventorying others.
49. As Fiona Mountford wrote, 'David Edgar has provided a linguistically robust new version of Ibsen's original, highlighting in particular Hilde's vigour and the threat she poses to the subdued Solness household'. 'The Master Builder Reconstructs Ibsen', *Evening Standard*, 17 September 2010.
50. David Edgar, 'Ticket to Milford Haven', *London Review of Books*, 21 September 2006, p. 12.
51. Interestingly for our discussion of agitprop and realism, Edgar criticizes Shaw's view of his own plays as 'accept[ing] a fundamentally false dichotomy between the didactic and dramatic elements of his plays'. Introduction to *Plays Unpleasant*, by George Bernard Shaw (Harmondsworth: Penguin, 2000), p. ix.
52. Christopher Innes, '"Nothing but talk, talk, talk – Shaw talk": Discussion Plays and the Making of Modern Drama' in *The Cambridge Companion to George Bernard Shaw*, ed. Christopher Innes (Cambridge University Press, 1998), p. 163.
53. David Edgar, *How Plays Work* (London: Nick Hern, 2009), p. 27.
54. *Ibid.*
55. *Ibid.*
56. *Ibid.*
57. Paul Taylor, 'An evening with the tutor', *Independent*, 20 July 2001; see also *Theatre Record*, 21.15, 16–29 July 2001, p. 973.
58. John Peter, 'Conflicts of interest', *Sunday Times*, 10 February 2002, p. 19.

59. Dominic Cavendish, 'The power of words', *Daily Telegraph*, 20 July 2001, p. 24.
60. An exception can be seen in the case of Peter Jenkins (see Chapter 2 below).
61. *The Times*, 28 October 1994, p. 33.
62. *Ibid.*
63. Although the space is large, the Evidence Room is also only a 99-seat house, like the New York venue; thus, in this case, the space is experientially extremely different.
64. F. Kathleen Foley, 'Art, politics and dissent in sweeping "Pentecost"', *Los Angeles Times*, 31 May 2002, pp. F25 ff.
65. Reinelt interview with Tony Taccone, Berkeley Repertory Theatre, 27 April, 2010.
66. Reinelt interview with Michael Attenborough, 2 September 2010.
67. While we discuss Islamophobia in detail in Chapter 2 below, we will not return to the issue of weight and the NHS. Edgar addressed this in 'These medical moralizers might as well try banning sex', *Guardian*, 7 June 2007.
68. Oakeshott, *Rationalism in Politics*.

## 2 Intervening in public discourse: Edgar as commentator and activist

1. Edgar points out that his childhood ambition was to be a performer, though he discovered early on that the initial form he thought that would take – as an actor – was not to be for him. He has spoken/written about this often, for example in an address to the Oregon Shakespeare Festival patrons in connection with the premiere of *Continental Divide*, 1 March 2003 (typescript copy, courtesy of David Edgar).
2. For an excellent profile of Edgar, see John O'Mahony, 'Enter stage left', *Guardian*, 20 March 2004.
3. Edgar has been, since 2007, president of the Writers' Guild.
4. An estimate shared by an earlier assessment of his work through 1996. See Painter's summary treatment of his range, variety, and quantity of performative activities, *Edgar: the Playwright*, pp. 9–10.
5. David Edgar, 'Ways of seeing', *Guardian*, 13 March 2010, p. 46 (also reprinted as the introduction to the playscript of *Arthur and George)*.
6. Misha Glenny, 'Letters', *Guardian*, 24 September 2005, p. 31.
7. These are cited as we refer to them throughout the text.
8. Edgar joined with Reinelt, Dan Rebellato, Steve Waters, and Julie Wilkenson to form the British Theatre Consortium in 2007, with the aim to organize the British Theatre Conference series, conduct and publish

research, and act as consultants and advocates for British theatre in all its forms. In 2009 it was commissioned by Arts Council England to conduct the research that eventually became 'Writ Large: New Writing on the English Stage, 2003–2009'. This is published on the Arts Council England website: www.artscouncil.org.uk/.

9. For a brief summary of these findings, see David Edgar, 'Shock of the new play', *Guardian*, 12 December 2009, p. 34. For the entire Arts Council report, see 'Writ Large'. See also David Edgar, 'Enter the new wave of political playwrights', *Observer*, 22 February 2010, p. 20.
10. Edgar, *Second Time as Farce*, p. 9.
11. *Ibid.*, p. 12.
12. 'Public intellectual' is a term we apply to him. Being British, he probably would not presume to apply it to himself.
13. David Edgar, 'I'm a traffic light voter', *Guardian*, 5 May 2010, p. 34.
14. Published in several newspapers, and fully entitled 'Government and the Value of Culture', it is available online at http://webarchive.nationalarchives.gov.uk/ and at www.culture.gov.uk/.
15. David Edgar, 'Where's the challenge?', *Guardian*, 22 May 2004, p. 18.
16. *Ibid.*
17. *Ibid.*
18. *Ibid.*
19. Steve Waters, 'The case of complexity', *Guardian*, 30 June 2004; James Fenton, 'Down with this access pottiness', *Guardian*, 29 May 2004.
20. This event was covered in the *Guardian*, and the arguments repeated: Charlotte Higgins, 'Outrage is central to art says dramatist', *Guardian*, 22 June 2004.
21. David Edgar, 'A shortsighted view of the defectors' decades', *Guardian*, 29 October 1983, p. 12.
22. *Guardian*, 19 April 2008, Saturday Review, p. 4.
23. *Ibid.*
24. *Ibid.*
25. *Ibid.*, p. 6.
26. *Ibid.*
27. Andrew Anthony, 'Defective logic', *Guardian*, 19 April 2008.
28. David Edgar, 'My misspelling their misrepresentation', *Guardian*, 25 April 2008.
29. It is difficult not to seem elitist in dismissing a good deal of the blogging that comes from a few repeated voices, so maybe the best indication of the richness of this exchange is to contrast two opposite comments that were both thoughtful and principled on Commentisfree.guardian.co.uk: Comment 1302556,'HankScorpio': 'You have fallen into the same trap

as Anthony and the rest in believing that if those on the Left criticize the disproportionate nature of the US response to 9/11 that we are somehow siding with the "terrorists"' (26 April 2008, 2.48); and on the other side, Comment 1302678, 'winchmorehillbilly': 'Andrew Anthony is a good bloke, by the way. There's a lot of sense in his book *The Fallout.* You'd probably disagree with fair bits of it but it's worth reading because it deals directly with the kind of changes which make thinking about yourself as on the left so different now from the late 60's. I identified with it because it's quite painful seeing what's happened to beliefs and principles we once thought secure' (26, April 2008, 6.45).

30. Chantal Mouffe, *The Return of the Political* (London: Verso, 1993), p. 4.
31. John Bull, *Stage Right: Crisis and Recovery in British Contemporary Mainstream Theatre* (London: Macmillan, 1994), *passim*; Stephen Lacey, 'British Theatre and Commerce, 1979–2000' in *The Cambridge History of British Theatre,* Vol. III, ed. Baz Kershaw (Cambridge: Cambridge University Press, 2004), pp. 434–5; Simon Jones, 'New Theatre for New Times: Decentralization, Innovation and Pluralism, 1975–2000' in Kershaw, *Cambridge History,* vol. III, p. 450; Baz Kershaw, 'Alternative Theatres, 1946–2000', *Cambridge History.* vol. III, p. 365.
32. Saunders, *Cool Britannia*, pp. 1–15. We discuss the topic of faction much more extensively in Chapter 6 below.
33. From Edgar's address, 'Playwriting Studies: Twenty Years On', at 20/20 Playwriting/Pedagogy, a conference of the British Theatre Consortium, University of Birmingham, 13–14 March 2010. Quotes from MS, courtesy of David Edgar.
34. Edgar, *State of Play.* pp. 1–34.
35. Lacey, 'British Theatre and Commerce', pp. 434, 440, 446.
36. Edgar, 'Provocative Acts', p. 7.
37. David Edgar, 'Ideology in the red', *Guardian,* 3 May 1990, p. 34.
38. To see the sections of 'Writ Large' for which Edgar was primarily responsible, see pp. 25–40.
39. Quoted in Painter, *Edgar: the Playwright,* p. 16.
40. Painter covers this period in her study. See *ibid.,* pp. 13–27.
41. David Edgar, interview printed in Billingham, *At the Sharp End,* pp. 38–9.
42. Painter, *Edgar: the Playwright,* p. 49.
43. *Socialist Challenge,* 21 July 1977, pp. 113–14 (emphasis in original title).
44. David Edgar, 'Achtung!', *New Review* (June–July 1977), pp. 69–71.
45. David Edgar, 'Britain's National Front', *Present Tense* (spring 1978), pp. 17–22.

46. The speech was published as 'The International Face of Fascism', *Urgent Tasks* (fall/winter 1982), pp. 1–7. This quotation appears on pp. 6–7. This journal was a publication of the Sojourner Truth Organization, a Chicago-based anti-racism organization active during the 1970s and 1980s.
47. The Annan Committee on the Future of Broadcasting of 1977 was a public inquiry focused on a number of issues concerning television. David Edgar, 'Why the Front is beyond the pale', *Sunday Times*. 1 October 1978, n.p.
48. These reviews appeared in *New Review* (January/February 1977), pp. 69–71 (Martin Walker); *New Statesman*. 20 November 1981, pp. 19–20 (Paul Wilkinson); *New Statesman*, 16 April 1982, n.p. (Stan Taylor); and *Race & Class* (spring 1981), pp. 427–31 (Nigel Fielding).
49. Interview with Edgar, 'Play for Today', *Fabian Review*, (winter 2001), pp. 6–7.
50. A domestic comedy in form, the play revisits the miners' strike of 1984 to investigate the false optimism of the early strike period. While not generally well received by critics, Christopher Edwards describes it succinctly in a sentence that would work for most of Edgar's oeuvre: 'His position is . . . that of elegist at the court of revolutionary commitment'. 'Culture Clash', *Spectator*, 25 July 1987, p. 37.
51. David Edgar, 'Why Live Aid Came Alive', *Marxism Today* (September 1985), pp. 26–30; and 'How Live Aid revived the Sixties Message', *Guardian*. 2 September 1985, p. 34.
52. *Guardian*, 7 July 1986, p. 25.
53. For an excellent account of this case and a richly subtle and complex analysis of the issues involving formal and informal theatre censorship in Britain, see Helen Freshwater, *Theatre Censorship in Britain: Silencing, Censure and Suppression* (Houndmills: Palgrave Macmillan, 2009), especially chapter 8.
54. Delivered first as a paper at Gagging, a conference at the University of Hull on 25 March 2006, then revised and published in *Race & Class*, 48.2 (October/December 2006), pp. 61–75, as 'Shouting Fire: Art, Religion and the Right to be Offended'.
55. For an account of the rehearsal process and director Janet Steel's negotiation of the play's aesthetics, see Freshwater, *Theatre Censorship*, pp. 150–1.
56. Freshwater reports 'thousands of pounds' worth of damage. *Ibid.*, p. 139.
57. *Ibid.*, p. 148.
58. Edgar, 'Shouting Fire', p. 72.
59. *Ibid.*, p. 72.
60. David Edgar, 'Hear the people sing', *Guardian*, 28 January 1988, p. 32.

61. *Ibid.*, pp. 72–4.
62. Freshwater, *Theatre Censorship*, p. 149.

## 3 Things fall apart: after ideology in *Maydays* and *Contriental Divide*

1. The Frankfurt Declaration is the general name that refers to the set of principles entitled '*Aims and Tasks of Democratic Socialism*' issued by the Socialist International in Frankfurt, Germany, on 3 July 1951. See www.socialistinternational.org/ [accessed 8 August 2010].
2. In addition to the 'regular' CP, there were also the CP (Marxist Leninist), the CP of Britain (Marxist-Leninist), the CP of Great Britain (Marxist-Leninist), the CP of Great Britain (Provisional Central Committee), Alliance for Workers Liberty, Democratic Socialist Alliance, Independent Socialist Group, New Communist Party of Britain, Permanent Revolution (UK), Red Party, Revolutionary Communist Group, Revolutionary Communist Party (Marxist-Leninist), and at least seven groups with names beginning 'Socialist'. See Electoral Commission, Register of Parties, http://registers.electoralcommission.org.uk/ [accessed 8 August 2010].
3. The statistics in this section come from A. J. Davies, *To Build a New Jerusalem* (London: Abacus 1996), and David Butler and Gareth Butler, *British Political Facts 1906–1994, 7th edn.* (Houndmills: Palgrave Macmillan, 1994).
4. For a recent and comprehensive history of the British Communist Party in the context of national and international politics, see Keith Laybourn, *Marxism in Britain: Dissent, Decline and Reemergence 1945–c. 2000* (London: Routledge, 2006). For another insightful account of the Thatcher years, written close to the time of *Maydays*, see Stuart Hall, *The Hard Road to Renewal: Thatcherism and the Crisis of the Left* (London: Verso, 1988).
5. The National Association for the Advancement of Colored People, Southern Christian Leadership Conference, and the Student Non-Violent Coordinating Committee, respectively, all major US civil rights leadership groups.
6. For a full discussion of the relationship of the civil rights movement to the Left in the US, see Glenda Elizabeth Gilmore, *Defying Dixie: The Radical Roots of Civil Rights: 1919–1950* ( New York: W. W. Norton, 2008); also see Taylor Branch's comprehensive trilogy, *Parting the Waters: America in the King Years, 1954–1963* (New York: Simon and Schuster, 1988), *Pillar of Fire: America in the King Years, 1963–1965* (New York: Simon

and Schuster, 1998), and *At Canaan's Edge: America in the King Years, 1965–1968* (New York: Simon and Schuster, 2006).

7. Michael Billington, 'Coming back into form', *Guardian*, 30 December 1983, p. 11.
8. David Roper, 'The RSC at the Barbican', *Plays and Players* 1.1 (1984), p. 31.
9. Painter, *Edgar: the Playwright*, p. viii.
10. The Social Democratic Party, active from 1981 to 1988, was a breakaway party from Labour led by moderates who feared the party had moved too far to the left and had been infiltrated by Trotskyites; David Edgar himself could be perceived to be an instance of this trend.
11. Peter Jenkins, already mentioned above, in Chapter 1 note 60, was a regular contributor to the *Guardian* and a strong supporter of the recently formed Social Democratic Party, which had broken away from Labour because of what it saw as Labour's leftward drift.
12. David Edgar, *Plays: Three* (London: Methuen, 1991), 'Introduction', p. xi. All further citations to this work in the text will be to this edition.
13. Edgar, *How Plays Work*, pp. 154–67.
14. Painter goes further in pointing out the parallelisms Edgar uses in his scenic structure. Painter, *Edgar: the Playwright, p.* 95.
15. *Ibid.*, p. 100.
16. Edgar, 'Political Theatre 1968–78', reprinted in *Second Time as Farce*, pp. 43–4.
17. *Ibid.*, p. 46. Certainly, this essay not only describes the development and changes in socialist theatre during the ten-year period; it also explains Edgar's own path from General Will and agit-prop to a form that combines epic structure with some conventions drawn from realism, seen from *Destiny* onwards in his work for major subsidized and commercial venues – see above, Chapter 1. The essay takes up, in prose rather than theatrical form, the issues behind the controversy over *Maydays*: what was the responsibility to the class struggle for socialist theatre-workers (who should be represented, in what forms, and on what stages)?; what did working in new media such as television mean for artists committed to socialist outputs?; what audiences should be identified and targeted for new dramatic forms?; what were the emergent dramatic forms uniquely appropriate to the times? It seems to us from hindsight that the journalism around *Maydays* functioned as an indication of the liveliness and importance of issues that required more sophisticated formulations than those that were geared to the newspapers. In fact, John McGrath's criticism came through an academic journal. For an extended account, see Tony Mitchell, 'Popular

Theatre and the Changing Perspective of the 80s', *New Theatre Quarterly*, 1.4 (1985), p. 395 ff.

18. There is one additional reference to the Lenin quote; it punctuates the end of Act 1, Scene 8, when Crowther, whose office has been rubbished by demonstrators occupying his building, picks up the phone to ask for directory assistance: 'Hallo, could you get me Directory – I'm sorry? The revolution is the festival of *what*?' (emphasis in the text, p. 232).
19. Act 2 begins with Phil's stencilled statement outlining a basically situationist position (p. 241).
20. James Fenton, 'The long march to conformity', *Sunday Times*, 23 October 1983, pp. 24–5; Bernard Crick, 'Dogdays and Maydays for Edgar at the Barbican', *Times Higher Education Supplement*, 12 February 1983, p. 13.
21. Paul Allen, 'Passing the baton', *New Statesman*, 28 October 1983, Robert Cushman, 'A matter of tryanny', *Observer*, 23 October 1983, p. 34.
22. Crick, 'Dogdays'.
23. Painter, *Edgar: the Playwright*, pp. 104–9.
24. Pam Brighton, 'Elitist, dismal and ignorant', *City Limits*, 10–16 February 1984, p. 7.
25. *Ibid.*
26. *Ibid.*
27. Reinelt, interview with Tony Taccone, Berkeley Repertory Theatre, 27 April 2010.
28. Reinelt, interview with Robyn Rodriguez, 25 January 2010.
29. In the US, 'Continental Divide' ordinarily refers to the ridge line of the Rocky Mountains, dividing the continental US into east and west. Political divisions do not follow geography in this way, but do show a definite split, in this case between coastal (both east and west) and northern areas, which tend to be 'liberal' and more supportive of the Democratic Party, and interior and southern regions, which tend to be 'conservative' and more 'Republican'.
30. Chad Jones, 'Berkeley Rep takes a big risk with massive two-play project', *Oakland Tribune*, 16 November 2003.
31. Ben Winters, 'How political is the American theatre?', *Performink Online, Chicago's Entertainment Trade Paper*, 23 May 2003.
32. In the first decade of the twenty-first century the strongest presentation of 'political theatre' in the US was not to be found in the theatre at all, but came in the form of the television drama *West Wing*, which had the financial support necessary to sustain a large cast and major production,

and which had a sure-handed ability to explore basic issues within 'everyday' politics.

33. Gray Davis was recalled – the second governor ever to be recalled in the US – principally as a result of voter irritation with his performance during the electricity crisis in California in 2000/1, when large-scale blackouts turned out to be the result of price manipulation involving Enron. Davis declared a state of emergency, but ended up absorbing voter anger. This was also the time of a bad financial downturn following the dot.com collapse, propelling California's budget into crisis, for which Davis was blamed. Schwarzenegger, a popular Hollywood celebrity, mounted a surprisingly effective campaign and became governor on 17 November 2003.
34. Several of the newspaper reviews of *Continental Divide* mentioned this adjacency. For example, Leslie Katz opened her review, 'A theatrical gubernatorial race is going on at Berkeley Repertory Theatre that is more intelligent, provocative and engaging than the real-life fiasco in California'. '"Daughters" droops; "mothers" satisfies', *Oakland Tribune*, 18 November 2003. Pat Craig writes, 'Anyone looking for even a hidden Arnold Schwarzenegger reference will be disappointed', 'Politics, struts, frets onstage', *Contra Costa Times*, 18 November 2003.
35. Reinelt interview with Tony Taccone.
36. Elderhostel is a programme of brief, basic seminars for retired individuals, at various locations around the US and abroad, often making use of staff and facilities at universities available in vacation times.
37. Reinelt, interview with Robyn Rodriguez.
38. Robert Hurwitt, 'Parts better than sum in pair of plays on politics', *San Francisco Chronicle*, 18 November 2003, p. D1.
39. The description of the play below and several other passages have been incorporated within this chapter from a previous essay: see Janelle Reinelt and Gerald Hewitt, 'Principles and Pragmatics in Political Theatre: David Edgar's *Continental Divide*', *Theatre Forum*, 25 (2004), pp. 3–14.
40. For a detailed discussion of the British adaptations of Brecht's methods, see Janelle Reinelt, *After Brecht: British Epic Theatre* (Ann Arbor: University of Michigan Press, 1994).
41. Lorri Holt, 'Winner Takes All', *American Theatre*, 20 (October 2003).
42. Pam Brighton, 'Elitist, dismal and ignorant', *City Limits*, 10–16 February 1984, p. 7; Michael Billington, 'New maps of revolution', *Guardian*, 21 October 1983, p. 11.

43. David Edgar, *Daughters of the Revolution* in *Continental Divide* (London: Nick Hern, 2004) – all subsequent references in the text are to this edition.
44. David Edgar, *Mothers Against* in *Continental Divide* (London: Nick Hern Books, 2004) – all subsequent references in the text are to this edition.
45. Vine, 1,681 votes; McKeene, 915 votes; Write-ins, 117. Email from Susie Falk, Berkeley Repertory Theatre staff, to Reinelt, 26 January 2004.
46. The real-life Proposition 54, a referendum issue, was another ideological litmus test for candidates, as its passage would have required the state to stop collecting and using racial and ethnic information. It was voted down in the actual election.
47. The proposition appears in the published text as well. Edgar, *Continental Divide*, p. 11.
48. Reinelt and Hewitt were present at this talk in Ashland, Oregon, on 1 March 2003. The quotations come from a typescript copy of the address, courtesy of David Edgar.

## 4 Governing memberships: *Destiny, Playing with Fire,* and *Testing the Echo*

1. Mouffe, *Return of the Political*, p. 18.
2. Kenan Malik, *From Fatwa to Jihad: The Rushdie Affair and its Legacy* (London: Atlantic, 2009), p. 70.
3. Etienne Balibar, *We, the People of Europe* (Princeton University Press, 2003), p. 8.
4. *Ibid.*
5. David Edgar, *Destiny* (London: Methuen, 2005), p. vii – all subsequent page references are to this edition.
6. This statement from Prime Minister Margaret Thatcher came the day before the television broadcast of *Destiny*, although that coincidence was accidental.
7. See the obituary for Enoch Powell by Mike Phillips and Norman Shraprel, 'Enoch Powell: An enigma of awkward passions', *Guardian*, 7 February, 2001.
8. Tony Judt, *Postwar: A History of Europe since 1945* (Harmondsworth: Penguin, 2006), p. 336.
9. *Ibid.*
10. For 'bare life' see, for example, Giorgio Agamben, *Homo Sacer: Sovereign Power and Bare Life* (Stanford University Press, 1998). See also his *State of Exception* (University of Chicago Press, 2005).

11. Quoted in Katrin Sieg, 'The Ambivalence of Antifascist Rhetoric: Victims, Artists, and the Masses in Elfriede Jelinek's *Stecken, Stab und Stangl'*, *New German Critique*, 92 (summer 2005), p. 139.
12. Edgar, 'Thirty Years On' in *Destiny*, p. ix.
13. *Destiny* was playing during Elizabeth II's silver jubilee celebrations (when most houses were dark), and was boisterously picketed by a small break-away group from the National Front. That led to counter-pickets, some confrontations, and some national publicity for the play, enhancing the campaign against the National Front.
14. Indeed, in a recent retrospective on the theatre and race in the UK, *Guardian* critic Michael Billington said: 'David Edgar's *Destiny*, which explored the muddled motives that drive people into ultra-right groups, remains the best play on the subject.' 'A Day at the Racists', *Guardian*, 10 March 2010, p. 36,.
15. Tristram Hunt, 'Election 2010: Stoke Rejected the BNP, but immigration is still the issue,' *Guardian*, 9 May 2010.
16. Painter, *Edgar: the Playwright*, p. 43.
17. As described by Edgar in an interview with Painter, *ibid.*, pp. 45–6.
18. *Ibid.*, p. 35. Thomas Bernhard, in *Vor dem Ruhestand* (*Eve of Retirement*) had in 1979 dramatized an incestuous Austrian family who celebrated Hitler's birthday every year with a savage attack on Austria's failure to come to terms with their Nazi past . The style of the play is very different from Edgar's –it is an horrific, almost surreal nightmare of repetition and exaggeration making an absurd yet compelling picture of a dysfunctional society/family.
19. Painter, *Edgar: the Playwright*, pp. 38–9 shows clearly the centrality of this scene to the overall play.
20. Interviewed by Painter, *ibid.*, p. 44.
21. David Edgar, 'From Far Right to New Labour', *StageWrite* (National Theatre, autumn 2005), p. 4.
22. Judt, *Postwar*, p. 545.
23. *Ibid.*, p. 543.
24. Deliberately patterned by Edgar on the 'tribunal plays' produced at the Tricycle Theatre, and recalling in particular the Macpherson Inquiry into the murder of Stephen Lawrence and the Tricycle's *The Colour of Justice*, which dramatized it. See David Edgar, *Playing With Fire* (London: Nick Hern, 2005), p. 83 – all subsequent references in the text are to this edition.
25. Malik, *From Fatwa*, p. 76.
26. Niccolò Machiavelli, *The Prince*, trans. Luigi Ricci (New York: Modern Library, 1940), chapter 6.
27. It played to houses 72 per cent full on average, respectable enough, but somewhat disappointing for a play in the 10 Pound season, which is

expected to top 80 per cent. Data from David Edgar email, 9 September 2010.

28. Read, *Theatre, Intimacy*, pp. 38–9.
29. *Ibid*, p. 38.
30. Michael Billington, 'Tale of racial tension in the north that fails to add up', *Guardian*, 22 September 2005, p. 38; Kate Bassett, 'Something rotten in the boroughs', *Independent*, 25 September 2005, p. 8; Mark Shenton, 'The melting pot of mankind', *Sunday Express*, 25 September 2005, p. 31; Jane Edwardes, 'Playing with fire', *Time Out*, 28 September 2005, p. 71.
31. Paul Taylor, 'New Labour fingers burnt', *Independent*, 23 September 2005, p. 52.
32. Edwards, 'Playing with fire'; Billington, 'Tale of racial tension'.
33. Georgina Brown, 'A fire that left me cold', *Mail on Sunday*, 25 September 2005, p. 69.
34. Sheridan Morley, 'Clash of race and politics', *Express*, 22 September 2005, p. 32.
35. Reinelt, interview with Tony Taccone.
36. Susannah Clapp, 'We get the message', *Observer*, 25 September 2005, p. 10.
37. Bassett, 'Something rotten'.
38. Brown, 'Fire that left me cold'.
39. Email to Reinelt, 9 August 2010.
40. Mouffe, *Return of the Political*, pp. 65–6.
41. Malik, *From Fatwa*, p. 59.
42. Martha Kearney, 'Brown seeks out "British values"', *BBC Newsnight*, 14 March 2005.
43. Rosalind Ryan, 'Goldsmith unveils proposals to strengthen citizenship', *Guardian*, 11 March 2008.
44. Quoted on the immigration advice website, *Workpermit.com*, 6 April 2010.
45. For example, the Tricycle Theatre brochure (spring 2008) describes the play thus: 'Written with wit and passion, *Testing the Echo* is a fascinating tapestry about the twisting road to becoming British.'
46. David Edgar, *Testing the Echo* (London: Nick Hern, 2008), p. 10 – all subsequent page references in the text are from this edition.
47. Data taken from email from David Edgar, 9 September 2010.
48. Shuttleworth, 'Testing the Echo', *Financial Times*, 7 April 2008.

## 5 'A legend in your own time': *The Jail Diary of Albie Sachs*, *Mary Barnes*, and *Albert Speer*

1. Edgar, 'Adapting Nickleby', in *Second Time*, p. 145.
2. Edgar discusses this in a witty opening to the 'Adapting Nickelby' essay, saying he 'did not view my function as being no more than the oil in

which the chips fried' (*ibid.*, p. 144). See also Painter's discussion in *Edgar: the Playwright*, pp. 51–3.

3. David Hare, *Obedience, Struggle and Revolt* (London: Faber and Faber, 2005), pp. 76–7.
4. Edgar, 'Adapting Nickleby', p. 144.
5. John Grierson, 'First Principles of Documentary' in *Grierson on Documentary*, rev. edn, ed. Forsythe Hardy (New York: Praeger, 1966), p. 201.
6. Janelle Reinelt, 'The Promise of Documentary' in *Get Real: Documentary Theatre, Past and Present*, ed. Chris Megson and Alison Forsythe (Houndmills: Palgrave Macmillan, 2009), pp. 6–23.
7. Heinar Kipphardt wrote *In the Matter of J. Robert Oppenheimer* (1964) and Peter Weiss wrote *The Investigation* (1965). Edgar's comments are from a typescript copy of his remarks to the University of Reading, March 2004 (courtesy of the author).
8. David Edgar, 'Between Fact and Fiction', University of Birmingham, 5 September 2007, p. 5. See this characterization and link in the earlier talk at the University of Reading, March 2004, p. 15, reappearing in Reinelt's interview with Edgar published *in Contemporary Theatre Review* in 2004.
9. *Ibid.*
10. See pp. 208–9.
11. Christian, Jewish, and Islamic thinkers all addressed this.
12. Allister Sparks, *The Mind of South Africa: The Story of the Rise and Fall of Apartheid* (London: Mandarin, 1991), p. 194.
13. *Ibid.*, p. 200.
14. One difference between Sachs's and Speer's memoirs is that Sachs wrote his after the experience of imprisonment, looking back, while Speer (partially) wrote his in prison and smuggled out the manuscript. Speer was, of course, in prison far longer.
15. David Edgar, *The Jail Diary of Albie Sachs* in *Plays: One* (London: Methuen, 1987) – all subsequent page references are to this edition.
16. Albie Sachs, *The Jail Diary of Albie Sachs* (London: Harville, 1966), p. 61. In order to avoid confusion, all page references in the text are to Edgar's playscript; references to Sachs's actual published diary will be identified in the endnotes.
17. *Ibid*, p. 84.
18. *Ibid.*, p. 190.
19. *Ibid.*, p. 123.
20. *Ibid*, p. 124.

21. *Ibid.*, p. 207.
22. *Ibid.*, p. 92.
23. *Ibid.*, p. 95.
24. Described in Sachs's second book, *Stephanie on Trial* (1968).
25. Albie Sachs, *Running to Maputo* (New York: Harper Collins, 1990), p. 198.
26. Jill Dolan, *Utopia in Performance: Finding Hope at the Theater* (Ann Arbor: University of Michigan Press, 2005).
27. The Eureka went on to stage a number of successful productions by these authors, including Churchill's *Cloud 9* and *Top Girls* and Trevor Griffiths's version of *The Cherry Orchard*.
28. Reinelt interview with Tony Taccone, 27 April 2010.
29. *Ibid.*
30. David Edgar, interviewed by Richard Slayton in *L. A. Weekly*, 18–24 February 1983, p. 25.
31. R. D. Laing, *The Divided Self* (London: Routledge, 1971), p. 15.
32. Brenda, in *Mary Barnes*; Edgar, *Plays: One*, p. 164.
33. Actually, the book is a *double* memoir. Mary Barnes and Joe Berke did not 'write the book together'; each wrote her/his separate account of the same events, and those accounts were then printed as alternating chapters.
34. David Edgar, 'Towards a Theatre of Dynamic Ambiguities', *Theatre Quarterly*, 9.33 (spring 1979), p. 20, as quoted in Painter, *Edgar: the Playwright*, p. 54.
35. David Edgar, note to *Mary Barnes*, in *Plays: One*, p. 91 – all subsequent references are to this edition.
36. R. D. Laing, *The Politics of Experience* (New York: Ballantine, 1967), p. 58.
37. Daniel Burston, 'R. D. Laing and the Politics of Diagnosis', *Janus Head*, 4.1 (2001).
38. Michael Coveney, 'Mary Barnes', *Financial Times*, 1 September 1978.
39. David Edgar, 'My Hero', *Independent Magazine*, 3 June 1989, p. 62.
40. Kingsley Hall was the first of a number of 'community households' where similar therapies were practised. Laing founded the Philadelphia Association in 1965 as the umbrella organization. It still exists and does some similar work. See www.philadelphia-association.co.uk/ [accessed 10 August 2010].
41. Arguably, Laing's work, especially *The Politics of Experience*, contributed to the growing perception that the personal *was* political, which was so crucial to second-wave feminism.

42. Simon Callow, *Being an Actor* (Harmondsworth: Penguin, 1985), pp. 90–1.
43. 'Patient' is very deliberately what persons like Beth and Mary are *not* called in the community. We use that term here to keep some distinction between those on the reception end of therapy, and the therapists themselves.
44. Reinelt, interview with Tony Taccone. The play did very well at the Eureka; the *San Francisco Chronicle* reviewer, Bernard Weiner, wrote: 'the play is loaded with powerful, touching scenes, which director Richard E. T. White and his talented cast handle with dignity and care' (3 March 1981, p. 3).
45. David Edgar, *Albert Speer* (London: Nick Hern, 2000), p. 146 – all subsequent references are to this edition.
46. For example, in addition to the Sereny biography, see Matthias Schmidt, *Albert Speer: The End of a Myth* (1984), Henry T. King, *The Two Worlds of Albert Speer: Reflections of a Nuremberg Prosecutor* (1997); Dan van den Wet, *The Good Nazi* (1997); and Joachim Fest, *Speer: the Final Verdict* (1999).
47. The design team included Ian MacNeil (sets), Rick Fisher (lights), Chris Laing (video), and Chris Shutt (sound), as well as Joan Wadge (costumes).
48. Michael Billington, 'Staging Speer', *Guardian*, 31 May 2000.
49. *Ibid.*,
50. Gitta Sereny, *Albert Speer: his Battle with Truth* (New York: Vintage, 1996), p. 13.
51. Albert Speer, *Inside the Third Reich*, trans. Richard and Carla Winston (New York: Macmillan, 1970), p. 616.
52. David Marshall, *Celebrity and Power: Fame in Contemporary Culture* (University of Minnesota Press), p. 70.
53. Speer told Sereny they were 'dreams of his knowing what I did, dreams of his saying that I wanted to kill him. They went on for years, and even now they sometimes come back. Sometimes he isn't even in the room in these dreams, but he is in the dreams, or he is the dream' (Sereny, *Albert Speer*, p. 544).
54. *Ibid.*, p. 707.
55. *Ibid.*, p. 708.
56. It is significant that it is Marlowe and not Goethe that Edgar cites – while Goethe is mentioned in the quotation from Speer, Edgar is weaving an English reference through the play, echoed in the choice of military titles from the English and other details such as costume design of uniforms.

57. 'June 1940 at the fall of France. When in defiance of the whiners and moaners, he had the world before him. And he laid it at my feet' (Edgar, *Albert Speer*, p. 42).
58. This, too, is partially invented. Neither Sereny nor Speer himself report the scene in this specific way (linking the command to a triumphal tour of Paris). Speer reports the key conversation coming after the outing to the city of Paris, when they had returned to Hitler's temporary headquarters in a small village, Bruly le Peche (Speer, *Inside the Third Reich*, pp. 206–7). Sereny discusses the plans for the rebuilding of Berlin starting from an earlier moment in 1936, when Hitler fist assigned Speer to redesign and build Berlin and also from the time in January of 1937 when Hitler appointed Speer inspector-general for the reconstruction of Berlin. Paris does not figure in Sereny's account of this commission (pp. 140–4).
59. Sereny, *Albert Speer*, p. 720.
60. This is the same David Irving who lost a libel suit he brought against American historian Deborah Lipstadt in 1996. The court agreed with her that he was indeed a Holocaust denier, a racist and an anti-Semite.
61. Sereny, *Albert Speer*, pp. 227, 681.
62. Joachim Fest, *Speer: The Final Verdict*, trans. Ewald Osers and Alexandra Dring (London: Harvest, 2001).
63. Quoted in Sereny, *Albert Speer*, p. 393. Interestingly, Joachim Fest, a more recent biographer than Sereny, has quoted the fraudulent Goldhagen statement slightly differently: 'Speer is not a philo-Semitic politician obstructing the Final Solution. He and I will jointly snatch the last Jew living on Polish territory from the hands of the Wehrmacht generals, send him to his death, and thereby conclude the final chapter of Polish Jewry.' Fest, *Speer*, p. 187. Unfortunately, the archives of *Midstream Magazine* do not go back beyond 1999, so we are unsure of the exact citation. This might be simply a translation question.
64. Sereny, *Albert Speer*, p. 401.
65. Kate Connolly, 'Wartime reports debunk Speer as the good Nazi', *Daily Telegraph*, 11 March 2005.
66. Irving, Wardle, 'A soul in search of salvation', *Sunday Telegraph*, 28 May 2000, taken from *Theatre Record*, 20.11 (20 May–2 June 2000), p. 684.
67. Charles Spencer, 'Hitler on stage', *The Times*, 14 June 2000, p. 31.
68. Charles Spencer, 'Speer provides new building blocks for Nunn', *Daily Telegraph*, 26 May 2000, p. 23.
69. *Sunday Telegraph*, 28 May 2000, taken from *Theatre Record*, 20.11 (20 May–2 June, 2000), p. 684.
70. Edgar, 'Shouting Fire', p. 65.

## 6 Socialism's aftermath: *The Shape of the Table, Pentecost*, and *The Prisoner's Dilemma*

1. See Caryl Churchill, *Mad Forest* (1990) and Howard Brenton and Tariq Ali, *Moscow Gold* (1990).
2. According to Edgar, 'They weren't conceived as a trilogy, but they're all about being European and about nationhood, and in each case there's a conflict between theory and practice. And I guess each play has dealt with the unfinished business of the play before.' Quoted in Sarah Hemming, 'Thinking big about the big issues', *Financial Times*, 16 July 2001.
3. Francis Fukuyama, *The End of History and the Last Man* (New York: Free Press, 1992), p. 4.
4. Richard Woolfenden, 'A Dramatic Loss of Faith', *Living Marxism* (June 1995), p. 43.
5. Edgar develops this idea in several places, but this quotation comes from a talk he gave at the University of Reading, in March 2004. His earliest formulation of this concept with regard to these plays appears in 1990 concerning *The Shape of the Table*: 'What I hope people will accept is the idea of a world parallel to the real world where you have fictional people who are clearly based on real people, but have different names and different histories. You enter into a deal with the audience, which says this person is like that historical person, but they're not the same. So you're not setting up to be an advocate, nor indeed a prosecuting counsel for that historical person.' Quoted in Painter, *Edgar: the Playwright*, p. 132. Edgar is making no claim to have originated the concept of 'faction', a term used fairly loosely in literary analyses for many years and reflecting a practice traced back at least as far as Geoffrey of Monmouth. Instead, he is simply crystallizing his own understanding of the genre, and why it is particularly useful for political theatre. He thinks it essential for an audience to find the play's action plausible. 'Domestic' dramas come with built-in plausibility tests, because most of the audience has a direct experience of domestic life, against which the performance can be measured. Political plays, however, do not have the advantage of personal familiarity – likening their action to events/persons already 'known' from current events bridges this gap.
6. Kiš was responding to accusations of plagiarism and misuse of documentary sources. He responded that combining fact and fiction was a common practice, citing Jorge Luis Borges, Thomas Mann, Ivo Andrić, and Arthur Koestler, among others. For details about his case, see Vasa D. Mihailovich, 'Faction or Fiction in *A Tomb for Boris Davidovich*: A Literary Affair', *Review of Contemporary Fiction*, 14.1 (1994), pp. 169–73.

7. For an extensive analysis of the background of this historical development, see Larry Wolf, *Inventing Eastern Europe: The Map of Civilization on the Mind of the Enlightenment* (Stanford University Press, 1994). For discussion of the symbolic discourse surrounding the Balkans, see Dušan Bjelić and Obrad Savić, *Balkans as Metaphor: Between Globalization and Fragmentation* (Cambridge, MA: MIT Press, 2002).
8. Milica Bakič-Hayden, 'Nesting *Orientalism:* The Case of the Former Yugoslavia', *Slavic Review*, 54.4 (1995), pp. 917–31.
9. Patrice C. McMahon, *Taming Ethnic Hatred: Ethnic Cooperation and Transnational Networks in Eastern Europe* (Syracuse University Press, 2007), p. 24.
10. Quoted in Will Kymlicka and Magda Opalski (eds), *Can Liberal Pluralism be Exported?: Western Political Theory and the Ethnic Relations in Eastern Europe* (Oxford University Press, 2001), p. 371.
11. *Ibid.*, pp. 371–2.
12. Boris Tsilevich, 'New Democracies in the Old World: Remarks on Will Kymlicka's Approach to Nation-building in Post-Communist Europe', in Kymlicka and Opalski (eds), *Liberal Pluralism*, p. 165.
13. David Edgar being interviewed in Martyn Clement, 'Table Talk', *Plays and Players* (November 1990), p. 7, as cited in Painter, *Edgar: the Playwright*, p. 179.
14. See above, p. 156.
15. And, in fact, Edgar specifies in the script the dates of the play. For anyone familiar with the sequence of events in 1989 (only a year before the play's initial performances), these dates not only point to Czechoslovakia, they indicate a time period in which Poland and Hungary have already thrown off their Communist regimes, Germany is doing so (the Berlin Wall has already fallen), Tiananmen Square has happened, and Czechoslovakia has already served for months as a transit camp for thousands of Germans fleeing through to Hungary and from there to the West.
16. Yugoslavia and Albania, though 'Communist' EC countries, were not a part of the Soviet bloc (for quite different reasons), and did not have the same kinds of experiences in 1989, though both were to undergo profound changes over the next several years.
17. Called the 'French and Indian War' in the US.
18. Edgar, *The Second Time*, p. 58. See also a more recent formulation of these points: 'By drawing on a wide variety of examples of the same thing, the faction writer is able to present not what's happening (the job of a journalist) nor what happened (the role of the historian) but what

happens, in a particular process, whenever it occurs.' 'In the line of fire', *Guardian*, 22 July 2010, p. 19.

19. David Edgar, *The Shape of the Table* (London: Nick Hern, 1990) – all subsequent references will be to this edition.
20. Reinelt saw the original production at the Cottesloe Theatre in 1990. The dynamism of Dermot Hayes's shifting set design enabled the spatial dynamics to team up with the verbal dynamics to provide an experience of chimerical fast-changing action through a fully realized *mise en scène*.
21. Painter, *Edgar: the Playwright*, pp. 138–9.
22. Lynne Truss, 'He's talking about a revolution', *Independent on Sunday*, 4 November 1990, p. 4.
23. Clement, 'Table Talk' p. 7.
24. Painter, *Edgar: the Playwright*, p. 133.
25. It is important to remember that many of the proposed economic changes here – proposals coming from the opposition, not the Communists – were changes already being put in place – by Communists – in the Soviet Union.
26. Michael Coveney, 'Theatre', *Observer on Sunday*, 11 November 1990, p. 62.
27. David Edgar, 'With friends like these', *Guardian*, 19 April 2008, Review, p. 4.
28. Alone among reviewers, the one Czech writer points out the importance of this encounter between Prus and Spassov. See Martin Hilský, 'The Prus and Cons', *Times Higher Education Supplement*, 23 November 1990, p. 16.
29. Sheridan Morley, 'Lear in Eastern Europe?', *International Herald Tribune*, 14 November 1990, p. 33.
30. Hilský, 'Prus and Cons', p. 16.
31. Marvin Carlson, *Speaking in Tongues: Language at Play in the Theatre* (Ann Arbor: University of Michigan Press, 2006), p. 54.
32. Although it is most often compared to a detective story or whodunnit, and even Edgar himself has called it thus: 'The play uses a detective story about art and restoration to analyse what it means to be European today.' See Aleks Sierz, 'Stages of Struggle', *Red Pepper* (November 1994), p. 42.
33. All quotations are taken from the programme edition of *Pentecost* (London: Nick Hern, 1995).
34. Stanton B. Garner Jr, 'Rewriting Europe: *Pentecost* and the Crossroads of Migration', *Essays in Theatre/Études Théâtrales*, 16. 1 (1997), p. 6.

35. An excellent example occurs in Vello Pettai's discussion of liberal political theories of ethno-cultural justice with specific application to Estonia and Latvia. While the thrust of Pettai's essay makes the macro-point that normative conceptual thinking is possible and valuable in relation to central and eastern Europe, 'a critical causal puzzle piece remains missing if we do not complement these *definitions* [of ethnopolitical justice] with the *discourses* ethnocultural groups use to wage their ethnopolitical struggles' (original italics). He divides his essay into two parts, and in the second, examines the case study of Estonia and Latvia to point out the specificities of their discourses crucial to understanding their particular situation. 'Definition and Discourse: Applying Kymlicka's Models to Estonia and Latvia', in Kymlicka and Opalski (eds), *Liberal Pluralism*, p. 259.
36. Tsilevich, 'New Democracies', p. 165.
37. Carlson, *Speaking in Tongues*, p. 53.
38. Pentecost is related to the Jewish commemoration of Shavuot.
39. Sean Carney, 'Capitalism's *Pharmakos:* David Edgar's *Destiny* and *Pentecost*', *Essays in Theatre/Études Théâtrales* 18.2 (May 2000), p. 143.
40. Quoted in the playscript before Act 2, p. 77. We use this epigraph with some deliberate irony, since Izebegovic is also one of the figures responsible for building that 'mountain of corpses'.
41. Spoken by Jan, Gina's 12-year-old son, a droll and sometimes wise commentator on the scene. The page reference, and all subsequent references, is to David Edgar, *The Prisoner's Dilemma* ( London: Nick Hern, 2001).
42. Lynn Gardner, 'The Prisoner's Dilemma', *Guardian*, 31 January 2002, p. 16.
43. McMahon, *Taming Ethnic Hatred*, p. 20 (emphasis in the original).
44. George Schöpflin, 'Liberal Pluralism and Post-Communism', in Kymlicka and Opalski (eds), *Liberal Pluralism*, pp. 121–2.
45. Premiere on 11 July 2001 at The Other Place, Stratford, England.
46. Several reviewers noted the topicality of the play in the shifting scene: Rachel Halliburton, for example, remarked on the change of reception climate between the Stratford premiere and the Barbican transfer, when 'the Afghanistan conflict gave renewed relevance to aspects of Edgar's script' and made a comparison between Edgar's pointing of the struggle over terminology and George Bush's 'inflammatory misuse of the word "crusade"'. 'Mind your language', *Evening Standard*, 30 January 2002, p. 44. John Peter also opened his review of the Barbican production with the comment, 'The 21st century started on September 11, 2001: a late

start, but it looks as if it means to go on as it has begun'. 'Conflicts of Interest' p. 19.

47. Diplomacy in the period had mixed results: the Oslo accords (1993) were judged by their subsequent failure to improve the Palestinian–Israeli conflict, while the recent success of the Good Friday accords in Northern Ireland (1998) was hailed as a significant landmark agreement.
48. Ian Shuttleworth, 'No winners in a war of words', *Financial Times*, 20 July 2001.
49. See Janelle Reinelt and Gerald Hewitt, 'The Prisoner's Dilemma: Game Theory, Conflict Resolution, and the New Europe', *Contemporary Theatre Review*, 13.2 (2003), pp. 41–55. The description of the play below is taken from this essay and several other passages are incorporated within this chapter.
50. Merriam Webster dictionary online.
51. Edgar, *How Plays Work*, p. 139.
52. The term appeared in Rudyard Kipling's novel *Kim* (1900), but had been used during the previous half-century to describe the triangulation of the competition between the Russian and British empires with Afghanistan as the third term. Thus it is a term of empire in which the third country is purely instrumental.
53. David Edgar, 'Making drama out of crisis', *Guardian*, 7 July 2001, Saturday Review, p. 2. Edgar cites Howard again in his acknowledgements to the printed version of the play, p. vii.
54. In fact, the idea for the play came to Edgar after watching Jane Corbin's *Panorama* television documentary of the secret negotiations that made possible the 1993 Oslo Accords. See Elizabeth Stewart, 'Deconstructing Diplomacy', *Diplomat* (July/August, 2001), p. 48.
55. Shuttleworth, 'No Winners'.
56. Lila Abu-Lughod, 'Do Muslim Women Really Need Saving? Anthropological Reflections on Cultural Relativism and its Others', *American Anthropologist*, 104.3 (2002), p. 789.
57. *Ibid.*
58. Paul Taylor, 'An evening with the tutor', *Independent*, 20 July 2001.
59. Michael Billington, 'The Prisoner's Dilemma', *Guardian*, 20 July 2001, p. 22.
60. Peter, 'Conflicts of interest'.

## Afterword

1. David Edgar, 'Patriotism games', *Guardian*, 27 February 2010, p. 18.
2. David Edgar, 'If only the BBC behaved less like bankers and more like my local council', *Guardian*, 17 February 2010, p. 17.

3. David Edgar, 'Enter the new wave of political playwrights', *Observer*, 28 February 2010, p. 20.
4. David Edgar, 'I'm a traffic light voter', *Guardian*, 4 May 2010.
5. David Edgar, 'Labour must stay committed to civil liberties', *Guardian*, 7 July 2010.

# Selected bibliography

## Primary sources

While only twelve of Edgar's plays make up the main focus of this study, we have listed all his published plays below, partly because many of the other plays and writings contributed in minor ways to our research, and partly in order to provide a record of many of these works. There has simply not been enough space to list all his work for television, and radio, and his writings on theatre and more general commentary, so we have limited this list to those works cited in the text or directly used in this study.

### *Published plays*


*Albert Speer* (London: Nick Hern, 2000).

*Arthur & George* (London: Nick Hern, 2010).

*Baby Love* in *Edgar: Shorts* (London: Nick Hern, 1989).

*Ball Boys* (London: Pluto Press, 1978); in *Edgar: Shorts* (London: Nick Hern, 1989).

*Black Tulips* in *The Great Game* (London: Oberon, 2009).

*Blood Sports* in *Edgar: Shorts* (London: Nick Hern, 1989).

*Continental Divide* (London: Nick Hern, 2004).

*Destiny* (London: Methuen, 1976; 2005); in *Plays: One* (London: Methuen, 1987).

*Dick Deterred* (New York: Monthly Review Press, 1974).

*Ecclesiastes* in *Plays: Two* (London: Methuen, 1990).

*Entertaining Strangers* (London: Methuen, 1985); in *Plays: Two* (London: Methuen, 1990).

*Heartlanders* (with Stephen Bill and Anne Devlin) (London: Nick Hern, 1989).

*Mary Barnes* (London: Methuen, 1979); in *Plays: One* (London: Methuen, 1987).

*Maydays* (London: Methuen, 1983); in *Plays: Three* (London: Methuen, 1991).

*Nicholas Nickleby Parts One and Two* (New York: Dramatists' Play Service, 1982); in *Plays: Two* (London: Methuen, 1990).

*O Fair Jerusalem* in *Plays: One* (London: Methuen, 1987).

*Our Own People* (London: Methuen, 1988); in *Plays: Three* (London: Methuen, 1991).

*Pentecost* (London: Nick Hern, 1995).

*Playing with Fire* (London: Nick Hern, 2005).

*Saigon Rose* in *Plays: One* (London: Methuen, 1987).

*Teendreams* (London: Methuen, 1979); in *Plays: Three* (London: Methuen, 1991).

*Testing the Echo* (London: Nick Hern, 2008).

*That Summer* (London: Methuen, 1987); in *Plays: Three* (London: Methuen, 1991).

*The Jail Diary of Albie Sachs* (London: Rex Collings, 1978); in *Plays: One* (London: Methuen, 1987).

*The Midas Connection* in *Edgar: Shorts* (London: Nick Hern, 1989).

*The National Theatre* in *Edgar: Shorts* (London: Nick Hern, 1989).

*The Prisoner's Dilemma* (London: Nick Hern, 2001).

*The Shape of the Table* (London: Nick Hern, 1990).

*The Strange Case of Dr Jekyll and Mr Hyde* (London: Nick Hern, 1992).

*Two Kinds of Angel* in *The London Fringe Theatre*, ed. V.E. Mitchell (London: Burnham House, 1975).

*Vote for Them* (London: BBC Publications, 1989).

*Wreckers* (London: Methuen, 1977).

## *Theatre\television writing*

'Adapting Nickleby', *The Dickensian*, spring 1983, reprinted in Robert Giddings (ed.), *The Changing World of Charles Dickens* (London and New York: Vision, 1983).

'The best performance I've ever seen: David Edgar', *Observer*, 18 July 2010, p. 35.

'Come together', *Guardian*, 10 January 2005, www.guardian.co.uk/stage/ [accessed 18 July 2010].

'Enter the new wave of political playwrights', *Observer*, 28 February 2010, p. 20.

*How Plays Work* (London: Nick Hern, 2009).

'Introduction' to George Bernard Shaw, *Plays Unpleasant* (Harmondsworth: Penguin, 2000).

'The National Front', review of Nigel Fielding's *The National Front* (London: Routledge and Kegan Paul, 1981), *Race & class* (spring 1981), pp. 427–31.

'The National Front in English Politics', review of Stan Taylor's *The National Front in English Politics* (London: Macmillan, 1981), *New Statesman*, 16 April 1982, n.p.

'The perils of populism', *Guardian*, 19 February 2000 (revised\edited version of 'Provocative Acts: British Playwriting in the Post-war Era and Beyond') in *State of Play*, ed. David Edgar (London: Faber and Faber, 1999), pp. 1–34.

'Political Theatre 1968–1978', *Theatre Quarterly* (winter 1979) and *Socialist Review* (April/May 1978).

*The Second Time as Farce: Reflections on the Drama of Mean Times* (London: Lawrence and Wishart, 1988).

'Secret lives', *Guardian*, 19 April 2003, www.guardian.co.uk/stage/ [accessed 19 July 2010].

'Shock of the new play', *Guardian*, 10 December 2009, p. 34.

'A shortsighted view of the defectors' decades', *Guardian*, 29 October 1983, n.p.

'Something Rotten in the State of Drama' in *The Month in Yorkshire*, (February 1972), pp. 4–5.

'Ticket to Milford Haven', *London Review of Books*, 21 September 2006, p. 10–13.

'Ways of seeing', *Guardian*, 13 March 2010, p. 16.

'Where's the challenge?', *Guardian*, 20 May 2004, p. 18.

## General articles

'Achtung!', *New Review* (June-July 1977), pp. 69–71.

'Britain's National Front', *Present Tense* (New York) (spring 1978), pp. 17–22.

'How Live Aid revived the sixties message', *Guardian*, 2 September 1985, p. 34.

'I'm a traffic light voter', *Guardian*, 5 May 2010, p. 34.

'If only the BBC behaved less like bankers and more like my local council', *Guardian*, 17 February 2010, p. 17.

'The International Face of Fascism', *Urgent Tasks* (fall/winter 1982), pp. 1–7.

'It wasn't so naff in the 60s after all', *Guardian*, 7 July 1986, p. 21.

'Labour must stay committed to civil liberties', *Guardian*, 7 July 2010, www.guardian.co.uk/commentisfree/libertycentral/ [accessed 26 September 2010].

'My hero', *Independent Magazine*, 3 June 1989, pp. 60–3.

'My misspelling their misrepresentation', *Guardian*, 25 April 2008, www.guardian.co.uk/commentisfree/david_edgar/2008/04/ [accessed 20 July 2010].

'The National Front *is* a Nazi Front', *Socialist Challenge*, 21 July 1977, pp. 113–14.

'Patriotism games', *Guardian*, 27 February 2010, p. 18.

'Shouting Fire: Art, Religion, and the Right to be Offended', *Race & Class* (October/December 2006), pp. 61–75. Revised and republished as 'From the Nanny State to the Heckler's Veto: The New Censorship and How to Counter It', *Contemporary Theatre Review*, 17.4 (November 2007), pp. 33–47.

'When the Hardline is Right', *Marxism Today* (February 1988), pp. 23–4; see also 'Hear the people sing', *Guardian*, 18 January 1988, p. 32.

'With friends like these', *Guardian*, 19 April 2008, Review, p. 4.

'Why Live Aid came Alive', *Marxism Today* (September 1985), pp. 6–30.

'Why the Front is beyond the pale', *Sunday Times*, 1 October 1978, n.p.

## Secondary sources

Abu-Lughod, Lila, 'Do Muslim Women Really Need Saving? Anthropological Reflections on Cultural Relativism and its Others', *American Anthropologist*, 104.3 (2002), pp. 783–90.

Agamben, Giorgio, *Homo Sacer: Sovereign Power and Bare Life* (Stanford University Press, 1998).

*State of Exception* (University of Chicago Press, 2005).

Allen, Paul, 'Passing the Baton', *New Statesman*, 28 October 1983.

Anthony, Andrew, 'Defective logic', *Guardian*, 19 April, 2008, www.guardian.co.uk.commentisfree/andrew_anthony/2008/04/defective-logic.html [accessed 20 July 2010].

Bakič-Hayden, Milica, 'Nesting *Orientalism:* The Case of the Former Yugoslavia', *Slavic Review*, 54.4 (1995), pp. 917–31.

Balibar, Etienne, *We, the People of Europe?* (Princeton University Press, 2003).

Bassett, Kate, 'Something rotten in the boroughs', *Independent*, 25 September 2005, p. 8.

Bernhard, Thomas, *The President and Eve of Retirement* (London: PAJ Publications, 1991).

Billingham, Peter, *At the Sharp End: Uncovering the Work of Five Leading Dramatists* (London: Methuen, 2007).

Billington, Michael, 'Coming back into form', *Guardian*, 30 December 1983, p. 11.

'A day at the racists', *Guardian*, 10 March 2010, p. 36.

'The Prisoner's Dilemma', *Guardian*, 20 July 2001, p. 22.

'Staging Speer', *Guardian*, 31 May 2000, www.guardian.co.uk/culture/2000/may/31/artsfeatures#history-link-box [accessed 15 August 2010].

*State of the Nation: British Theatre since 1945* (London: Faber and Faber, 2007).

'Tale of racial tension in the north that fails to add up', *Guardian*, 22 September 2005, p. 38.

Bjelić, Dušan, and Obrad Savić, *Balkans as Metaphor: Between Globalization and Fragmentation* (Cambridge, MA: MIT Press, 2002).

Branch, Taylor, *At Canaan's Edge: America in the King Years, 1965–1968* (New York: Simon and Schuster, 2006).

*Parting the Waters: America in the King Years, 1954–1963* (New York: Simon and Schuster, 1988).

*Pillar of Fire: America in the King Years, 1963–1965* (New York: Simon and Schuster, 1998).

Brighton, Pam, 'Elitist, dismal and ignorant', *City Limits*, 10–16 February 1984, p. 7.

Brown, Georgina, 'A fire that left me cold,' *Mail on Sunday*, 25 September 2005, p. 69.

Brown, Gordon, 'Speech on Immigration Measures', www.workpermit.com/news/2010-04-06/uk/uk-minister-speech-on-immigration-measures.htm [accessed 9 August 2010].

Bull, John, *Stage Right: Crisis and Recovery in British Contemporary Mainstream Theatre* (London: Macmillan, 1994).

Burston, Daniel, 'R. D. Laing and the Politics of Diagnosis', *Janus Head*, 4.1 (2001), www.janushead.org/4-1/burstonpol.cfm [accessed 10 August 2010].

Butler, David, and Gareth Butler, *British Political Facts 1906–1994*, 7th edn (Houndmills: Palgrave Macmillan, 1994).

Callow, Simon, *Being an Actor* (Harmondsworth: Penguin, 1985).

Carlson, Marvin, *Speaking in Tongues: Language at Play in the Theatre* (Ann Arbor: University of Michigan Press, 2006).

Carney, Sean, 'Capitalism's *Pharmakos:* David Edgar's *Destiny* and *Pentecost*', *Essays in Theatre/Études Théâtrales*, 18.2 (May 2000), p. 143.

Cavendish, Dominic, 'The power of words', *Daily Telegraph*, 20 July 2001, p. 24.

Clapp, Susannah, 'We get the message', *Observer*, 25 September 2005, p. 10.

Clement, Martyn, 'Table Talk', *Plays and Players* (November 1990), p. 7.

Collini, Stefan, 'On Variousness; and on Persuasion', *New Left Review*, 27 (June 2004), pp. 65–97.

Comment 1302556, 'HankScorpio', Commentisfree, *Guardian*, 26 April 2008, 2.48, www.guardian.co.uk/commentisfree/ [accessed 6 August 2010].

Comment 1302678, 'winchmorehillbilly', Commentisfree, *Guardian*, 26 April 2008, 6.45, www.guardian.co.uk/commentisfree/ [accessed 6 August 2010].

Connolly, Kate, 'Wartime reports debunk Speer as the good Nazi', *Daily Telegraph*, 11 March 2005, www.telegraph.co.uk/news/worldnews/ [accessed 14 August 2010].

Coveney, Michael, 'Mary Barnes', *Financial Times*, 1 September 1978.
'Theatre', *Observer on Sunday*, 11 November 1990, p. 62.
Craig, Pat, 'Politics, struts, frets onstage', *Contra Costa Times*, 18 November 2003, p. 22, www.bayarea.com/mld/cctimes/entertainment/performing_arts/ [accessed 7 August 2010].
Crick, Bernard, 'Dogdays and Maydays for Edgar at the Barbican', *Times Higher Education Supplement*, 12 February 1983, p. 13.
Cushman, Robert, 'A matter of tyranny', *Observer*, 23 October 1983, p. 34.
Davies, A.J., *To Build a New Jerusalem* (London: Abacus, 1996).
D'Monté, Rebecca, and Graham, Saunders, *Cool Britannia?: British Political Drama in the 1990s* (Houndmills: Palgrave Macmillan, 2008).
Dolan, Jill, *Utopia in Performance: Finding Hope at the Theater* (Ann Arbor: University of Michigan Press, 2005).
Edwards, Christopher, 'Culture clash', *Spectator*, 25 July 1987, p. 37.
Edwards, Jane, 'Playing with fire', *Time Out*, 28 September 2005, p. 71.
Fenton, James, 'The long march to conformity', *Sunday Times*, 23 October 1983, pp. 24–5.
Fest, Joachim, *Speer: The Final Verdict*, trans. Ewald Osers and Alexandra Dring (London: Harvest, 2001).
Foley, F.Kathleen, 'Art, politics and dissent in sweeping "Pentecost"', *Los Angeles Times*, 31 May 2002, pp. F25 ff.
Freshwater, Helen, *Theatre Censorship in Britain: Silencing, Censure and Suppression* (Houndmills: Palgrave Macmillan, 2009).
Fukuyama, Francis, *The End of History and the Last Man* (New York: Free Press, 1992).
Gardner, Lynn, 'The Prisoner's Dilemma', *Guardian*, 31 January 2002, p. 16.
Garner, Stanton B. Jr, 'Rewriting Europe: *Pentecost* and the Crossroads of Migration', *Essays in Theatre/Études théâtrales*, 16.1 (1997), pp. 3–14.
Gilmore, Glenda Elizabeth, *Defying Dixie: The Radical Roots of Civil Rights: 1919–1950* (New York: W.W. Norton, 2008).
Glenny, Misha, 'Letters', *Guardian*, 24 September 2005, p. 31.
Grierson, John, 'First Principles of Documentary' in *Grierson on Documentary*, rev. edn, Forsythe Hardy (New York: Praeger, 1966).

Hall, Stuart, *The Hard Road to Renewal: Thatcherism and the Crisis of the Left* (London: Verso, 1988).

Halliburton, Rachel, 'Mind your language', *Evening Standard*, 30 January 2002, p. 44.

Hanks, Robert, 'Speaking in tongues', *Independent*, 26 October 1994, p. 2.

Hare, David, *Obedience, Struggle and Revolt* (London: Faber and Faber, 2005).

Higgins, Charlotte, 'Outrage is central to art says dramatist', *Guardian*, 22 June 2004, www.guardian.co.uk/uk/2004/jun/22/arts.artsnews1 [accessed 20 July 2010].

Hilský, Martin, 'The prus and cons', *Times Higher Education Supplement*, 23 November 1990, p. 16.

Holt, Lorri, 'Winner Takes All', *American Theatre*, 20 (October 2003), www.tcg.org.am_theatre/at_articles/ [accessed 10 June 2003].

Hunt, Tristram, 'Election 2010: Stoke rejected the BNP, but immigration is still the issue', *Guardian*, 9 May 2010, www.guardian.co.uk/politics/ [accessed 27 July 2010].

Hurwitt, Robert, 'Invading the mind and heart: "Pentecost" gets Berkeley Rep off to powerful start', *San Francisco Examiner*, 19 September 1997, p. C1.

'Parts better than sum in pair of plays on politics', *San Francisco Chronicle*, 18 November 2003, p. D1.

Innes, Christopher, '"Nothing but talk, talk, talk – Shaw talk": Discussion Plays and the Making of Modern Drama' in *The Cambridge Companion to George Bernard Shaw*, ed. Christopher Innes (Cambridge University Press, 1998).

Jones, Chad, 'Berkeley Rep takes a big risk with massive two-play project', *Oakland Tribune*, 16 November 2003, http://nl.newsbank.com/nlsearch/we/ [accessed 7 August 2010].

Jones, Simon, 'New Theatre for New Times: Decentralization, Innovation and Pluralism, 1975–2000' in *The Cambridge History of British Theatre*, Vol. III, ed. Baz Kershaw (Cambridge University Press, 2004).

Judt, Tony, *Postwar: A History of Europe since 1945* (Harmondsworth: Penguin, 2006).

Katz, Leslie, '"Daughters" droops; "Mothers" satisfies', *Oakland Tribune*, 18 November 2003, p. 23.

Kearney, Martha, 'Brown seeks out "British Values"', *BBC News*, 14 March 2005, http://news.bbc.co.uk/2/hi/programmes/newsnight/ [accessed 9 September 2009].

Kelleher, Joe, *Theatre and Politics* (Houndmills: Palgrave Macmillan, 2009).

Kershaw, Baz, 'Alternative Theatres, 1946–2000' in *The Cambridge History of British Theatre*, Vol. III, ed. Baz Kershaw (Cambridge University Press, 2004).

Klein, Alvin, 'Linguistic games, theory of art', *New York Times*, 26 November 1995, http://theater.nytimes.com/mem/theater/treview [accessed 27 June 2010].

Kymlicka, Will, and Magda Opalski (eds), *Can Liberal Pluralism be Exported?: Western Political Theory and the Ethnic Relations in Eastern Europe* (Oxford University Press, 2001).

Lacey, Stephen, 'British Theatre and Commerce, 1979–2000' in *The Cambridge History of British Theatre*, Vol. III, ed. Baz Kershaw (Cambridge University Press, 2004).

Laing, R.D., *The Divided Self* (London: Routledge, 1971).

*The Politics of Experience* (New York: Ballantine, 1967).

Laybourn, Keith, *Marxism in Britain: Dissent, Decline and Reemergence 1945–c. 2000* (London: Routledge, 2006).

Lukács, Georg, *Studies in European Realism* (New York: Grosset and Dunlap, 1964).

Machiavelli, Niccolò, *The Prince and the Discourses* (New York: Modern Library, 1940).

McMahon, Patrice C., *Taming Ethnic Hatred: Ethnic Cooperation and Transnational Networks in Eastern Europe* (Syracuse University Press, 2007).

Malik, Kenan, *From Fatwa to Jihad: The Rushdie Affair and its Legacy*, (London: Atlantic, 2009).

Malvery, Sharon, 'Pentecost powerful portrait of modern times', *Stratford Beacon Herald*, www.stratfordbeaconherald.com/ [accessed 21 August 2007].

Marmet, David, 'Why I am no longer a "brain-dead" Liberal', *Village Voice*, 11 March 2008, www.villagevoice.com/ [accessed 19 July 2010].

Marshall, David, *Celebrity and Power: Fame in Contemporary Culture* (Minneapolis: University of Minnesota Press, 2007).

Megson, Chris, and Alison Forsythe (eds), *Get Real: Documentary Theatre, Past and Present* (Houndmills: Palgrave Macmillan, 2009).

Mihailovich, Vasa D., 'Faction or Fiction in *A Tomb for Boris Davidovich*: A Literary Affair', *Review of Contemporary Fiction*, 14.1 (1994), pp. 169–73.

Mitchell, Tony, 'Popular Theatre and the Changing Perspective of the 80s', *New Theatre Quarterly*, 1.4 (1985), p. 395 ff.

Morley, Sheridan, 'Clash of race and politics', *Express*, 22 September 2005, p. 32.

'Lear in Eastern Europe?', *International Herald Tribune*, 14 November 1990, p. 33.

Mouffe, Chantal, *The Return of the Political* (London: Verso, 1993).

Mountford, Fiona, 'The Master Builder Reconstructs Ibsen', *Evening Standard*, 17 September 2010, www.thisislondon.co.uk/theatre/ [accessed 21 September 2010].

Nightingale, Benedict, 'History below the surface', *The Times*, 28 October 1994, p. 33.

Oakeshott, Michael, *Rationalism in Politics and Other Essays* (London: Basic Books, 1962).

Painter, Susan, *Edgar: the Playwright* (London: Methuen, 1996).

Peter, John, 'Conflicts of interest', *Sunday Times*, 10 Feburary 2002, p. 19.

'Politics in the Picture', review of *Pentecost*, *Sunday Times*, 30 October 1994.

Pettai, Vello, 'Definition and Discourse: Applying Kymlicka's Models to Estonia and Latvia' in *Can Liberal Pluralism be Exported?: Western Political Theory and the Ethnic Relations in Eastern Europe*, ed. Will Kymlicka and Magda Opalski (Oxford University Press, 2001), pp. 259–69.

Phillips, Mike and Norman Sharprel, 'Enoch Powell: An enigma of awkward passions', *Guardian*, 7 February 2001, www.guardian.co.uk/politics/ [accessed 27 July 2010].

Read, Alan, *Theatre, Intimacy and Engagement: The Last Human Venue* (Houndmills: Palgrave Macmillan, 2009).

Rebellato, Dan, 'Can theatre change the world?', *Guardian*, 12 April 2010, www.guardian.co.uk/stage/theatreblog/ [accessed 17 July 2010].

'From the State of the Nation to Globalization: Shifting Political Agendas in Contemporary British Playwriting' in *A Concise Companion to Contemporary British and Irish Drama*, ed. Nadine Holdsworth and Mary Luckhurst (Oxford: Blackwell, 2008).

Reinelt, Janelle, *After Brecht: British Epic Theatre* (Ann Arbor: University of Michigan Press, 1992).

'"Politics, Playwriting, Postmodernism": An Interview with David Edgar', *Contemporary Theatre Review*, 14.4 (2004), pp. 42–53.

'The Promise of Documentary' in *Get Real: Documentary Theatre, Past and Present*, ed. Chris Megson and Alison Forsythe (Houndmills: Palgrave Macmillan, 2009).

Reinelt, Janelle, and Gerald Hewitt, 'Principles and Pragmatics in Political Theatre: David Edgar's *Continental Divide*', *Theatre Forum*, 25 (2004), pp. 3–14.

'The Prisoner's Dilemma: Game Theory, Conflict Resolution, and the New Europe', *Contemporary Theatre Review*, 13.2 (2003), pp. 41–55.

Ridout, Nicholas, *Stage Fright, Animals, and Other Theatrical Problems* (Cambridge University Press, 2006).

Roper, David, 'The RSC at the Barbican', *Plays and Players*, 1.1 (1984), p. 31.

Ryan, Rosalind, 'Goldsmith unveils proposals to strengthen citizenship', *Guardian*, 11 March 2008, www.guardian.co.uk/politics [accessed 9 September 2009].

Sachs, Albie, *The Jail Diary of Albie Sachs* (London: Harville, 1966).

*Running to Maputo* (New York: Harper Collins, 1990).

Schöpflin, George, 'Liberal Pluralism and Post-Communism' in *Can Liberal Pluralism be Exported?: Western Political Theory and the Ethnic Relations in Eastern Europe*, ed. Will Kymlicka and Magda Opalski (Oxford University Press, 2001), pp. 109–25.

Sereny, Gitta, *Albert Speer: his Battle with Truth* (New York: Vintage, 1996).

Shenton, Mark, 'The melting pot of mankind', *Sunday Express*, 25 September 2005, p. 23.

Shuttleworth, Ian, 'No winners in a war of words', *Financial Times*, 20 July 2010, http://globalarchive.ft.com/globalarchive/ [accessed 21 July 2010].

'*Testing the Echo*, Tricycle Theatre, London', *Financial Times*, 7 April 2008 www.ft.com/ [accessed 9 August 2010].

Sieg, Katrin, 'The Ambivalence of Antifascist Rhetoric: Victims, Artists, and the Masses in Elfriede Jelinek's *Stecken, Stab und Stangl*', *New German Critique*, 92 (summer 2005), pp. 123–40.

Sierz, Aleks, *In-Yer-Face Theatre: British Drama Today* (London: Faber and Faber, 2000).

'Stages of Struggle', *Red Pepper* (November 1994), p. 42.

Sparks, Allister, *The Mind of South Africa: The Story of the Rise and Fall of Apartheid* (London: Mandarin, 1991).

Speer, Albert, *Inside the Third Reich*, trans. Richard and Carla Winston (New York: Macmillan, 1970).

Spencer, Charles, 'Hitler on stage', *The Times*, 14 June 2000, p. 31.

'Speer provides new building blocks for Nunn', *Telegraph*, 26 May 2000, n.p.

Taylor, Paul, 'An evening with the Tutor', *Independent*, 20 July 2001, www.independent.co.uk/arts-entertainment/theatre-dance/revienws [accessed 22 July 2010].

'New Labour fingers burnt', *Independent*, 23 September 2005, p. 52.

Tricycle Theatre, *Brochure* (spring 2008).

Truss, Lynne, 'He's talking about a revolution', *Independent on Sunday*, 4 November 1990, p. 4.

Tsilevich, Boris, 'New Democracies in the Old World: Remarks on Will Kymlicka's Approach to Nation-Building in Post-Communist Europe' in *Can Liberal Pluralism be Exported?: Western Political Theory and the Ethnic Relations in Eastern Europe*, ed. Will Kymlicka and Magda Opalski (Oxford University Press, 2001), pp. 154–70.

Wardle, Irving, 'A soul in search of salvation', *Sunday Telegraph*, 28 May 2000, n.p.

Weiner, Bernard, 'Mary Bames', *San Francisco Chronicle*, 3 March 1981, p. 3.

Welsh, Anne Marie, '"Pentecost" unfolds at the Old Globe', *San Diego Union Tribune*, 2 June 2003.

Winn, Steven, 'A weighty "Pentecost" opens rep season', *San Francisco Chronicle*, 19 September 1997, p. C1.

Winters, Ben, 'How political is the American theatre?', *Performink Online, Chicago's Entertainment Trade Paper*, 23 May 2003, www.performink.com/Archives/ [accessed 7 August 2010].

Wolf, Larry, *Inventing Eastern Europe: The Map of Civilization on the Mind of the Enlightenment* (Stanford University Press, 1994).

Woolfenden, Richard, 'A Dramatic Loss of Faith', *Living Marxism* (June 1995), pp. 43–4, http://web.archive.org/web/ [accessed 13 August 2010].

# Index


42-day detention bill, 140
Abu-Lughod, Lila, 262
Adams, Gerry, 249
African National Congress, 160
Agamben, Giorgio, 109
*Albert Speer*, 3, 19, 188–204
  and admission of guilt, 202
  and Faust, 195–7
  and the *Chronik*, 198–201
  as celebrity, 193
  as humanizing evil, 204
Ali, Tariq, 69, 205
Allam, Roger, 203
Althusser, Louis-Pierre, 159
Amin, Idi, 107, 108
Amis, Kingsley, 44, 45
Anthony, Andrew, 44, 45
*Arthur & George*, 154, 267
Attenborough, Michael, 31, 87, 137, 264

Bakič-Hayden, Milica, 209
Balibar, Etienne, 12, 104, 109
Barnes, Mary, 156, 175, 181, 188
Bassett, Kate, 138
Baudrillard, Jean, 7
Beckett, Samuel, 4, 21
Beloff, Max, 44
Berke, Joe, 156, 178, 181, 189
Berkeley Repertory Theatre (BRT), 85, 87
Bhatti, Gurpreet Kaur, 57
Billingham, Peter, 16, 271
Billington, Michael, 13, 69, 154, 191, 193, 264, 283
Birmingham Repertory Theatre, 58, 151, 154
Blair, Tony, 124
Bosnia, 207
Bradford, 127
Brecht, Bertolt, 4, 19, 39, 90, 193
Brenton, Howard, 11, 14, 15, 112, 205
Brighton, Pam, 83
British National Party (BNP), 109, 111
British Nationality Act (1948), 107
Britishness, 109, 112, 127
Brown, Georgina, 136, 138
Brown, Gordon, 112, 139
Bull, John, 47
Burnley, 127
Burston, Daniel, 177
Butterworth, Jez, 7

Callow, Simon, 179
Carlson, Marvin, 230, 241
Carney, Sean, 242
*Caucasian Chalk Circle, The*, 231
Chalfont, Alun, 44
Chekhov, Anton, 21
Churchill, Caryl, 13, 14, 112, 151, 173, 205

Clapp, Susannah, 138
Clinton, Bill, 249
Cohen, Nick, 44
Collini, Stefan, 10
Commission on Racial Equality, 1
Commonwealth Immigration Act (1962), 107
communism, 21, 64, 206
in the UK, 67
in the US, 67
constitutionalism, 158
*Contemporary Theatre Review*, 47
*Continental Divide*, 2, 28, 84, 280
and Edgar's own evolution, 99
and Latina/o characters, 93
and means vs ends in politics, 97–9
and negotiation and retrieval, 93, 102
and utopian visions, 95
*Daughters of the Revolution*, 3; and comedy, 95, 97
*Mothers Against*, 3; and tragedy, 95, 96
Crick, Bernard, 151
Cushman, Robert, 82

Daniels, Ron, 87
Davis, Gray, 87, 281
Davis, Jim, 138
Deleuze, Gilles, 20
*dēmos*, 12, 14, 15, 104, 108, 111
Derrida, Jacques, 20, 189
*Destiny*, 3, 19, 23, 110–23
and citizenship, 117
and Edgar's dramaturgy, 111
and fascism, 110, 113, 115, 129
Dolan, Jill, 173
Downie, Penny, 264
dramadocs/docudramas
and truth claims, 157
Dubček, Alexander, 214, 215
Dunster, Matthew, 151
eastern and central Europe (ECE)
and definitions, 209
and discussion of, 209
Edgar, David, 174
and adaptation, 154
and agitprop, 18
and art as provocation, 41
and arts policy, 40–2
and awards, 3, 70
and basic political questions, 17
and 'Black Tulips', 57, 267
and Brecht, 19, 71, 111
and 'Britishness', 38, 105
and cause and effect in politics, 133–4
and censorship, 38, 60
and centrality of class, 52, 65
and characterization, 118
and complexity in playwriting, 31, 136
and conflict resolution, 245
and 'defections' from Left to Right, 2, 42–7, 72
and documentary, 155
and drama's representations of evil, 204
and dramaturgy of asymmetrical balance, 91
and early years, 35
and faction, 47, 154–6, 175, 208, 217, 247, 249, 289
and game theory, 250
and gender, 85, 179
and General Will, 18
and genres and politics, 90
and idealism vs pragmatism, 91, 217
and intercommunal conflict, 123
and Islamophobia, 45, 57, 61
and 'Kronstadt moments', 44
and Labour Party, 2
and libertarianism, 72, 270
and Margaret Thatcher, 41
and Marxism, 1, 15, 53
and multiculturalism, 56, 57, 103

Edgar, David (cont.)
and negotiation and retrieval, 4, 23, 73, 131–3, 194, 230
and neo-conservatism, 2
and New Labour, 41
and political disillusionment, 16, 69, 70, 206
and political leadership, 187, 188
and political membership, 103, 105
and political resistance, 171
and political theatre, 5, 85
and public intellectuals, 35, 37
and revolution, 2, 51
and revolutionary socialism, 2
and rhetorical playwriting, 5, 22, 23, 65
and romance, 231
and Shaw, 24–5
and social democracy, 2, 63
and social realism, 20, 22, 159
and state-of-the-nation plays (SON), 12, 112
and teaching playwriting, 36, 38
and the academy, 47–9
and the *Behzti* affair, 57–60
and the critics, 28, 71
and the Left, 2, 11, 51, 64
and the political process, 18
and the Right, 123, 129
and the Theatre Writers' Union, 48, 50
and the University of Birmingham, 48
and the Writers' Guild, 50
and theatricalization of politics, 87
and Trotskyism, 2, 270
and union activities, 36
and utopian communities, 4, 175
and verbatim theatre, 155, 156, 163
and 'Writ Large', 50, 275
as advocate and activist, 37, 39, 50–60
as analyst and commentator, 37, 38, 40–2
ethnic conflict
and definitions, 210
*ethnos*, 12, 14, 15, 104, 108, 109, 110, 111, 125, 139
Eureka Theatre, 173, 188
Eustis, Oscar, 173
Evidence Room, The, 29

Fabian Society, 1
fascism, 4, 106
and democracy, 110
Faust, 195, 196
feminism, 56, 120, 184
Fenton, James, 42
Fest, Joachim, 200
Foucault, Michel, 159
Fukuyama, Francis, 206

Gandhi, Mahatma, 179
Gardner, Lynn, 245, 247
Garner, Stanton B. Jr, 232
Gibbs, A. M., 25
Giotto di Bondone, 231, 237
Glenny, Misha, 37
globalization, 109, 113
Goethe, Johann Wolfgang von, 196
Goldhagen, Erich, 200, 201
Goldsmith Report, 139
Gorbachev, Mikhail, 212, 265
Grierson, John, 155
Griffin, Nick, 109
Griffiths, Trevor, 173
Grosso, Nick, 7
*Guardian*, 11, 13, 32, 38, 40, 41, 42, 43, 47, 50, 271, 272, 274, 275, 276, 277, 279, 281, 284, 287, 291, 292, 293, 294
Guattari, Felix, 20

Hare, David, 11, 14, 112, 154
*Stuff Happens*, 14
Havel, Vaclav, 214
Heath, Ted, 106
Hobbes, Thomas, 158
Holbrooke, Richard, 250

Holroyd, Michael, 25
Holt, Lorri, 91
*How Plays Work*, 23, 48, 71, 251, 252
Howard, Nigel, 255
Hughes, Mary, 91
Hurwitt, Robert, 89
Husain, Ed, 44
Husák, Gustav, 215

Ibsen, Henrik, 17
immigration, 106–7, 109, 112, 205
Imperial Typewriters, 108
*Independent*, 38
Innes, Christopher, 24
Institute for Public Policy Research, 42
in-yer-facers, 7
Irving, David, 199
Izetbegovic, Aliya, 245

*Jail Diary of Albie Sachs, The*, 3, 22, 160–73
  and impact of play in UK and US, 172–3
  as political performative, 172
  in relation to original source, 164, 167
Jenkins, Peter, 69, 70
Jennings, Alex, 203
Johnson, Paul, 44
Jones, Chad, 85
Jones, Simon, 47
Jowell, Tessa, 40
Judt, Tony, 107, 124

Kane, Sarah, 7, 48
Kearney, Martha, 139
Kelleher, Joe, 10
Kennedy assassination, 165
Kershaw, Baz, 47
Kingsley Hall, 176, 179
Kiš, Danilo, 208
Kosovo, 207
Kramm, Oliver, 45
Kristol, Irving, 45
Kymlicka, Will, 211

Labour, 125
Lacy, Stephen, 47, 49
Laing, Ronald David, 156, 174, 176, 177, 178
Layman, Terry, 94
Led Zeppelin, 241
Left, the, 211, 270
  history, 65–9
Lehmann, Hans-Thies, 5
liberal, 210
libertarianism, 158, 176
*Listener*, 47
Locke, John, 158
*London Review of Books*, 32, 38
Love, Patti, 179
Lukács, Georg, 15, 20, 21, 160, 203
Lyotard, Jean-François, 7, 20

Machiavelli, Niccolo, 10, 129, 158
MacShane, Denis, 45
Major, John, 124, 206
Malik, Kenan, 103, 127, 128, 139
Mamet, David, 17, 18, 43
Mandela, Nelson, 160, 189
Marlowe, Christopher, 195
Marshall, David, 193, 200
Marx, Karl, 10
Marxism, 15
*Marxism Today*, 38, 47
*Mary Barnes*, 3, 22, 174–88
  and alternative communities, 175, 176, 188
  and female characterization, 184–6
  and liberal constitutionalism, 176
*Master Builder, The*, 267
*Maydays*, 2, 14, 19, 84
  and critique of the Left, 79
  and generational difference, 73, 76
  and political resistance, 73
  and public debate over, 82, 280
  and public performance, 81
  and revolutions as festivals, 77, 78
McCarthy, Joseph, 67

McDiarmid, Ian, 122
McGrath, John, 83
McMahon, Patrice C., 210
*Midstream Magazine*, 200
Morley, Sheridan, 136
Mouffe, Chantal, 46, 103, 138, 141
multiculturalism, 127, 128
Murphey, Mark, 94

National Campaign for the Arts, 42
National Front, 52, 54, 56, 110, 112, 283
National Theatre, 1
New Labour, 124, 125, 126
  critique of in *Playing with Fire*, 129–31
*New Statesman*, 38, 42
*New Theatre Quarterly*, 47
*Nicholas Nickleby*, 3, 24, 154, 178
Nightingale, Benedict, 204
Norton-Taylor, Richard
  and *The Colour of Justice*, 154, 283
Nottingham Playhouse, 154
Nunn, Trevor, 193

Oakeshott, Michael, 9, 10, 128, 175, 266
*Observer*, 82
Oldham, 127
Oregon Shakespeare Festival (OSF), 85, 87
orientalism, 207
Oslo Accords, 258, 293
Out of Joint (theatre company), 140
Oxford University Research Group on Conflict Resolution, 249

Painter, Susan, 18, 71, 83, 117, 120, 219, 221
Pavis, Patrice, 7, 16
*Pentecost*, 3, 19, 28, 205, 245
  and the 'Pentecost scene', 241
  and tragedy, 242
  as faction, 234–5
  as romance, 231–4
Peres, Shimon, 249
Peter, John, 1, 264
Phillips, Melanie, 44
physical theatre, 5
Pinter, Harold, 21, 191
Piscator, Erwin, 19
*Playing with Fire*, 3, 28, 110, 113, 123–38
  and change, 129
  and citizenship, 108, 127
Podhoretz, Norman, 45
political theatre, 5, 271
  definition of, 6–17
  in the US, 85
politics
  definition of, 8–11
Powell, Enoch, 106, 107, 282
Prentice, Reg, 44
*Prisoner's Dilemma, The*, 14, 19, 28, 205, 245–64
  and critique of 'gaming', 252–4
  and ethnic conflict, 247
  and ethnicity, 246
  and faction, 249
  and the Prisoner's Dilemma game, 251

*Race & Class*, 38, 47, 57
Race Relations Act (1965), 107
racism, 107–9
Ravenhill, Mark, 7, 15
Read, Alan, 135, 136
*Rebel Without a Cause*, 251
Rebellato, Dan, 7, 11, 13, 15, 19
  and nation-state, 12
  and political theatre, 8
  and state-of-the-nation (SON) plays, 11
refugees, 4, 205
Reich, Wilhelm, 184
Reinelt, Janelle
  and documentary, 155
restoration
  vs revolution in central and eastern Europe, 207, 216
Ridout, Nicholas, 9
Right, the, 270
Rodriguez, Robyn, 85, 87, 88

Roper, David, 69
Royal Shakespeare Company (RSC), 1, 3
Royal Society of Arts, Manufacturing and Commerce, 1

Sachs, Albie, 155, 156, 160, 162, 165, 166, 172, 173
  and *Home Affairs* vs *Fourie*, 189
Salisbury Playhouse, 151
Salisbury Theatre, 151
Samuel, Raphael, 267
Saunders, Graham, 7, 8, 15
Schöpflin, George, 246
Schwarzenegger, Arnold, 87
*Second Time as Farce: Reflections on the Drama of Mean Times, The*, 47, 49
Sereny, Gitta, 118, 157, 191, 192, 200
  and *Albert Speer: his Battle with Truth*, 189
Seyd, Richard, 173
Shakespeare, William, 232
*Shape of the Table, The*, 3, 24, 205, 212–30
  and 'actually existing socialism', 213
  and faction, 214, 215
Sharpeville Massacre, 161
Shaw, George Bernard, 17, 24–5
Shuttleworth, Ian, 153, 250, 256
Sieg, Katrin, 109
Sierz, Aleks, 7, 271
Slane, Andrea, 109
socialism
  defined, 63
*Socialist Worker*, 42
Soweto Uprising, 161
Sparks, Allister, 161
Speer, Albert, 157, 188, 189, 191, 192, 200, 201
  *Inside the Third Reich*, 189, 192
  *The Spandau Diaries*, 189, 192
Stafford-Clark, Max, 140, 151
Stalin, Josef, 67
Stalinism, 42
*State of Play: Playwrights on Playwriting*, 49
*Sunday Times*, 54, 82

Taccone, Tony, 29, 85, 87, 137, 173, 188, 270
Taylor, Paul, 135, 264
*Testing the Echo*, 3, 14, 28, 30, 110, 113, 138–53
  and Britishness, 139, 140
  and citizenship, 141
  and negotiation and retrieval, 141–5
*That Summer*, 56
Thatcher, Margaret, 106, 124, 206
'Third Way', 215
*Times Higher Education Supplement*, 82
*Times Literary Supplement*, 47
Tower of Babel, 241
Tricycle Theatre, 151, 154
Truth and Reconciliation Commission, 160
Tsilevich, Boris, 211, 239

United Kingdom Independence Party (UKIP), 112

Voltaire (François-Marie Arouet), 60

Wardle, Irving, 203
Warwick Arts Centre, 151, 152
Waters, Steve, 41
Weeden, Derek Lee, 87
Willems, Susanne, 202
Winters, Ben, 86
Wolters, Rudy, 200

Yaqoob, Salma, 151

CPSIA information can be obtained
at www.ICGtesting.com
Printed in the USA
LVHW03s1929200918
590806LV00011B/217/P

9 781108 701617